THE COMPLETE IDIOT'S GUIDE® TO

Surviving Divorce

Third Edition

by Pamela Weintraub and Terry Hillman

ALPHA

A member of Penguin Group (USA) Inc.

We dedicate this book to all members of the Divorce Central.com community
(www.divorcecentral.com), who have taught us so much
about the challenges and realities of divorce.

ALPHA BOOKS

Published by the Penguin Group

Penguin Group (USA) Inc., 375 Hudson Street, New York, New York 10014, U.S.A.

Penguin Group (Canada), 10 Alcorn Avenue, Toronto, Ontario, Canada M4V 3B2 (a division of Pearson Penguin Canada Inc.)

Penguin Books Ltd, 80 Strand, London WC2R 0RL, England

Penguin Ireland, 25 St Stephen's Green, Dublin 2, Ireland (a division of Penguin Books Ltd)

Penguin Group (Australia), 250 Camberwell Road, Camberwell, Victoria 3124, Australia (a division of Pearson Australia Group Pty Ltd)

Penguin Books India Pvt Ltd, 11 Community Centre, Panchsheel Park, New Delhi—110 017, India

Penguin Group (NZ), cnr Airborne and Rosedale Roads, Albany, Auckland 1310, New Zealand (a division of Pearson New Zealand Ltd)

Penguin Books (South Africa) (Pty) Ltd, 24 Sturdee Avenue, Rosebank, Johannesburg 2196, South Africa

Penguin Books Ltd, Registered Offices: 80 Strand, London WC2R 0RL, England

Publisher: *Marie Butler-Knight*
Editorial Director: *Mike Sanders*
Senior Managing Editor: *Jennifer Bowles*
Senior Acquisitions Editor: *Randy Ladenheim-Gil*
Development Editor: *Jennifer Moore*
Production Editor: *Janette Lynn*

Copy Editor: *Sarah Cisco*
Cartoonist: *Shannon Wheeler*
Cover/Book Designer: *Trina Wurst*
Indexer: *Heather McNeil*
Layout: *Angela Calvert Johnson*
Proofreading: *Mary Hunt*

Contents at a Glance

Appendixes

Contents

Foreword

As the American family approached the new millennium, the statistic that half of all marriages in the United States end in divorce, unfortunately, has become a cliché. The staggering truth is that over two and a half million men and women, with more than one million children, struggle through divorce each year in this country. If you are going through a divorce, it may be the most grueling, emotionally exhausting, and expensive experience you will ever have. This book that you hold in your hands recognizes that though your divorce is a time of turmoil, you want to be informed and you need to make the best possible decisions to protect your interests.

With a title like *The Complete Idiot's Guide to Surviving Divorce*, I did not know what to expect. What I am pleased to find is a superb, practical, realistic, yet compassionate manual to guide men and women through the minefield of the divorce process. Whether yours will be an uncontested divorce or a high-conflict divorce, this book will help you understand the process and minimize your apprehension and anxiety. This book is filled with professional advice, interesting stories about real people, and a variety of strategies for negotiating the divorce experience. This book begins with a discussion of the pros and cons of deciding to divorce and ends with support for re-creating your life after your divorce. The chapters explain the divorce process step by step and answer your questions about numerous legal issues, including child custody, child support, alimony, and property division. Straightforward, sensible guidance is provided on a wide range of topics and concerns, such as how to select an attorney who is right for you, helping your children cope with the changes in their lives, and ensuring that you are protected after the divorce is final. The in-depth discussions about the alternatives for resolving your divorce through mediation and settlement, as well as litigating your case in court, will help you to have a better understanding of what is happening and to have more control of your case.

As President of the American Academy of Matrimonial Lawyers, I represent more than 1,500 lawyers, who are recognized by their peers as leading experts in the field of family and matrimonial law. On behalf of the Academy, I welcome this book, not to replace your lawyer, but to complement your working relationship with your lawyer. From my perspective, this book will help you to be a better client, and from your perspective, this book will help you to be a more informed consumer of your lawyer's services.

Your divorce may be the most stressful experience of your life, and the outcome may be the most important to your life. You deserve every benefit available to you. I recommend that you read this book from cover to cover at the very beginning of your divorce and re-read sections as the topics become relevant to your own situation. The understanding you will gain will make you stronger and more confident. In short, this book will help you to survive your divorce. In closing, I wish you well.

George S. Stern

George S. Stern is a senior partner in the Atlanta, Georgia law firm of Stern & Edlin, P.C, which limits its practice to complex family law cases. As a nationally recognized authority, he is a frequent lecturer and panelist at matrimonial law seminars, and a frequent contributor of articles on matrimonial law. Mr. Stern is the President of the American Academy of Matrimonial Lawyers, a prestigious organization consisting of the top family law attorneys in the country.

Preface to the Third Edition

In revising *The Complete Idiot's Guide to Surviving Divorce, Third Edition,* for this third edition, we were struck by the many changes and improvements the divorce procedure has undergone. Our overall impression, from researching the 50 states, is that most have taken great care to facilitate the process, make it as fair as possible for all parties, protect the children, and tend to the psychological needs of those involved.

One of the most useful undertakings of the states has been to put almost everything you need to know about divorce laws and related services on their websites. If you can't find what you're looking for on your state's website, you might find it on the website of your state's Bar Association, the professional association of lawyers. In most cases, you will be able to find the divorce laws, or statutes, including child custody, visitation (time sharing), and support guidelines. You may also find a child support calculator, a direct link to child support enforcement, and a link to information on domestic violence. We were also struck by the many new faces emerging in the divorce process. In response to expensive, convoluted, and emotion-laden divorce procedures, consumers now have an array of legal options beyond the customary full-service attorneys who represent clients in adversarial mode. Choices include mediators; "collaborative lawyers," who embody the ideal of cooperation instead of dissent; and "unbundled divorces," where people can hire attorneys for certain aspects of their divorce while handling the simpler steps themselves. And most states now have personnel to help individuals acting as their own attorneys, handling their own cases in the legal trend known as *pro se* divorce.

The trend toward shared custody (as opposed to sole custody) has continued to increase in the United States as well. Parenting plans are now being used in many states to help parents devise a shared time strategy that puts the children's needs first but that is fair to the parents as well.

We suggest you glance through the entire book before focusing on a particular chapter. There are useful tidbits that might help you in your search for sanity during this unsettling time.

Finally, if you would like to commiserate with others in the same boat, try Pam and Terry's website, www.divorcecentral.com, which has an active community bulletin board. See you there!

Introduction

One of the most striking facts about divorce is its sheer frequency. The statistics are staggering—more than 50 percent of all marriages end in failure. There are 1.2 million divorces, involving some 2.4 million adults and more than a million children each year. The number of people dealing with fallout from past divorces registers in the tens of millions. Ongoing battles over spousal and child support, custody, and visitation are issues for untold numbers of American families. And the new American family—defined by singleparents, stepparents, stepsiblings, and alternating homes—are more common than the nuclear family of the recent past.

Over the past eight years, we have had ample opportunity to serve the divorced and divorcing through our website, www.divorcecentral.com. Our intimate work with this community forms the basis for the utilitarian approach in *The Complete Idiot's Guide to Surviving Divorce, Third Edition*. First and foremost, members of this huge and often-disenfranchised group are in need of basic information and expertise. The divorced and divorcing are often confused about their legal rights, intimidated at the prospect of finding an attorney, and baffled by the array of choices—from seemingly peaceful mediation to ferocious, litigation-based war. Frequently in the dark about how to even begin the process of divorce, they seek answers piecemeal through printed material and websites, high-priced attorneys, and the nightmare stories of friends.

The Complete Idiot's Guide to Surviving Divorce, Third Edition, aims to fill this void. One of the few books covering divorce in its entirety, this volume is a step-by-step primer on the legal, financial, and emotional terrain. Written for the person who may be too shell-shocked or upset to develop elaborate strategies themselves, this Idiot's Guide presents a strategic plan of action for those in crisis. It also lays out useful solutions for the spectrum of day-to-day issues likely to emerge in the months and years after the divorce has been decreed.

In an effort to cover the range of divorce issues, we have divided our volume into four distinct sections: deciding to divorce, legal issues, financial issues, and life after divorce, ranging from parenting issues to the stepfamily. Whatever your concerns, we have attempted to cover the basics. Because divorce is one of the most complex and emotionally loaded situations you will ever face, we have written this book as a bastion of simplicity. In the end, of course, you will make decisions with the help of your attorney— but you'll find *The Complete Idiot's Guide* a useful touchstone and the essential place to start.

How to Use This Book

As you read this book, you will find that many topics are universal—reestablishing self-esteem, making the best possible settlement, and managing your money—affect divorcing people across the board. Other areas are more specialized. Not all divorced people, for instance, have children or wage custody wars; not all receive alimony; and not all must navigate the complexity of the step-family.

We suggest, however, that you read this book thoroughly. We have tried to include enough anecdotes to make this book a page-turner. We suggest you turn every page.

Also, pay special attention to the sidebars scattered throughout. These provide real-life anecdotes, help you avoid common pitfalls of the divorce process, and familiarize you with the legal lingo. They will get you going in a positive direction and will give you some comfort when you need it the most. You'll come to recognize these icons as you read:

You Can Do It!
Don't wallow in your misery. Instead, take positive steps to regain control of your life and move on.

Silver Linings
Every dark cloud has a silver lining. In these boxes, you'll find some ways to look on the positive side.

Divorce Dictionary
Here, you'll find definitions of commonly used legal terms in divorce.

Red Alert
Know these pitfalls and you will be ahead of the game.

Acknowledgments

We want to thank Marlene M. Browne, Esq. and Elayne Kesselman, Esq., who supplied the legal background for this guide, psychologist Mitchell A. Baris, Ph.D., for sharing his ideas on the psychology of divorce, children of divorce, and parenting in the face of divorce; pioneering psychologist Janet Johnston, Ph.D. for her insight and input; psychologist Carla Garrity, Ph.D. who, along with Dr. Baris, and other experts in this field, pioneered the concept of the Parenting Coordinator; and financial analyst Ted Beecher, who helped make our chapters on money management and settlement as detailed and timely as possible. Special thanks to our editors, Jennifer Bowles, Randy Ladenheim-Gil, Jennifer Moore, Janette Lynn, Sarah Cisco, and to our literary agent, Wendy Lipkind.

Special Thanks to the Technical Reviewer

The Complete Idiot's Guide to Surviving Divorce, Third Edition, was reviewed by an expert who double-checked the accuracy of what you'll learn here, to help us ensure that this book gives you everything you need to know about divorce. Special thanks are extended to Marlene M. Browne, Esq.

Trademarks

All terms mentioned in this book that are known to be or are suspected of being trademarks or service marks have been appropriately capitalized. Alpha Books and Penguin Group (USA) Inc. cannot attest to the accuracy of this information. Use of a term in this book should not be regarded as affecting the validity of any trademark or service mark.

Part 1

Making the Decision

For those of you who have picked up this book because you can't see your way out of a marriage gone stale, or because you've forgotten who you are, or perhaps because you've let yourself slip into a romantic relationship you were unable to resist, we urge you to take a step back and look again at what you now have. Perhaps you should be reading a guide to salvaging your marriage, not one on divorce.

The decision to divorce, or to stay together and work it out, is the most important you may ever make. In Part 1, we help you grapple with the decision to end or attempt to save your marriage, and we help you deal with the rejection if the decision to divorce has been thrust upon you by your spouse. Either way, we suggest some ways you can navigate your way to a new beginning.

Saving Your Marriage: When There's Hope

In This Chapter

◆ When it's appropriate to try to save your marriage

◆ What therapy can do for you

◆ The pros and cons of divorce

◆ Telltale signs that your marriage should end

When you married a decade ago, it seemed to be for all the right reasons. Both outdoor enthusiasts, you spent your weekends hiking and camping. Back in town during the week, your needs were simple—a night at home watching a video with a bowl of microwave popcorn or take-out Chinese food was all you needed to feel happy and at one with each other and the world. But somewhere along the line things changed—with you desirous of material comforts and symbols of success and your spouse devoted to simplicity no matter what. You want a *new* sofa, not one from the Salvation Army, you have come to realize, and you'd like to store your books and stereo in a wall unit, not atop boards and cinder blocks toted home from a lumberyard down the road.

Your diverging tastes are reflected in your careers. A high school biology teacher, your husband loves nothing more than helping his students protect the ecosystem of a local lake. You, on the other hand, have gravitated to the corporate world. You started out as a secretary and assistant, but over the years you have worked your way up to management. Your salary is still modest, but your ambition is not. As for those vacations, you want the Hilton next time, thank you very much, not a tent in the woods. You still like each other, but you've grown apart. Your relationship has changed.

Or perhaps the following scenario more accurately describes your situation: At first you thought it was exciting, that fiery temper that flared up whenever she sensed a universal injustice or personal slight. At a restaurant, she was the most demanding customer, protesting if her table was too close to the kitchen and conducting an angry dialogue with the chef when her *coq au vin* was seasoned with off-the-shelf spices instead of fresh sprigs of parsley and thyme. Yet now her discerning nature has begun to feel compulsive, and the passion has turned to venom—and it has turned on you. Whenever you leave your coat in the living room or whenever you disagree with her politics or her taste in film, her eyes widen in anger, and before you know it, a book or shoe has flown across the room. You'd like to work it out, but she wants a divorce. What, if anything, can you do?

Or does the following better describe your dilemma? You thought you would be faithful forever, but suddenly, at the cusp of middle age, you have fallen in love. The new object of your affections is irreverent, exciting, forever into something exotic or new. An insatiable world traveler, she's spent years abroad, with extended periods in Sao Paulo, Jerusalem, Osaka, and Madrid. Or, a jack-of-all-trades, he's worked as a photographer, gardener, stock broker, and now—in his latest incarnation—masseur. Oh, those massages! It's wonderful now, of course, but will you really abandon your reliable, loving spouse—the father or mother of your children—for this?

The Most Difficult Decision You Will Ever Make

The decision to divorce is never easy, and as anyone who has been through it will tell you, this wrenching, painful experience can leave scars on adults as well as children for years. Before you and your spouse decide to call it quits, consider whether your marriage can be saved.

Colorado clinical psychologist and divorce expert, Mitchell Baris, Ph.D, co-author of *Caught In the Middle: Protecting the Children of High-Conflict Divorce*, has some guidelines for those wrestling with this difficult decision. When is it possible, through diligent, hard work, perhaps in counseling, to save a marriage? And when is it generally impossible? When—despite the kids—are you doing the right thing by throwing in the towel?

There are, of course, many reasons for divorce, including sexual infidelity or abandonment, a lack of interest, a difference in values, and even abuse. When are these chasms just too wide to bridge? When can bridges be mended and relationships restored? "The decision to divorce is personal," states Dr. Baris. "But I think the point of no return comes with the loss of respect and trust. Those two feelings are particularly difficult to rekindle. Trust can be built back, but it takes years. Often, if trust and respect are gone, rebuilding the marriage is hopeless."

Dr. Baris also feels it might be difficult to rebuild a marriage when the animosity between two people builds to the breaking point. "I find couples are most likely to split when the intensity of negativity between them escalates." One couple, for instance, fought relentlessly about their son's bedtime, his eating habits, the duties of the cleaning service they had hired, and even the cable TV bill. For such couples, discussion on any topic—from the children to the brand of dog food they buy— might erupt into a negative and angry emotion. "These people will continually make destructive remarks about each other or just bring up the past," states Dr. Baris. "In therapy with them, you see this intense negativity and anger just pouring out."

What if children are involved? Dr. Baris explains the studies show that whether or not parents stay married is less important than whether they engage in fighting or conflict—and whether or not they drag the children into their disagreements. The degree of conflict in the environment is the critical factor that determines the ultimate psychological health of a child.

Silver Linings

As painful as it may be to admit that your marriage is at an end, sometimes ending a painful or difficult marriage is the only way you can empower yourself to move forward toward emotional health and growth. We know that leaving a familiar relationship for the possible isolation and stress of single life (and perhaps single parenthood) is a rough road to travel. But after you have made the transition, you will find that you are open to new experiences and new relationships never before possible. If your marriage has been demeaning, painful, or even boring, take comfort in the knowledge that divorce might signify the beginning of something, not just the end.

In other words, don't keep your marriage together for the children if that means exposing them to constant conflict and wrath. It's better for your children if you divorce amicably than if you stay together and continue at war.

Divorce often means relinquishing the creature comforts that defined your life in the past. Families who lived in the suburbs as a unit may now have to sell their house, leave the neighborhood, or move out to less expensive (and possibly less desirable) areas. Divorce means divesting the accoutrements of a shared life and starting out again—diminished in strength and number, and often alone. The death of a marriage inspires, among other emotions, anger, grief, and fear.

Resolving Conflicts and Saving Your Marriage

Your marriage is at the brink of dissolution. You and your spouse have lost trust and faith in each other; your mutual anger is so palpable that you can no longer go out as a couple without breaking into a verbal sparring match or an out-and-out fight. Past hurts and wrongs haunt both of you, coloring your interpretation of the present; and perhaps most damaging, one or both of you have engaged in an extramarital affair.

Despite such problems, couples can and do put their marriages back together, although only through extremely hard work. But both members of the couple must do the work, or it will be doomed from the start. Generally, the best approach is finding a marriage counselor to help you.

Therapists come in as many styles as this year's wall calendar. The question is, what should you look for in a marriage counselor? What kind of therapist is right for you?

Some of the best advice we've heard comes from Dr. Mitchell Baris, who works with the divorced and the divorcing every day. Couples should look for someone who can help them restructure their communication and react to their partner in terms of the real situation, not ghosts of the past, Dr. Baris advises. "Some counselors look into the couples' deep past; they help them go over their own childhood experiences, their early family dynamic. Couples might explore the impact their past had on their marital choice and on the negative (and positive) patterns they carried into their marriage and up to the present."

Divorce Dictionary

Conflict resolution is a peaceful and mutually satisfactory way to end or significantly—and hopefully permanently—de-escalate a conflict.

Although different marriage counselors emphasize different strategies, we have seen the highest levels of success among those who focus on *conflict resolution*. When one spouse gets excited or angry, the ideal strategy for the other is to try to defuse the anger by soothing his or her partner. Going to war—or worse yet, dredging up the past—will only fuel the fires of conflict and weaken the relationship already on its last legs.

Couples in trouble might also benefit from lessons in fair fighting. In this technique, each partner listens to the other without being vicious or defensive—or striking back with hurtful insults or references to the past. One well-known doctor, who pioneered the technique of "restructuring" couples so that they can fight fairly, has this amusing approach: He keeps a piece of linoleum in his office and hands it to one person at a time. "Here, you hold the floor," he says to the person holding the linoleum. The other person cannot speak until the linoleum is handed over. The lesson for couples here: learn how to hear the other one through, and do *not* interrupt, especially to escalate the conflict.

How do you find the right therapist? The best way, our experts tell us, is to get referrals from satisfied friends. Make sure, of course, that you select someone who specializes in couples and relationships and that he or she is well-regarded by other professionals. Make sure that whoever you choose feels "right." Is there a rapport among all three of you? Can you communicate easily with the therapist? Sometimes one spouse will come to feel the therapist has allied with their partner against them; if your spouse feels this way, perhaps it would be best to seek help from another counselor, one who can strike a better sense of neutrality as the sessions go on.

Once you find a therapist who meets these criteria, give therapy a fair chance. Be open to the possibility that your marriage can be saved—and be ready to do the work that it requires. Remember, therapy isn't always easy, especially if you're carrying painful emotional baggage from your childhood. But, if you and your partner truly love each other and are willing to alter some basic patterns, therapy can succeed.

Point of No Return

Sometimes, the best-laid plans are laid to waste. Despite all your hopes and dreams in the beginning, and all your good intentions now, it seems impossible to continue your marriage. For many of us, the twentieth-century notion of "till death do us part" has become an anachronism. When life becomes too painful, with too many battles and battle scars, few of us question the notion, at least intellectually, of moving on.

Sometimes, Dr. Baris notes, so much hurt has been engendered over the years that it is simply impossible to get beyond it—at least in the context of your current relationship. When people harbor deep, abiding anger, and when, despite therapy, that anger cannot be resolved, it could be time to let go.

Even in the absence of anger, one or both partners might start to lose respect for the relationship and a spouse. That might signal the end as well. One couple we know, for instance, divorced after the husband made some poor investments and lost his business and the family home. The woman, who insisted she bore no anger, said she could no longer remain married to someone for whom she had "no respect." In another instance, a man divorced his wife, who he'd met in the fiction-writing workshop at the University of Iowa, after she gave up her artistic career for a high-paying job at a public relations firm.

Sometimes, people divorce because they grow apart. A couple from the Chicago area spent 20 years in a traditional marriage; he went off to work, and she stayed home in the role of homemaker. They had it all, from the two kids to the house in the 'burbs to the cars. When the youngest child left for college and the couple had untold hours to spend together, focusing not on child or family issues but on each other, they found they had little in common. His involvement in business and marketing was simply boring to her, and he couldn't relate to her interests in gourmet cooking and international travel. Their taste in movies and even friends had become widely divergent. There were no affairs and no long-simmering anger or resentment issues. It's just that when both people reached this new crossroad, marked by the departure of their children, his arrow pointed east and hers west.

Younger people with relationships of much shorter duration often reach this juncture as well. When people get married too young, they might find they have gone through enormous changes during the relationship and have grown apart. They've simply gone through more personal development; they have a stronger sense of identity, and in light of that, they would not make the same marriage choice today. Frequently, in such cases, the decision to divorce is mutual. Often, these people can walk away from marriage without feeling particularly angry, especially if they don't have any children. They both just throw up their hands, shrug their shoulders, and say "This doesn't work."

When Is It Over?

How do you know when you've finally reached the point of no return, when putting your relationship together again is simply too much of a stretch? In the end, of course, the answer is personal. But if your answers to the following questions are irrefutably "yes," it might be time to let go:

♦ Does every situation, no matter how seemingly trivial, evolve into a fight?

♦ Do you or your spouse continually refer to hurtful events in the past?

♦ Is all the respect gone from your relationship? Do you feel it is impossible to bring that respect back?

♦ Have your goals and directions changed whereas your partner's have stayed the same? (Or vice versa.)

♦ Is your partner no longer fostering your individual growth?

♦ Have you and your partner both changed so much that you no longer share moral, ethical, or lifestyle values?

♦ Have you and your spouse lost the art of compromise? When you disagree, are you unable to forge a path together that is acceptable to both?

♦ Do you and your spouse have a basic sexual incompatibility? Do you feel completely unattracted to each other? Despite help from professional therapists, have you stopped making love?

Don't Burn Your Bridges: Be Absolutely Certain

The decision to divorce should never be made in the aftermath of a fight. Divorce is final and should be considered carefully, not just for its impact on you, but also for its impact on your children. When you divorce, what ramifications will reverberate through your life and the life of your family? Will you have enough money to sustain your lifestyle—including important small details such as trips to the movies, piano lessons, or your weekly take-out Chinese food? Are you ready to leave the family house for a tiny apartment? Are you ready to divide the Impressionist paintings you've collected over the last 20 years, your mint collection of rock 'n' roll singles, or the living room set you bought from the furniture master in Milan?

The answers, for many, might be straightforward: The emotional relationship with their spouse is largely negative, for one or more of the reasons listed previously. Why else would divorce be in the air?

Nonetheless, sometimes couples in conflict can overlook the positives. For instance, if you have a child, have you considered how difficult it might be to take total responsibility, on the one hand, or restricted visitation on the other? Will you miss your in-laws, friends who might have to choose your spouse over you, or neighbors you might have to leave? Have you considered the stress of the dating scene? Perhaps most important, will you be relieved or paralyzed by the solitude you might be subject to, day in and day out, once you and your partner split?

Should you decide that divorce is your best option, we suggest that you proceed with caution and be aware of what you could lose. If you move forward heedlessly, you might lose more than you need to, or more than you can bear. During her years at college, Melanie was famous for her outgoing nature, flirtatious affect, and pure love of life. Yet when she met Brad, an accountant from the Midwest, she thought she had found a balance. Sober and sane, Brad seemed to have everything organized—where to buy a house and how much to pay for it; how many children to have, and when; where to vacation and when to buy a car. But it soon became clear that Brad had an agenda for Melanie, too. He always seemed to know where she might get her hair cut, and what style she might request; when she should ask for a raise; what committees she should volunteer for; and, in almost every situation, what she should say, think, and feel. It was Brad who insisted she work out of the house, spending less time with the kids, since it was so easy for him to conduct his business from home. Soon Melanie found playing Eliza to Brad's Doolittle a heavy load to bear. Repressed and confused, she suffered depression and self-doubt, all the while living the so-called dream. Despite her love for her children—at Brad's insistence, there were three—she felt strangely disenfranchised. No longer comfortable with her instinct and spontaneity, she felt like a stranger to herself.

It's no wonder she responded so strongly to Rick, an old flame from her glory days at school. He contacted her soon after his divorce—and seemed to love whatever she said or did. With a new love in her life, her motivation for divorcing Brad was high. Yet the price she paid to be rid of Brad was high, too. As the work-at-home parent (who had a higher income), he maintained sole custody of the children. In his usual, controlling fashion, he encouraged their animosity toward their mother. And he managed to secure a significant portion of Melanie's salary for child support.

There's no question that Melanie needed out of this marriage. But her haste caused her to suffer irretrievable losses, most notably her relationship with her children. Her relationship with Rick was never able to compensate her for the grief she experienced as her children increasingly shut her out. There's a lesson in this for most of us. When it comes to divorce, there is always a cost. You must calculate the cost/benefit ratio before you move forward with your divorce. If the price is too high, you may decide to hold off—or at least wait until you've positioned yourself in such a way as to rebalance the equation and come out ahead.

Take some time to consider your losses—and there are sure to be some—before your decision to divorce is set in stone.

When Divorce Is Urgent

We end this chapter with one final caveat. Occasionally, the decision to divorce is mandatory. In instances of spousal or child abuse (mental or physical)—in fact, whenever your safety is in jeopardy—you don't have the luxury of merely considering separation. If your life, limb, or sanity are threatened, it's important to make a quick and abrupt break. If you or your child is in danger, do not wait to organize your finances, collect your valuables, or even see a lawyer. Just get out.

One woman we know had been abused for years when, in the aftermath of one final, brutalizing battle, she phoned her oldest friend and one-time college roommate. The friend came over with her husband and a couple of shopping bags and gathered what she could: some clothes, a toothbrush, and spare cash. Then, the friend and her husband escorted the badly beaten woman out the door. The woman never went back; however, to this day, she states that if she had not been ushered out by her friend, she might still be in that abusive relationship.

> **CAUTION**   **Red Alert** _____
>
> Sometimes, people in destructive relationships have trouble removing the shackles and setting themselves free, and for good reason. Studies reveal that the most dangerous time for a domestic violence victim exists when he or she first tries to leave—or does leave—the abusive relationship. If you're in this situation, call the National Domestic Violence Hotline (800-799-SAFE) or 911 for your protection and safety.

When it comes to domestic violence, women are victimized most. There are millions of such victims annually, according to the National Domestic Violence Hotline, with a woman battered every nine seconds. Almost 5 percent of battering victims are men, and trauma can be similar regardless of the victim's gender. At the center of abusive relationships are issues of power, with the batterer using violence to maintain control over the relationship and his partner. Victims are often in denial about their situation, but it is hard to deny some typical battering tactics:

- **Isolating the victim from family and friends.** This helps keep the victim locked into the relationship because she is kept away from her support system.

- **Intimidation.** The abuser intimidates the victim through looks, actions, and gestures. As an example, perhaps the couple is at a party and the wife is talking to a man across the room. The batterer looks across the room and clenches his fist. She sees this gesture and knows the subtext: She will be assaulted when they get home. He might also intimidate her by destroying her personal property or displaying weapons around the house.

- **Name calling.** This is a prime feature of emotional abuse.

- **Threats.** Batterers might threaten their partners as a means of coercion. Threats might be directed at the victim, at the victim's family and friends, or even at the batterer himself. Threatening to commit suicide if the victim leaves is not uncommon.

◆ **Economic abuse.** Batterers often control family finances and might keep the victim on a weekly allowance to take care of the household. Victims of abuse might not have access to family bank accounts or might be prevented from taking or keeping a job.

◆ **Minimizing the violence.** Almost universally, batterers minimize violence they perpetrate by saying such things as, "What's the big deal? I didn't really hit you; I just slapped you." They will often deny the violence outright and tell their victims that it was all imagined.

◆ **Blaming the victim.** Batterers will blame their partners for the violence, saying they were provoked.

◆ **Using the children.** Batterers think nothing of using the children to relay intimidating messages or harassing the victim during child visitation.

You Can Do It!

If you are the victim of verbal abuse from your spouse or ex, you should move to de-escalate the situation immediately. As soon as you notice the first sign of verbal abuse, put up your hand and say "stop." If the verbal abuse continues, you should deal with your spouse or ex only through a third party. Be aware that "verbal abuse," depending on the circumstances, can be considered "harassing" or "threatening" criminal conduct, and as such, could support the issuance of a protective order.

What can family and friends do if they think someone's in an abusive relationship? First, provide unconditional support. And second, provide a safe haven so the victim has somewhere to go.

What can you do if you are being abused? The first step is recognizing the telltale signs, and the second is seeking help and removing yourself from the situation as quickly as you can. Domestic violence resources are listed in Appendix B.

The Least You Need to Know

◆ Think long and hard before you move forward with your decision to divorce. Once you announce the decision to your spouse, it might be impossible to reverse.

◆ If you want to save your marriage, therapy based on conflict resolution might help.

◆ If your marriage is rife with conflict, don't stay together for the children. The conflict is worse for them than a divorce.

◆ If your physical or mental safety is threatened, separation from your spouse is mandatory.

Planning for Divorce

In This Chapter

◆ Twenty-one things you can do to strengthen your position before telling your partner

◆ How to protect your legal position as soon as you learn divorce is in the cards

◆ Financial posturing: how to protect your money and reduce your liability before the legal maneuvering begins

◆ How to strengthen your right to custody and visitation

There comes a time when you have to bite the bullet and admit that your marriage is at an end. You've tried living together and sorting things out; you've tried couples therapy; and you've tried living apart. The truth is, unless you sever the ties and go your separate ways, you'll never have a shot at the happiness you both deserve.

Think Before You Act

Before you move forward with divorce, the savviest attorneys would advise you to make some preparations. It might seem heartless, but if you plan to ask your spouse for a divorce, or if you think your spouse might want one from you, there are some matters you should take care of first. Attend to these issues before you or your partner decide to call it quits, and you'll be ahead of the game during legal negotiations.

We know that the notion of a pending divorce—even one not yet discussed with your spouse—can send you into a tailspin. The mere thought of divorce might evoke a range of emotions, including relief, fear, disappointment, excitement, and dread. After years of frustration, you're finally ready to divest yourself of some old and uncomfortable life choices for a world of new possibilities and, you hope, lower levels of conflict and pain. But no matter what you feel, you must push these emotions aside and take some practical and highly strategic steps before anyone gets the ball rolling.

1. Consider Your Legal Options

Until you have embarked upon the journey of divorce yourself, you might have some unrealistic notions about what is involved. Ideas about the painful process derive not just from family and friends but also Hollywood movies and tabloids that focus, often, on extraordinary circumstances or the extraordinarily rich and famous. When you read about divorce in the newspaper, the principals are enduring pop icons like Donald and Ivana Trump—not Mary and Tom from down the street. Movie divorce is typified by the classic drama-cum-comedy-cum-nightmare, *The War of the Roses*, the 1980s farce about Barbara and Oliver Rose, the perfect, wealthy couple with all the accoutrements, from the spectacular house to designer cars and clothes to the real art. Neither wants to part with all the luxuries, so when divorce becomes inevitable, they and their attorneys fight to the death—literally. The Roses end up dead on the floor of their magnificent home after a final battle royale atop the crystal chandelier. Although most protagonists like these manage to come out alive, divorce for the wealthy and well-to-do has always been a high stakes game involving costly attorneys, each negotiating (and sometimes litigating) for a client's part of the marriage "pie." For the richest Americans, much about divorce remains the same.

For many years, middle-class divorce was a less-costly version of the battles waged by the rich, with each party hiring an attorney—albeit a less illustrious one—who negotiated for assets and other rights on the client's behalf. But in the twenty-first century, that has changed. Most middle-class divorces today are conducted through a variety of venues, often veering significantly from the lawyered-up model of the past. Indeed, over the past couple of decades, according to the American Bar Association, the process of divorce has undergone radical changes in the United States.

For one thing, large numbers of middle-income Americans hire attorneys for just part of the process and increasingly handle paperwork and logistics themselves. Many others opt for low-conflict resolutions. This includes not just mediation, in which a neutral third party—the mediator—helps the parties reach a compromise, but also the newer method of "collaborative divorce." In collaborative divorce, each party has an attorney, but the adversarial milieu is replaced by a philosophy of harmony and the goal of getting along. In collaborative divorce, the two attorneys work together as a team, with the goal of problem-solving, not duking it out.

The well-to-do may always divorce the traditional way. They simply have too much at stake to do it any other way; given all their assets, the process must be technical and involved if everyone's interests are to be served.

But for the middle-income couple, the options have widened. From the do-it-yourself divorce (referred to as *pro se* or *pro per*) to the mediated divorce to all the variations in-between, divorce has become a consumer's marketplace. If you have limited funds, you no longer have to spend them all on your attorney just to sever your marriage. On the other hand, extra choice means extra risk and responsibility. Should you stop at a storefront and offer your credit card for a $99 divorce, leaving the details to an attorney (or more likely, a paralegal)? One thing is certain: You should educate yourself so you can make sure you are fully protected. As you begin to investigate divorce logistics, stay alert and remain skeptical. The choices you make now could impact your financial and familial situation for years or even decades, so make sure you are doing things right.

2. Consult and Hire an Attorney

As soon as you think you will be seeking a divorce, you must speak with an attorney. This is the first step in your journey, and an essential one. Even if you have been married for only a short time, even if you have no property or children, and even if you plan to mediate your divorce or handle it all yourself, you still need to take this step. An initial consultation with a divorce lawyer can be free, but even if it costs you a couple of hundred dollars, it's better not to be penny wise and pound foolish.

You may think your situation is so simple, or your assets so negligible, that you have nothing to worry about, and nothing to lose except for the attorney fee. But you could be wrong. From lingering debt to funds in a pension or retirement plan, there are many assets and liabilities even the most modest couple is sure to have. You may make fatal errors before you have a chance to tell your spouse what's on your mind. Should you move to another apartment now? Might you lose your chance at custody of the children? Can you date? Should you take money out of your bank account? In short, are you at risk in any way?

A qualified divorce attorney will help you avoid traps you could never know about on your own. (Don't rely on advice from your divorced friend—every case is different.) During the meeting, the lawyer will ask you questions that will allow him or her to evaluate your case. Building on this knowledge and knowing the law and the court system, the lawyer will be able to answer your questions and offer appropriate strategies. Whether you end up hiring this lawyer or not, you will gain a better strategic sense of what's ahead.

Although the wealthiest individuals often pay their full-service attorneys hefty retainers to start work, those of more modest means may now purchase legal services à la carte through a new style of practice called "unbundled" law. In this method, an attorney will look over your shoulder if you can't afford "full service," and no retainer may be necessary. He or she can help you strategize, write a legal letter, or review a mediated settlement agreement. Should you decide to handle many of the details and do the bulk of the work yourself, it is nevertheless in your best interest to have an attorney on tap who is familiar with your case. Even if you and your spouse have "worked everything out" or have chosen a mediator, your own lawyer will advise you about rights you probably don't know you have. You don't need a Marvin Mitchelson or a Raul Feldman, but you should find someone who has handled divorces before, someone you can afford, and someone with whom you feel comfortable. You are going to have to live with your divorce settlement for the rest of your life. Make sure you don't sell yourself short. More about this later on.

How do you find an attorney? Word of mouth is usually a good way to begin, but don't go by recommendations alone. Other resources are your local Bar Association (see Appendixes B and D), or if you are really strapped for cash, you can try legal aid. Don't settle for the first attorney you meet. You must find someone you like, and that individual must practice the kind of law that meets your needs. If you want someone to offer services by menu, then a full-service powerhouse may not be for you. Meet with a few lawyers before making up your mind. Even if you have to pay for these consultations, you'll learn a little about the differences in legal style and hone in on the qualities you prefer.

3. Know Your Spouse's Annual Income

One of the first issues you'll be settling in your divorce agreement or in court relates to money. Whether for spousal support or child support, you will have to know your spouse's earnings and assets to calculate a reasonable figure. If it doesn't make sense to ask your spouse, you might have to do some digging before that information becomes unavailable.

If your spouse has a salaried position or is paid by the hour, the information should be on a recent pay stub. Alternatively, look at last year's tax return. If your spouse is self-employed, a tax return might not tell you the full story. Do a little detective work. Be creative, but be careful not to break state or federal privacy rules. Perhaps you can enlist the help of another person. Does your spouse have a business partner? Are you friendly with the partner's spouse? He or she might know about the business and be willing to share what he or she knows over a friendly lunch. Is someone else in the partnership divorced? Make an ally of that partner's former spouse, who will probably be full of information from his or her divorce and only too eager to share it.

Red Alert _____

Be on the lookout for financial information that is distorted or intentionally incomplete. If you suspect any shenanigans on the part of your spouse, consult a forensic accountant.

Red Alert _____

When fishing for information about your spouse, do not explain, explicitly, why you need this information. Whoever you're asking might well figure out your motivation. Therefore, you must make it understood that discretion is essential. But do so subtly; the less said, the better. Remember, even a friend can be forced to testify against you under oath.

Ultimately, you might have to rely on your spouse to furnish this information, but it's prudent to know as much financial information as possible before taking it up with him or her. One wife we know happened to be enrolled in a course on money management when she decided to move ahead with her divorce. Before she informed her husband, she asked him to help her fill out an income-disclosure form—ostensibly her "homework." When she began divorce proceedings, she had the information she needed—in her husband's handwriting, no less. Even if you're not enrolled in a class, requesting such information should be fairly straightforward. Why do you want the details? In this day and age, our financial status is something we must all be on top of. Just tell your partner you feel foolish without a handle on the economic underpinnings of your life.

4. Realistically Assess What You Can Earn

Depending on the circumstances of your matter, you might have to go to work after the divorce. Have you been out of the job market for a while? Perhaps you need some time to get your skills up to speed before taking the plunge. Or, better yet, get a plan to make yourself more marketable and ask your spouse to support you while you go to school or get that extra training. Has business been off lately? Keep a record of that now so no one later accuses you of deliberately reducing your income to negotiate a more favorable settlement.

5. Learn About Your Family's Financial Holdings

Remember, as you wind your way through the divorce maze, you will only be able to share in assets you know about, so you must find out exactly what the two of you have. For most, that's probably easy. There's a house (with a mortgage), a car (maybe leased or encumbered by a loan), a pension or retirement plan (not yet vested), and a little bit of savings. But for some, property ownership is more complicated. For instance, businesses created during the marriage are assets to be valued, and a judge can distribute their value upon divorce. The same may go for an academic degree or even part of the value of a summer house—one you inherited during the marriage, depending upon the facts of your case.

6. Realistically Assess Your Family's Debt

Often, the allocation of debt is harder to prove or negotiate than the division of assets. What debts do you have? Credit card, personal loans, bank loans, car loans? How much does it cost to pay these debts each month?

As for tabulation of assets, a good source for this information is your family's tax return. Specifically, search under Schedule B for sources of interest income and jot down the information. If possible, locate the 1099 forms—the forms that banks use to report interest income each year. That form will have the name of the bank and the account number. If you don't have the tax return and are afraid of raising suspicions by asking for it, write the Internal Revenue Service. The IRS will provide you with a copy of the return (provided it was a joint return), but it takes several weeks to receive it. If you have a family accountant, you can also ask him or her to send you copies of returns and 1099 statements.

7. Make Photocopies of All Family Financial Records

Canceled checks, bank statements, tax returns, life insurance policies—if it's there, copy it. You might never need this information, but if you do, it's good to have it.

8. Take Stock of Your Family's Valuables

Inventory your safety deposit box or family safe, and take photographs of the contents. Do the same with jewelry or any furniture, paintings, or other items of value. You needn't list every worn-out piece of furniture, but anything with a value of more than $300 should be included. Property-insurance policies can be helpful here because many companies ask you to list the valuables you want insured. Some people keep a list of belongings in a safe, also for insurance purposes. If you've done that, start with that list. There's no need to reinvent the wheel.

What stocks, checking accounts, and savings accounts do either of you have? Do you have a stockbroker? What about life insurance and health insurance? Get detailed information on every policy you own, jointly or individually. Get the name and phone number of your insurance broker now.

9. Learn How Much It Costs to Run Your Household

Whether you plan to stay in the house or leave, you won't know how much money you need unless you know the monthly costs of running your household. If you pay the monthly bills, your job is easy. If you don't, look through the family computer files (if you pay online) or the checkbook—see how much you pay in monthly rent or on your mortgage; check utilities, including electricity, heat, and phone; and look at sundry costs from snow plowing in winter to lawn care and gardening in spring.

One woman we know, a well-educated social worker with a full-time career, didn't know the first thing about the family's monthly expenses because her husband's secretary made out the checks and paid the bills from the office. She was embarrassed to confess her "ignorance," but she is hardly alone. The point is, even if this woman hadn't been contemplating divorce, every adult should know these basic details.

10. Determine Where You Will Live Following Separation

If you're the spouse who plans to move out, decide where you're going to live and figure out how much it will cost, month-by-month, beforehand. Maybe you plan to move in with your romantic interest. Although that might be tempting—it might be the reason you want to divorce—it might also be a case of going from the frying pan into the fire. How is your spouse going to react when you want to bring the children there? Will this make your case a thousand times more difficult to settle? Will your spouse have an adultery claim that can hurt you later? If you answered any of these questions with a "yes" or an "I don't know," move somewhere else. Look through the real estate advertisements to learn about rents. Consider what it will cost to move, and calculate start-up expenses, including telephone installation and turning on electricity and cable.

11. Start Saving Money

One unemployed wife of an electrician wanted a divorce immediately. Her friend, a paralegal who worked in a law firm specializing in divorce, convinced her to hold off for a while. Instead, the friend advised her, it would be best to wait a solid year before starting the divorce action. During that time, she was instructed to save money—enough, hopefully, to be able to pay the rent for a place of her own after she asked for a divorce. It wasn't easy, but the wife saved enough to move out and pay rent for a year. As it turned out, the judge ordered the husband to pay her monthly rent until the divorce was final; but without the initial savings, she wouldn't have been able to move out in the first place.

12. Build Up Your Own Credit

If you don't have credit cards in your own name, apply for them now. You might be able to get them based on your spouse's income, and you will probably need credit later. Use the cards instead of cash and pay the entire balance by the due date every month. Don't charge more than you can pay; you'll be creating even more problems for yourself!

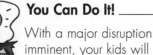

You Can Do It!

With a major disruption imminent, your kids will need the reassurance of your extra attention. Fear of abandonment by one or both parents is the number-one reaction of children faced with divorcing parents. On the legal front, the more involved you are with your kids now, the more chance you will have to stay involved—by court order, if necessary.

13. Stay Involved with Your Children

First of all, this is important for your children—especially because they will need all the support and reassurance they can get during the turbulent times ahead. In addition, because courts consider the depth and quality of your relationship when making custody and parenting time decisions, such involvement now could translate to more time with your children and the likelihood of shared custody after the divorce.

Do a self-check: Have you been so busy earning a living that you've let your spouse bear the brunt of child rearing? If so, now is the time to reallocate your

priorities. If you have school-age children, help get them off to school in the morning, help them with homework at night, and help get them to bed. Learn who their
teachers are, who their pediatrician is, who their friends are. If your children are not
yet in school, spend as much time with them as you can before and after work. Be an
involved parent—for now and for your future together.

14. Withdraw Your Money from the Bank

If you fear your request for divorce will send your spouse straight to the bank, withdraw half of the money in all your savings accounts first. Place the money in a new
account, and keep it there until you and your spouse can work out the distribution
of property. Do not spend the money if at all possible. If the money is in a checking
account and you know the account is nearly emptied every month to pay bills, do not
withdraw any of that money; you'll create financial havoc if checks bounce.

15. Consider Canceling Charge Cards

If you pay the credit card bills, consider canceling your accounts—or at least reducing
the spending limit. In one case, the wife's announcement that she wanted a divorce
sent the husband on a $50,000 shopping spree—and she became liable for the home
entertainment system and the Jacuzzi (installed, incidentally, in a house she stood to
lose). If you cancel or reduce lines of credit, of course, you must inform your spouse
to save embarrassment and, later, anger. You can say the family needs to cut back,
which is probably going to be true.

16. Decide How to Tell Your Spouse

Here, you might need professional advice or advice from a battle-worn friend. Would
your partner accept the news more easily in a public place, such as a restaurant, or in
the privacy of your home? One husband we know delayed telling his wife he wanted
a divorce because she threatened suicide each time he mentioned separating. The
wife was an unsuccessful actress with a flair for the dramatic who dropped her suicide
threats once the husband agreed she could take over their apartment. Still, some
threats must be dealt with seriously. If you're afraid your announcement will send
your spouse off the deep end, be sure that you have consulted a professional counselor beforehand. Although there is often no way to lessen the hurt and rejection, a
professional therapist might be able to supply you with strategies for leaving your
spouse with as much of his or her self-esteem intact as possible.

17. Decide How to Tell the Children

You might want to consult with a professional. (For more details, see Chapter 22.) Would the news be best coming from the two of you together or from one of you alone? One husband we know planned to tell the children that he was moving out on Christmas. He thought that would be a good time because the whole family would be together. His lawyer tactfully suggested he choose a different day.

You Can Do It! _____

Before you start divorce proceedings, you might want to consider the legal difference between divorce and separation (see Chapter 4). If you want finality in your marital status, it is certainly preferable to be divorced. Alternatively, if you are not ready to be divorced, a judgment of separation is preferable. We suggest that, to the extent possible, you investigate these alternatives in advance.

18. Take Property That Belongs to You and Safeguard It

High school yearbooks, jewelry, computer disks, your collection of CDs, your grandmother's family heirlooms, whatever—if it indisputably belongs to you and you fear your spouse might take it for spite or leverage, move it out of the house. If you have several such items, move them out slowly, over time, before you announce your plans. Depending on the size of the objects, you might store them in a safe-deposit box, a storage facility, or the home of a trusted friend.

19. Don't Make Any Unnecessary Major Purchases

When there are suddenly two households to maintain, you might find your financial freedom drastically curtailed. The number of people who buy brand new cars while they're starting divorce proceedings is staggering. The payments could financially devastate you, and your spouse can use the existence of your new car as proof of your ability to pay for all sorts of other expenses. Sorry, guys and gals: Resist.

20. Make Sure That Your Spouse Is the First to Know Your Plans

Although you might consult with friends before you take the plunge, be sure that they know if word gets around before you have told your spouse you want a divorce, it could spell trouble for you down the road.

21. Stay in the Marital Residence If Possible

Depending on your circumstances and the laws of your state, you could weaken your position on custody and possibly your personal or *marital property* if you move out. You should discuss any plans to move from the marital residence with your lawyer before making a decision. As always, take immediate action if abuse is at issue.

> **Divorce Dictionary**
>
> **Marital property,** also called **joint property,** is generally what a husband and wife acquire during the marriage. In some jurisdictions, inheritances, disability awards, and gifts received from a third party—that is, not the spouse—are not considered marital or joint property, even if a spouse received them during the marriage. Other exceptions may exist as well.

When It Comes as a Shock ...

Every so often, the specter of divorce takes someone by surprise. Ted, a young man from Malibu, took his wife out to dinner with a couple of friends who were in town for the weekend. Halfway through the meal, she stood up, stretched and yawned, and announced, "I'm just so sleepy, I'll have to meet you guys back at home." When Ted arrived back at his beach house, guests in tow, his wife was nowhere to be found. Indeed, despite the embarrassment she caused her husband in front of his friends, she didn't return home that night at all. In the morning, she called to say she was in love with someone else and wanted a divorce.

Barbara found herself in a similar situation. She thought she and her husband were, for the most part, getting along well, with only some small disagreements. They had a beautiful one-year-old son whom they both adored. One night, her husband announced he wanted a divorce. At the same time, he refused to move out of the house for another year because he wanted to bond with his son. Barbara had no recourse. She lived under those strained circumstances until they worked out a settlement. Only then did he move out.

No matter what your circumstances, if your spouse's desire for divorce takes you by surprise, you will probably feel as if the bottom has dropped out from under you. You're likely to need months to lick your emotional wounds, restore your self-esteem, and start to heal. Nonetheless, as raw and beaten as you might feel, you will need to follow a plan of action if you want to protect your legal rights, financial assets, and access to your children. We know you'll have plenty of time to think the details through, but for now, when the pain is so enormous you can hardly think at all, the actions detailed below will shore up your strategic position for later.

Red Alert

Alberto was so furious at Sarah for divorcing him, and then suing for 90 percent of the estate, that he sent her a cockroach in the mail. Aware of her fear of insects, he chuckled to think of her reaction upon opening the clever "gift." But at trial, the so-called antic served merely to enrage the judge. He found the "trick" so reprehensible and Alberto's character and sense of justice so skewed that all discretionary decisions were made in favor of Sarah. Please keep your anger in check. Angry or aggressive acts can be used against you once the legal system is involved.

The second you're told you will be involved in divorce, hire a lawyer. Be sure to tell your lawyer about any problems that might require relief from the court: the need for money for yourself or your children; the need to decide, at least on a temporary basis, where the children will live and what the visitation arrangements will be; and in some cases, the need for protection from the other spouse.

If you are a parent, the most important thing to do is to consult your lawyer to make sure that you are doing everything possible to protect your rights with regard to your children.

You must also avoid trampling on the rights of your spouse, no matter how you feel about him or her. You may be furious, but don't make the fatal mistake of locking your spouse out of the house or abandoning your marital residence with or without the children. If you do so, you stand to damage your position with regard to custody and assets. If you leave, the judge could order that your spouse remain in the residence—with the kids—until things are settled. If you lock your spouse out, the judge could order you to let him or her back in. With emotions at peak levels, this situation would be uncomfortable at best.

Never act out of revenge. Do not put the children in a loyalty bind. Resist any urge to do "revenge spending." It might be used against you later if your case goes to court.

It goes without saying, of course, that if your spouse has asked for a divorce, you will also need to follow the 21 strategic tips provided at the top of this chapter. First, protect your financial position by learning all you can about your family's finances.

Be sure to photocopy all relevant documents and photograph your valuables, including those in the safe deposit box.

You must protect yourself against any preemptive moves your spouse may have taken without your knowledge. Directly ask your spouse for any papers that are suddenly missing. Make sure that the safe deposit box or family safe has not been raided. With your lawyer's help, you can get restraining orders against the use of specific bank accounts.

Now is the time for some financial strikes of your own. If it's not too late, collect any diaries, calendars, or other items and remove them from the house. If your spouse hasn't yet raided the bank accounts, withdraw half of the savings accounts and open a new account. Do not spend that money if at all possible. If the credit cards are in your name, or if you pay the credit card bills, cancel them. Tell your spouse you've cancelled the cards. Since he or she has announced plans to divorce, this should not come as a surprise. On the other hand, if you have not yet established credit in your own name, now is the time to do so; use your spouse's credit lines to build some credit of your own. Obtain and complete applications immediately.

If the two of you are going to live together until the divorce is final, decide where you'll sleep. Note that because your spouse told you that he or she wants the divorce, you have the upper hand and can probably successfully demand use of the bedroom. If you and your spouse can still have a civil conversation, decide how and what the two of you will tell the children.

Finally, consider therapy if you feel it might help. There are going to be many stresses in the future, emotional as well as financial, and the better you can cope with them, the smoother the divorce process will go for you.

Worksheet for Calculating Expenses

Item	Amount
Housing Expenses	
Rent	_____
Mortgage	_____
Property taxes	_____
Condominium charges	_____
Cooperative maintenance charges	_____

Worksheet for Calculating Expenses

Item	Amount
Outstanding loan payments	_____
Gardening	_____
Cleaning person	_____
Household repairs	_____
Painting	_____
Furniture, linens	_____
Cleaning supplies	_____

Utilities

Item	Amount
Water charges	_____
Electricity	_____
Telephone	_____
Cable	_____
Appliances and upkeep	_____

Transportation Expenses

Item	Amount
Car payments	_____
Car insurance	_____
Car repairs	_____
Fuel	_____
Public transportation	_____

Children

Item	Amount
Children's tuition	_____
Summer camp	_____
Babysitter/childcare	_____
Allowance	_____
School transportation	_____
Child support (from previous relationships)	_____
Lessons (music, dance, etc.)	_____
Sporting goods	_____

Personal Expenses

Item	Amount
Food	_____
Clothing	_____

Laundry _____

Dry cleaning _____

Books _____

Magazines _____

Newspapers _____

Cigarettes _____

Gifts _____

Beauty/salon _____

Lunches at work _____

Courses _____

Hobbies _____

Insurance

Life insurance _____

Personal property insurance _____

Fire, theft, liability insurance _____

Medical Expenses

Medical insurance _____

Medical _____

Dental _____

Optical _____

Pharmaceutical _____

Entertainment

Vacation _____

Movies _____

Video rentals _____

Theater _____

Dining out _____

Parties/entertaining _____

Miscellaneous Debts and Expenses

Credit card debt _____

Alimony (from
previous relationships) _____

Church or temple dues _____

Charitable contributions _____

Income taxes _____

Other (Have we missed something essential to your life? You fill in the blanks.)

_____		_____
_____		_____
_____		_____
Total: _____		_____

A quick glance at this chapter might turn your stomach in knots. The advice may seem aggressive and sometimes even adversarial, but you must protect yourself. Getting divorced is one of the great stressors in life, but you can get through this. Trust us. It may seem impossible right now, but time _will_ heal this wound.

The Least You Need to Know

- As soon as you know you will be involved in a divorce, consult an attorney.

- Find out your family's income and assets.

- Find out your family's expenses and estimate your future expenses.

- Photocopy all business records.

- Get any incriminating information—particularly personal diaries—out of the house. But be prepared to have your spouse ask you to produce this material during the discovery process.

- Care for your children. Their road will not be easy.

3

Love in Ruins

In This Chapter

◆ Understanding the emotional journey to divorce for the "dumper" and the "dumpee"

◆ How to tell your partner it's over and the importance of honesty

◆ How to work through the pain and get on with your life

◆ Protecting your custodial, property, and financial rights in the aftermath of separation

One of our friends was devastated when, during her last year of medical residency, her husband, a wealthy surgeon, left for someone else without explaining, even briefly, what went wrong. The couple became involved in a protracted court battle regarding finances and issues of child custody. As trial date after trial date was postponed, issues of spousal maintenance and child support, division of property, and a permanent custody decision were put on hold. In all that time, the ex-husband (by now living with his new partner) refused to tell his former wife why he'd left her, for fear it would weaken his case. But here's a tip: This woman would have traded untold thousands of dollars for a simple explanation. "I'll tell you after the case is closed," her former spouse often promised during their infrequent moments of civility. If only that moment had arrived.

In truth, it's impossible for you to shield your partner from pain if you are rejecting him or her. It's going to hurt—especially if you are forthright and direct in your communication. And yet, as you help your partner face this final stage of your relationship, the most important gift you can give is honesty.

Breaking the News

The inevitability of divorce is often experienced quite differently by the person who has done the rejecting (the "dumper" in divorce lingo) and the rejected individual (the "dumpee"). If you are the partner initiating the divorce, the emotional journey from your marriage toward a new life began long ago. However, your spouse, although sensing difficulties, might not realize how far you have traveled from the nucleus of your relationship. Your spouse might not feel just hurt and angry, but also shocked, when you announce the news.

You owe an honest explanation to the person you have married about why you want to leave. Again and again, divorce psychologists confide that the complaint they hear most is this: "I want one adequate explanation. I never knew what went wrong."

After you have provided your spouse with an explanation of what went wrong, expect powerful emotions ranging from sadness to anger to fear. Remember, the divorce might sadden you, too, but you have had time to get used to the idea. Your partner has not. You will have to give some time and some leeway for your spouse to catch up.

Oh, the Agony!

If you are on the receiving end of the divorce announcement, on the other hand, you might find yourself reeling with disbelief, pain, and, after the shock wears off, anger. You must remember that these feelings are entirely normal. Indeed, the grief one feels at divorce is in some ways comparable to the grief experienced when a beloved spouse dies. According to psychologist Mitchell Baris, Ph.D, the grief is experienced in phases.

"Initially," he explains, "You go through a phase of sadness, anger, and heightened feelings of rejection. There may be very different rates of acceptance for one partner than for another," Baris states. Eventually, even the rejected individual will come to see separation and divorce in a more positive light. The divorce decision, often pushed by one of you, becomes mutual.

It only makes sense that the person who initiated the decision comes to accept the reality of divorce sooner. "That individual is a little bit more advanced; they have been working through their initial feelings of acceptance, of realization that the relationship is over," says Dr. Baris. "The sadness, the sense of failure, has begun to fade, and he or she has already begun to envision the single life—whether as a single parent or as a single individual. By the time that person has announced a desire to divorce to a spouse, the idea of separation has already been worked through. The rejected individual, on the other hand, is typically several months behind in terms of working through the grief."

Famed death researcher Elizabeth Kubler-Ross defined the stages in the grieving process over the death of a loved one. Those facing divorce, say psychologists, can expect a similar, though perhaps not identical, process. Psychologist Mitchell Baris has altered the well-known Kubler-Ross list slightly in its application to divorce:

◆ **Denial.** This is your basic state of shock. You cannot believe it's true.

◆ **Anger.** The rejected individual, "the dumpee," will direct anger at the rejecting spouse and the world. Get it out. It's okay.

◆ **Guilt and Depression.** Feelings of guilt cannot help but rear their head, more often in the one initiating the divorce, but in the recipient as well. De-pression is a common emotion even in those who badly want to divorce and move on. After all, it is still the end of something that person once hoped would endure. It's important to turn guilt and depression into something constructive: an examination of the role you played in the breakup of your marriage. Life is about growth, after all, and if you can't see yourself clearly, you won't be able to move on.

◆ **Acceptance.** Reality has sunk in. It's not one of those bad dreams from which you will awaken; it's real. You accept this as your reality and move on—however awkwardly, however tentatively—with your life.

Envisioning the Future

If you have children, and often even if you don't, your relationship with your soon-to-be former spouse will change. As you both move on in your lives, the intense hurt and anger you are now experiencing will lessen. It is easy for us to say, "we've seen it before," but trust us, we have. Your feelings will change over time. You will meet new people and become involved in new interests or jobs. Other, unrelated issues will take center stage in your mind. Your children's activities will continue to engage you. Just watching them grow and change will give you immense pleasure as you rebalance your emotional life.

> **You Can Do It!**
>
> You will be involved with your former spouse regularly if you have children. For the children's sake, as well as your own sanity, civility is all-important during the break-up period of your marriage. Fostering bitterness will only root you in your current upset and pain. Instead, as you go through the beginning of the end, you must refocus your thoughts on your new life. This will hasten your healing, empowering you to move on.

At some point in the years to come, you'll be surprised to find that watching your son's baseball game with your ex-spouse just a few rows back or even on the same bench is not as painful as it had been. You might even be able to chit-chat about the kids. Who would have thunk!

> **Red Alert**
>
> Those who remain stuck in a morass of anger, self-pity, and self-imposed isolation might be helped by psychotherapy. The right counselor can do wonders for someone who needs to change his or her view of the world, embrace creativity in life, and, most important, start feeling good!

Right from the Start: Legal Implications Lurk Behind Every Emotional Wound

Even before the shock, disbelief, and confused feelings have abated, you are faced with a legal situation: What happens now for the two of you? Both of you will have to consider the legal implications of your behavior from now on.

Don't Let Your Feelings Impact Your Legal Standing

It's not fair, you say? Sorry, but the truth is that in many states courts are set up so that the circumstances leading one person to leave another have no bearing on the division of marital assets, child support, or parental time sharing. To repeat, if your spouse has left you for another love, in most cases, it will have no impact on the division of the worldly goods you have built up during your time together or on other issues in your separation and divorce. In a pure no-fault state, the dumper and the dumpee are on equal footing in the eyes of the law. (Check your state's laws, included in Appendix C.)

Despite common "no fault" divorce laws, the emotional turmoil of impending divorce often causes one partner to concede his fair share of the marriage spoils in a negotiated settlement. As you plan your separation and, ultimately, divide your marital assets and other arrangements, be aware that the emotional tenor created as your marriage crumbles and then dies can influence a divorce settlement in unforeseen and irrevocable ways.

Our friend Tonina provides the perfect cautionary tale. A seemingly reserved individual who has always wanted space and "more time for me," Tonina often felt overwhelmed by her outgoing, gregarious, and attention-seeking spouse, Leo. She'd been ambivalent about their marriage for years, spending much of her free time selling her homemade jewelry at craft shows, often far from home. Leo offered to accompany her, but Tonina explained that exhibiting jewelry was her only break from the pressure of the relationship, and requested he stay home. Because he truly loved Tonina, Leo—an aggressive salesman by day—consented to abide by her limits. But he realized his acquiescence had been a mistake.

Over time, the discontented Tonina found companionship through a recently-divorced fellow craftsman, a gentle bead-maker who also made the rounds of craft shows, and who decided to cry on her shoulder as they sold their wares. With so many hours together, their booths side by side, the friendship between Tonina and the sensitive bead-maker eventually blossomed into more. Finally, Tonina decided she'd found the gentle soul mate she had always needed. Though Leo had been good to her and truly loved her, and although he would be devastated, she felt she knew what she had to do: Tell him she had reached a fork in the road, and she could no longer travel his way.

In the days following "the announcement," Tonina moved into a spare room in the home of a female friend and participated in counseling with Leo. Leo had pressed for the sessions; his fervent hope was to use the counseling to convince Tonina to recommit to him. Tonina, on the other hand, hoped the therapist could convince Leo to let go. Eventually, that is just what occurred.

Six months after her announcement, Tonina had moved into her own apartment, a bastion of the space and solitude she had so long craved, but also a haven for nurturing her new romance. Leo, on the other hand, continued to live in the couple's home, where he often found the loneliness crushing. A regular at online dating services such as Match.com, he went out several times a week but found it hard to shake his fear that Tonina could never be replaced.

It was a full year after Tonina moved out that the divorce was finalized—a year of new awakenings for Tonina and agony for Leo. There was only one benefit to the underdog position that Leo could discern: Despite their 20 years of marriage, Tonina had demanded far less than her fair share of the marital estate than she was legally entitled to. Pressured by Leo at the outset not to obtain private counsel, but to work with a mediator of his choosing, Tonina agreed as part of her "penance."

In her desire to sever ties as quickly and cleanly as possible, she agreed to the stern terms Leo put forth in the mediation sessions each week. She literally (and knowingly) allowed Leo to shortchange her in settlement by waiving her rights to marital property belonging to them both. Not only did she agree to give Leo the house and the car free and clear, she also requested none of his 401-K, to which she was entitled. If Tonina had been less wracked by guilt and Leo had been less hurt during those months of separation, the division would have been more equitable. But with Tonina too guilty to hire a lawyer to negotiate on her behalf and with Leo too upset to abide by the standard of fairness he usually embraced, Tonina was left without a dime.

Our advice to those about to end a marriage is to be aware of how the emotional underpinnings of your initial breakup can affect the financial and legal terms of your final settlement. If you are the leaver, we beseech you to be emotionally kind to your soon-to-be-ex when you break the news. The angrier your spouse becomes during this delicate time, the more unyielding he or she will be in reaching a reasonable settlement.

This is not only the empathetic path, but also the strategic one. If you feel too much guilt, or if you are the object of too much anger, you may find yourself accepting unfair terms.

Even as you remain kind, you must also stay steadfast in your demand for what is your legal due. You are breaking up your marriage for a reason, after all. In the end, it takes two to ruin a marriage; if the law, generally, does not distinguish between dumper and dumpee, neither should you. It is tempting, in the interest of peace and economy, to go with a mediator. But if you feel so guilty you might cave during negotiations—for instance, if you have any doubt about your ability to demand economic fairness because you feel you inflicted emotional pain on your spouse by leaving—you would do well to hire someone to negotiate on your behalf.

If you are the one who's been left, on the other hand, this may be your best chance to strike the most favorable deal possible. Like Leo, you might be able to obtain greater concessions from your spouse in the early days of the announcement, when the hurt is still raw and the guilt most pronounced. This is all provided you keep your anger—but not your sense of disappointment and betrayal—to yourself. Remember that your spouse may be most likely to leave with less when you seem bereft and alone. Even if your partner has left for another love, he or she will be less likely to make concessions in settlement if you seem happily ensconced with a new love, too. This is just human nature. You have already been rejected; a better divorce settlement is hardly compensation, but you should still opt for whatever advantage you can.

The Least You Need to Know

- ◆ Be honest with your spouse about your reasons for moving on.

- ◆ Realize that although you are now in emotional turmoil, time will assuage your shock or your guilt. Life will move on and so will you, if you let it.

- ◆ The law, generally, does not distinguish between "dumper" and "dumpee" in terms of custody or distribution of wealth.

- ◆ Protect your financial and property interests through any legal means available to you, even if you feel guilty, as soon as it is clear that divorce is inevitable.

Chapter 4

Separation

In This Chapter

- ◆ Physically separating as a means to understanding what you really want
- ◆ Using the period of separation to come into your own
- ◆ Leaving the family home or staying until the divorce is final: pros and cons

Couples considering divorce often achieve a new balance during a period of separation—which can be one of the first emotional and legal steps down the road to divorce.

Separation (be it legal or physical) generally commences on the day a couple begins to live in separate residences with the intention of continuing to live apart. It is important to keep in mind, as you consider separation, the distinction between a legal separation, which requires formal filing, and mere physical separation, without court involvement. Needless to say, formal legal separation—and the specifics of the agreement rendered to formalize it—will have a far more profound impact on the ultimate disposition of your divorce.

Beginning of the End, or a New Beginning?

It merits saying up front that separation, physical or legal, does not always lead to divorce. Sometimes separation can be a time of forgiveness and renewed commitment. Many times, couples will separate in hopes of saving a marriage. Sometimes, this can work. After all, just getting distance from a painful, antagonistic situation can provide you with enough perspective to come back together weeks or months later and sort things out.

One couple we know did just that. The man, a newspaper reporter, left his wife in Boston and went on assignment in Russia for a year. Their marriage had been on the rocks, but during the year apart, the two developed an email correspondence that brought them new intimacy and understanding. When they came back together after 12 months apart, they were ready to really commit to the relationship and even decided to start a family.

In other marriages, separation—as opposed to divorce —becomes a permanent way of life. We know of a couple who stayed legally separate but married for some 25 years. (Indeed, they exist in that state to this day.) The woman, happily living in a town-house in Miami, plays tennis during the day and spends evenings with her lover, another woman. The man, who enjoys the city life in a Manhattan penthouse, runs a successful business and has pursued a series of monogamous relationships that fell apart, one by one, when he refused to commit to marriage. He had the perfect excuse. He was not yet divorced from his estranged wife. For this couple, divorce holds nothing positive. It would erode their joint fortune and diminish the money available to their children (they had two). In the man's case, getting a divorce would only make him available for remarriage, an idea he hardly relishes.

This estranged couple had their relationship formalized in a Separation and Property Settlement Agreement drafted by their attorneys. For them, it was the best route to new and separate lives.

Preamble to Divorce

As the name implies, separation can be the first step along the journey to separate lives. Not quite permanent or irrevocable, separation enables the two individuals to get a taste of what it would be like to exist apart—to manage separate households, separate finances, and separate selves.

Most of the time, separation is a preamble to divorce—even if that was not the original intent. A Dallas couple we know opted for a long-distance relationship as a means of gaining perspective. The decision to separate was facilitated when the woman was offered a job in Des Moines. Unfortunately, her husband began feeling so resentful when she really left that, ultimately, he could not accept her back into his life. He felt this way despite the fact that he was the one who had encouraged her to leave in the first place.

Red Alert

If you enter separation believing it is just what you need to heal your marriage, you may be kidding yourself. All too often couples who separate just to "get a little distance" find they like the distance just fine. The best way to work out marital problems is usually under one roof.

Another example involves a woman who married the first boyfriend she ever had right after college. As the marriage went on, he became increasingly critical and angry. (Psychological abuse is the term that comes to mind.) Yet because she'd never really been alone, she could not imagine life without him. Finally, through therapy, she was able to take what she thought would be a short hiatus from the marriage. She never imagined that during this break she would experience a return of self-esteem, enthusiasm, and even joy. This "brief" separation was just what she needed to realize she could go it alone over the long haul.

As a step before divorce, physical separation has emotional and legal implications that you need to understand. Decisions made during separation often become stamped in stone, and anyone separating without the appropriate strategizing and protections can suffer unpleasant repercussions for years. Indeed, the legal arrangements made for separation often cannot be renegotiated for the divorce; those who decide to let things go, believing they will have another chance at a fairer deal later, are sorely disappointed most of the time.

Remember what we said in Chapter 3: The emotional tenor of your break-up and, by extension, your separation can impact the legal outcome of your divorce. Separation is such a naturally turbulent and overwhelming period that it lends itself to rash decisions driven by emotions like guilt and anger. In a cooler moment, you may have made a more strategic deal, but you will not generally have the luxury of negotiating twice. If you are separating, you should attend to the fine print of your future life now.

There are couples who treat separation casually and live apart without any formal legal agreement. If you and your spouse are quite certain that your separation is temporary, and that you will be using the time to reconcile, a casual attitude may work well. You can date your spouse, even have sex with your spouse—because as far as you are concerned, divorce is not in the cards.

But please be careful. If you have filed for a fault divorce (covered in Chapter 6), you may lose grounds for divorce in your state if you date or have sexual relations with your spouse during a period of separation. If separation is likely to be the first step in your journey to single status, we suggest you enter it seriously and formally—with a signed agreement and full awareness of the potential errors, many of them impossible to reverse later on.

A Separate Peace

As with the decision to divorce itself separation is often experienced differently by the individual who initiates the separation and the one "informed" that an impasse is at hand. Whether you are the dumper or dumpee, remember that your future will be impacted by your decisions during this critical time.

It only makes sense that the person who initiated the divorce comes to embrace the single life of separation sooner; that individual has been living with the decision for quite a while. Given this fact, the individual who has initiated the divorce should see the separation as a means of providing his or her partner with time. Even though you might be saying, "Okay, we're going to end the relationship. Let's get working on the terms of the separation. Let's see if we can mediate this," your partner is still reeling from the pain. At first, he or she will not be nearly as ready to negotiate the terms of the agreement —certainly not in any sense that could be favorable to you.

If you have been rejected by your spouse, on the other hand, use the separation period to help yourself heal. As you go through the stages of grief we covered in Chapter 3, you will come to see yourself as a solo act. You might need to utilize this time to brush up on job skills, gain self-confidence, or simply come to know yourself as an individual who stands alone. You'll know you have arrived when you too can say, "Okay, I can see our incompatibility. This needs to end. At this point, I would also choose to end this relationship and go on in a new direction."

Remember, the process is painful. If you're like most people, you won't pass quickly through the emotional gauntlet of separation. Typically, psychologists say, the first year following separation is most difficult. During this period, you're most prey to mood swings, sadness, feelings of loss, and anger. If you remain on this emotional roller coaster for more than a year, however, you are not progressing fast enough. It is time to seek counseling or some other form of psychological help.

Published research bears this timetable out. According to a study from psychologist Joan Kelly, Ph.D., of the Center for Marital Transition near San Francisco, couples in conflict report that conflict drastically reduces after 12 months. Other research indicates that conflict and anger tend to diffuse after a period of separation, and if couples have not continued to interact, at the end of two years, most of the conflict will be gone.

Surviving Forced Togetherness

Sometimes, despite the positive impact of physical separation, couples stay together in the same physical space for legal and financial reasons until the day of the divorce decree. There are a number of reasons why this is often legally advisable. If you seek full or joint custody of the children—or if you just want a generous visitation schedule—staying in the house will help your cause. Leaving, in fact, often puts you at a tremendous disadvantage in any legal proceeding. Although the opinions expressed here, as in the rest of the book, do not constitute legal advice, the decision to stay or leave is so important that we strongly advise you to consult your attorney before you do anything.

Your leaving might make it easier for your spouse to delay the signing of divorce papers, putting you at a strategic disadvantage. Indeed, many times, a spouse will just want you out of the house but will be reluctant to move forward with divorce because of economic circumstances. Once you leave, your spouse will have little incentive to move quickly. The longer your spouse delays the divorce, the more frustrated you will become, and the more likely you will be to sign an agreement less favorable to you. On the other hand, if you stay in the home, your spouse will be the frustrated one; you will have the upper hand during negotiations.

> **CAUTION**
>
> **Red Alert** _____
>
> If you think you are going to divorce eventually and you might want custody of your children, some judges might hold your move from your children's house against you. Be careful. Don't let a short-term goal interfere with what you really want.

Finally, for those who are particularly money-conscious—and who isn't these days— the longer you and your spouse share the same home, the more money you will save.

If you've decided to stay in the house until the divorce is over, turn one section into your "camp." If you move out of the bedroom, do not—we repeat, do not—leave your clothes, jewelry, and other possessions in the dresser, especially if you plan to use them on a daily or weekly basis. Instead, choose a spot—the den, the guest room, or even the basement—and move all your clothes and possessions there so that you and your spouse have as little negative interaction as possible. (Workday mornings are pretty negative even in the happiest marriages!)

If you have been advised by your attorney to stay in the house, try to do so as amicably as humanly possible. One psychologist we have interviewed even suggests Yogic breathing exercises as a means of dealing with the stress this sort of situation brings. Remember, your code word is equanimity. Of course it will be difficult, but adding any more hatred or animosity to the marital pot is toxic.

Sayonara

If life in the house is intolerable and you know custody is not in the cards for you, a move might be wise. It could take one to three years for your divorce to be final, and neither you nor your spouse could cope with one to three more years of tension. More important, it's not good for the children. Again, check with a lawyer before making a decision.

Before you move, discuss the division of personal property with your spouse. You might not be able to take anything with you yet (one woman we know stayed with 10 friends during the 12 weeks it took her to locate an affordable apartment), but at least you'll both understand that by moving out, you're not giving up your rights to property. Your lawyer might want this in writing. If you don't have a lawyer, write down that you are not giving up any rights by moving out and ask your spouse to sign what you've written.

If life in the house is intolerable and you want custody of the children, talk to your lawyer about moving out with the children. Your lawyer might want to first obtain an order from a judge, giving you temporary custody of the children, thereby giving you the right to take the kids with you when you leave.

Silver Linings
During your first year of separation, you might find comfort and camaraderie in one of the myriad support groups for the divorced. As you go about choosing a group, however, do be cautious. Some divorce groups are wonderfully supportive and nurture healing. Others foster conflict and fan the flames of anger. It will not help you to associate with a group that feeds the anger. What you really need—and what should be available in most areas—is a support team that facilitates positive, constructive solutions for your life so you can get beyond your relationship and divorce and move on.

Reading the Fine Print

It's important to understand the legal implications of separation, including the difference between an informal break and a legally binding agreement. Remember that separation laws vary by state. In some jurisdictions, for instance, all assets and debts acquired after the date of the agreement are excluded from consideration as marital property. Without a legal agreement, you are considered married in every sense of the word—and held liable for every cent your partner spends.

For this reason, a formal separation agreement can go a long way toward protecting your financial assets, your custodial privileges, and your personal rights. After all, the separation agreement covers essentially the same ground as a divorce agreement: division of assets and debt, child support and custody, visitation, and spousal support. A separation agreement can be the blueprint for the divorce settlement, and is not easy to change after it has been set forth in a fairly drafted agreement. (Of course, terms of support and custody or visitation are subject to change upon proof of change in material circumstances.)

Remember, a separation agreement is a binding contract—one that is put in writing, signed by both parties, and typically notarized. Each separation agreement is different, based not only on the laws of the particular state, but also the circumstances of the couple involved.

As you and (hopefully) your lawyer render this document, you will establish the ground rules: Who stays in the marital home and who leaves; who pays support, and to whom; who has custody of the children and how each of you will contribute to their support and care; and how you will divide your marital assets and debts. These issues and a few others, including how you deal with income and debt accrued during separation, will be part of the boilerplate in any separation agreement.

But there are a few other points you may want to attend to as well:

- Continuation or cessation of certain benefits, ranging from medical and dental insurance to sharing a credit rating.

- The issue of who may deduct alimony payments on the tax return.

- College expenses. If you have toddlers, this is so far off as to seem irrelevant, but the years pass quickly. Unless this is spelled out, the noncustodial parent may not be required to contribute. (College tuition is not necessarily considered mandatory in every case. It usually depends on the lifestyle of the parents and the law of the state you are in.)

- Rights to a pension benefit.

- Access to liquid assets like cash, bonds, and credit cards.

- Ground rules for dealing with credit cards owned jointly.

> **You Can Do It!**
>
> The trend these days is for more and more couples to handle their divorces without attorneys, that is, *pro se* or *pro per*. Even if this is your plan, we urge you to consult attorneys at the outset and to put your separation agreement in their hands. In fact, we suggest that if you spend money anywhere it is up front, in drafting a separation agreement. A carefully constructed separation agreement may be the best investment you make; but if you aren't careful, a separation agreement can be your ruination as well. If your funds for legal assistance are limited, we urge you to do whatever you can—including using a credit card—to make sure that your separation agreement protects your assets, your income, your children, and your rights.

The Family Plan

For couples with children—who must interact with each other to co-parent, even in the face of divorce—a separation with a parenting plan goes a long way toward easing conflict. Only after time apart can these parents come back together and cooperate enough to co-parent again. A couple without children can make this break and need never come back together again. But for parents, this is impossible. If you're in this situation, you're stuck with your soon-to-be-ex-spouse for better or worse. You've got to figure out some way to manage the conflict and get over it so you can see your ex from time to time and reestablish a businesslike relationship that works. Psychologists advise these parents to create every opportunity for complete separation so that full emotional disengagement can take place. After a period of time—generally about a year—they can relax the separation. Without the hiatus, say psychologists like Baris, some parents may find it more difficult to end the conflict.

> **You Can Do It!**
>
> Make sure that even though you are moving out, your spouse understands you are not giving up the right to property. Some spouses, out of guilt, may give the other so much money that they have to move into a single room where they cannot bring the children to visit. Don't become one of them. Ask your attorney to protect you as vigorously as possible through a legally binding separation agreement.

In light of all the work you and your spouse will need to do during your physical separation, this is a poor time to invest in a new relationship. You must give yourself the time and space to find some new personal definition and direction. A time of separation is a perfect time to look inward, asking yourself how you contributed to the relationship's end. Some people have difficulty assuming responsibility for creating negative situations for themselves and so look to blame anybody or anything else. You must let go of this "victim" mentality if you want to avoid making the same mistakes again.

The Least You Need to Know

- Physical separation allows a time to assess your feelings about remaining married.

- While many couples see the value in remaining married, others find they are happier living on their own and begin the divorce process.

- If you think you will live apart for some time, a formal separation agreement negotiated with attorneys will protect you.

- If you are counseled by your attorney to remain in the home for legal reasons, but that situation becomes intolerable, ask your lawyer what you should do. Do not just leave, otherwise you might compromise your legal standing.

Chapter 5

When There's No Turning Back

In This Chapter

- ◆ Financial archaeology: documenting your life from year one
- ◆ When to hire a private investigator
- ◆ How to review your prenuptial agreement
- ◆ How to practice discretion if you decide to date
- ◆ How to craft your own settlement agreement

After the decision to separate and divorce is made, you must—each of you, alone—take some practical steps to protect your interests. As unfortunate and as heartless as it sounds, you have moved on to another stage. You have stopped trying to patch things up in the realm of the heart and have begun instead to negotiate the real world of lawyers and courts, bank accounts and mortgage payments, and, most critically, the custodial fate of your children.

Where to Begin the End

If you and your spouse still get along and you are both fully aware of the family's financial situation, you can sit down and work out an allocation of assets and liabilities. You might also be able to agree on custody and visitation. The two of you together could conceivably decide who takes the children when and for how long; how to structure visitation; how to arrange for childcare; and how to cooperate so that you are there to back up each other in the parental role, although you no longer function as husband and wife. Each of you can then find a mediator or lawyer. One attorney will draw up documents and the other will review them. Voilà, you're on your way.

The problem is, of course, things don't always go this smoothly. Even the best-intentioned couples find themselves arguing over anything from the custody of Rover to who gets the football season tickets. If you're like most people, sitting down over a cup of coffee and dividing up the hard-earned fruits of your marriage is just not going to happen.

What then? Follow the Scouting motto. Be prepared. In Chapter 6, we provide some additional tips to help you lay the groundwork for this preparation. We'll assume, of course, that you've already followed the steps recommended in Chapters 2 and 3. By now, you have consulted a lawyer and have taken stock of your family's financial situation, including any income, property, or outstanding debt. But as the dust begins to clear, as reality sets in, you will be dealing with the details—the accumulations, the detritus, the remains of your relationship, and the vestiges of your shared life. As you set out to settle the score—divest some baggage, work through pain, or simply clear the field—you'll need to attend to the special issues discussed in this chapter.

Gathering Your Financial Documents

You've already collected financial statements readily available around the house. In some cases, it's important to have copies of tax returns, bank statements, insurance policies, and loan applications going back in the marriage as far as possible. If you or your spouse have destroyed documents after a decade, as some people do, it could work against you. Such documentation might be especially critical if there's a gap between your reported income and your standard of living.

The Bright family, for instance, reported income of $50,000, but the two children attend private school ($20,000 per year total); the Brights take two very nice vacations a year ($5,000 total); the monthly mortgage on their house is $1,000 ($12,000 total); the monthly mortgage on their summer house is $500 ($6,000 total); and each party drives a leased car at a combined cost of $500 a month ($6,000 total). Grand total: $49,000. That leaves $1,000 for taxes, food, utilities, clothing, pet supplies, and so on. Clearly, there's more income than has been reported. Bank statements, credit card receipts, canceled checks, and the like all help prove real, as opposed to reported, income. You might also need tax returns simply to prove how much income you or your spouse earns, even if you work for someone else.

If you can't find any of these documents (or you never saved them), you can write the Internal Revenue Service for copies of joint returns, or you can ask your accountant for copies. The bank might keep copies of loan applications and might be willing to release a copy of your application to you. For a fee, although it tends to get expensive, you can obtain copies of canceled checks and your bank statements. (Before incurring that expense, check with your attorney. He or she might be able to get the same information directly from your spouse's attorney. In most instances, the divorce law of your state entitles you to this information if your spouse has it or has access to it.)

As you document your deep financial history, make sure that you include these assets:

Cash & Valuables

Savings accounts

Checking accounts

CD accounts

Options to buy stocks

403 accounts

401(k) accounts

Individual retirement accounts

Pens Cash value of life insurance

Businesses

Loans to others

Educational degrees

Security deposits

Bonds

Notes

Stocks

Real property

Jewelry

Antiques

Artwork

Vehicles

Business assets, including accounts receivable, work in process, inventory, hard assets, computer equipment, and software programs

---

The point is, once the dust has cleared and you can focus, you might need to do a little digging in preparation for the legal proceedings to come. A divorce trial can sometimes be like a war, and you want to go to battle fully armed. Who wouldn't?

The Price of Dating Before the Divorce

As you continue to plan strategically for your divorce in these early stages, you need to consider the impact dating will have during your day in court. You do not have to be a hermit just because you are divorcing, unless your attorney tells you otherwise. Usually, discretion is the key. For example, if your divorce is not yet final, never have a friend of the opposite sex sleep at your home or spend time alone with you in your bedroom while the children are home. Similarly, if you are claiming that your spouse was unfaithful, and it is important to your case that you have been faithful, do not become involved with anyone until the divorce is final.

Even if your lawyer tells you it's okay to date, avoid going places where you might run into your spouse. In one case, a husband took his new girlfriend to his wife's favorite restaurant. (She found out when the credit card charges came through.) She was furious and refused to cooperate in settling the case.

Don't bring the children along on a date and don't introduce your friend to them. Unless your case is over or it has been dragging on for many years, it's too soon for the children, and it will only make your spouse mad. (You can be sure that your kids will give your spouse a full report.)

Hiring a Private Eye

You might feel that you want to do some digging in a host of personal realms. Perhaps you suspect that your spouse is having an affair, and you want the goods on him or her. Should you hire a private eye?

The days when you needed compromising pictures of your spouse in the arms of another are long gone. In all states, you can get a divorce on grounds other than adultery. Still, there are people, and you might be one of them, who firmly believe that if you could catch your spouse "in the act," he or she would "cave in" and give you an enormous settlement rather than risk disclosure of the infidelity.

In our opinion, this works on television and in the movies, but not in real life. Sometimes, the two-timing spouse is relieved to have his or her relationship out in the open; other times, he or she just doesn't care. Paying a private eye, at a hefty hourly rate, usually is not worth it.

There is one exception. If custody is going to be an issue in your case, the work of a private investigator might pay off. If you suspect that your spouse ignores the children or relegates their care to someone else (ranging from grandparents to babysitters), or if there is an unknown person living with your spouse and your young children, you might consider calling a detective. Evidence for any of these scenarios could be vitally important in a custody case, particularly if you and your spouse are otherwise equally capable parents.

Finally, here's a word to the wise: Never conduct surveillance yourself. Secret tape recordings of your spouse might prove harmful. In one difficult case, the husband, who sought custody of his two young sons, provoked his wife into an argument while the children were in the same room. Secretly, he taped 10 minutes of his wife yelling and the children crying. The husband played the tape in court. The wife's voice filled the courtroom, sounding shrill on the recording, while the children wailed in the background. The husband lost custody. The wife testified that the husband had started the argument. What kind of father, her lawyer argued, would deliberately subject his children to an argument between their parents to create evidence for court?

Red Alert _____

You might worry that your spouse has hired a private detective or used other means to track you. Is your phone tapped? Are there hidden microphones in the walls? Sounds like paranoia, and for most people, it is. If you think your line is tapped, have the phone company check your line and phone. If you still feel paranoid, it might be worth your money to have your house checked, but never let your spouse know. (Do it when the children are away.)

Generally, it's against the law to tap a phone line, so don't do it unless you have permission from a court. Furthermore, there is not much to be gained from a phone tap. A recorded phone conversation probably won't do you much good, and could result in your prosecution, unless it somehow directly bears on the issue of custody.

One woman we know lost custody of her daughter because, following a benign voice mail message to her ex, she accidentally failed to turn her cell phone off. With her ex's tape still running, she said terrible things about him to her little boy. The tape was later produced in court—and provided the judge with all the evidence he needed to remove the child from his mother. As the "alienating parent," she was permitted to see the boy for just an hour a week, in therapy.

The moral here is simple. Always consult with your attorney before engaging in any scheme involving a tap or tape recorder. Be careful when leaving taped messages on machines—while secret tapings may be illegal in your state, your voluntary missives into the void are not. Even if taping is not against the law in your state, your plan might come back to haunt you.

Reviewing Your Prenuptial Agreement

If you and your spouse signed a *prenuptial agreement*, this is the time to pull it out. You might be surprised to read what the two of you signed in the throes of new love.

Divorce Dictionary

A **prenuptial agreement** is a written contract entered into by a couple before marriage to establish their rights in the event of a death or divorce. The validity of such agreements depends on state law. It is advisable to sign a prenuptial agreement only if you are sure that you have plenty of time to read and understand it, you know what assets your soon-to-be spouse has (and vice versa), and you have your own attorney review the document.

You Can Do It!

If you didn't have an attorney, you were unaware of your spouse's assets or liabilities, you did not understand the agreement, you were tricked into signing it, or you signed it very close to your wedding day, you might convince a judge to throw out the prenup.

Prenups, as lawyers call them, used to be popular mostly with older people who were marrying for the second time and wanted to protect the inheritance rights of their children in the event they died. However, provisions for what would happen in the event the parties divorced began to pop up, and now, young people marrying for the first time often inquire about having a prenup. Some stand to inherit money from parents, and the parents want the prenup. Others are wealthy in their own right and have heard so many divorce horror stories that they want to protect their assets.

If you signed a properly executed prenup or post-nuptial agreement (an agreement entered into after your marriage), there is little to discuss if the marriage fails. Judges will generally uphold the terms of the prenup with a couple of exceptions. In general, judges will not uphold provisions in a prenuptial agreement stating who is to have custody of children and how much child support is to be paid. The care and support of children is usually subject to court review. In addition, judges will not support your agreement if you can prove it was the product of fraud, coercion, distress, or some other unfairness the laws of your state allow you to assert.

What, exactly, will a judge consider unfair? Did you each have your own attorney when you signed the agreement? Did you each reveal how much money, assets, and debts you had before you signed the agreement? How close to your wedding date was the agreement signed? (Signing it on the day before might be construed as undue pressure.) Did you understand the agreement? Is it so unfair to one party that a court won't enforce it? Were you tricked into signing it? If you can prove any of these unfavorable conditions existed, a judge might invalidate the prenuptial agreement.

Starting the Divorce Action

To get the divorce process rolling, someone will need to file. The spouse who starts the legal proceedings is called the *plaintiff* or *petitioner*, and the one who responds is called the *defendant*, or *respondent*.

If you have hired a full-service attorney, he or she will decide when to start legal divorce proceedings, usually based on a number of different factors. Maybe you need some kind of immediate relief, such as support, and your spouse has refused to provide it. If you are fully represented, your lawyer must go to court and ask a judge to order your spouse to pay. The only way the lawyer can go to court is to first start a divorce action, and therefore you would be the plaintiff, or petitioner. If you are handling your case pro se, or if you have hired a lawyer to advise but not represent you, you will initiate the action yourself.

Perhaps you've decided to start your divorce action a few months before you get that bonus, thus excluding the money from marital property. Depending on the laws of your state, such strategy may or may not be completely effective. Even if a bonus is paid after the date of separation, it might be deemed joint property because it was earned during the marriage. If you have hired a full-service attorney, he will know just what you should do. If you are filing on your own, this is one of those areas where legal advice should be sought.

Whatever the details, if you and your spouse have worked out a mutually agreeable deal, when it's time to file, the lawyer (or individual) who has been doing the paperwork simply files. Either spouse can file first.

In short, who becomes plaintiff and who becomes defendant depends on a number of factors. Although it might not sit right with you to be the defendant or respondent, gone are the days when such labels mattered much.

Working Out a Settlement Agreement

Whether you call it a Separation Agreement or Divorce Settlement, in the best of all possible worlds, you and your spouse would sit down like two civilized adults and pound out a fair deal between yourselves.

In one difficult case, a 60-year-old man was divorcing his second wife. (His first wife died after 30 years of marriage.) Discussions between the lawyers went nowhere, and the parties' grown children from their first marriages weren't helping with their endless "suggestions." Finally, the husband met his wife for breakfast at a diner one Sunday morning. Monday, he came to see his lawyer with the details of a settlement scribbled on a napkin. The lawyers got busy writing up the settlement agreement.

The moral of the story? You and your spouse should do whatever you can to settle the case. You'll save legal fees and headaches. There is only one caveat. Do not sign anything until you speak to a lawyer.

Indeed, we conclude this chapter by stating the obvious. Always check with an attorney before signing any agreement or taking any major steps such as moving out, withdrawing money from joint accounts, stopping credit cards, hiring a private investigator, or trying to tape conversations.

The Least You Need to Know

- In the best of all possible worlds, you'll work out a settlement agreement with your spouse—but don't count on it.

- Photocopy all the financial documents you can find, particularly if actual income—as opposed to reported income—is going to be an issue.

- Be discreet if you date, and consider hiring a private investigator when appropriate in issues concerning child custody.

- Make sure to review your prenuptial agreement as early in the game as possible.

- Always check with an attorney before signing any agreement or taking any major steps such as moving out, withdrawing money from joint accounts, stopping credit cards, hiring a private investigator, or trying to tape conversations.

Part 2

Navigating the Law

After you digest the fact that your marriage is really ending, you must negotiate its conclusion as gracefully, efficiently, and inexpensively as you can—in a way that's advantageous to you. This simply won't be possible unless you learn all you can about matrimonial law. Only through such knowledge will you be able to protect your rights and your self-esteem.

Consider Part 2 your gentle introduction to divorce law. In the next several chapters, we help you take stock: Should you attempt to settle your case out of court, on your own, or with the help of an attorney? Should your legal counsel deliver services à la carte or in full? Should you seek a peaceable settlement through mediation, or proceed to the battleground of a trial, armed with attorney, financial documents, and more stamina than you have ever needed before?

Chapter **6**

The Art of the Deal

In This Chapter

- ◆ The no-fault divorce
- ◆ The quick divorce: when to pursue it and when to avoid it
- ◆ Constructive approaches to bargaining and compromise
- ◆ The cost of a quick divorce
- ◆ Your lawyer's role in a quick divorce

Most divorces end not with a bang, but with a whimper. After months or even years of negotiating, spouses reach agreements without anyone ever setting foot in a courthouse. This chapter tries to help you reach this goal quickly, saving tens of thousands of dollars and untold years.

"No-Fault" Divorce

In many states, provided you've resided in the state for a minimum amount of time (anywhere from six weeks, as in Nevada, to 18 months), you do not have to prove *grounds* to get divorced. All you have to plead is incompatibility or irreconcilable differences leading to the irremediable breakdown of the marriage, and a judge will grant you a divorce. This is quite a change from the days when private detectives hid in hotel room closets with cameras to prove adultery. Some states, however, still maintain a "fault" system. You have to prove one of several grounds to get divorced. Grounds usually include mental cruelty, abandonment, adultery, or imprisonment. When people living in "fault" states cannot prove grounds, they sometimes move to no-fault states to get their divorce.

Divorce Dictionary

Grounds are legally sufficient reasons why a person is entitled to a divorce. Although many states are "no-fault" states, where no grounds need be asserted other than incompatibility or irreconcilable difference, others require the plaintiff to prove grounds, including adultery, abandonment, or mental cruelty.

You might qualify for a no-fault divorce, but that doesn't mean the real issues—custody, support, visitation—are going to be easily resolved. If any of those areas presents a problem, you might still need a judge, even though the divorce itself is a given. Areas of fault, meanwhile, vary by state. For instance, in Illinois, desertion for two years and alcoholism for one year qualifies as fault. In Connecticut, insanity for five years is fault, as is imprisonment for life. In New York, insanity is grounds for annulment. With the specifics of each state so variable, and so subject to change, we hesitate to list every last detail here. Please be advised to educate yourself on the "fault" rules in the jurisdiction where you reside.

Quick and Easy

Regardless of whether you live in a fault or a no-fault state, the real measure of how quickly you'll get your divorce through the courts is how quickly you and your spouse agree on the issues that exist between you. If you have no assets or debt, if you have no children, and if you've only been married a short time, your divorce should be relatively quick and easy. We know several couples who lived together peacefully for years, got married, and were divorced two or three years later. Maybe it was being married, or maybe the relationship had run its course. Whatever the reason, for those individuals, the divorce was merely a matter of filling out the right papers and submitting them to the court. As long as you and your spouse agree that your marriage is over, you both know what assets and debt you have, and you agree on how you'll divide them, a quick divorce could work for you.

Not So Quick and Easy

A woman who had been married to a wealthy businessman for 12 years left him for her son's ninth-grade history teacher. She insisted that all she wanted was the

Farberware. Her lawyer begged her to demand a fairer deal, wrote her letters stating she was making a mistake, and even threatened to stop working as her attorney if she took the deal. But she ran off with her new love and the pots and pans. Four months later, when her relationship with the teacher ended, she wanted to reopen her case—but it was four months too late. She got a quick divorce, but hardly a fair one.

What's the moral of the story? A quick divorce works fine if it's fair, but not when it occurs because one side feels guilty or pressured. Remember, never sign papers dividing assets or debt without first consulting an attorney. Never sign such papers while you are in an overly emotional state. It's okay to sign papers if you feel sad or even somewhat depressed about the breakup, but if you're in a major depression, or you're enraged, spiteful, or blinded by love, wait until the sound and fury in your mind and heart have simmered down before you commit yourself to a deal you might regret later.

Working Through the Issues

What if you and your spouse just can't agree? What if issues ranging from custody of the children and ownership of the dog to an inability of one spouse to let go promise to complicate the situation for years to come? Can you get a quick divorce anyway? Sometimes you can, with the help of a judge, but it depends on where you live.

In major metropolitan areas, where the court dockets are crowded, it could be months, even as long as a year, before your case can be tried. In smaller communities, it is possible you can get your day in court much sooner.

Silver Linings

If you have gotten the short end of the stick in a divorce decision, you will almost always get another chance. If you haven't received what you want in the divorce decision in terms of custody or property, you will usually have the right to appeal. If you have been treated unfairly by the judge, the situation might be rectified. However, depending on how backlogged the appellate court is, it could take months or years to get back in front of a judge.

Bargaining and Compromise

It's difficult to negotiate for yourself, particularly when emotions are involved, as they tend to be in a divorce. For many couples, trying to negotiate is like reliving the worst moments of the marriage. After all, if the two of you got along well enough to work out a divorce, you might not be divorcing in the first place. Does this mean you have to abandon all hope and leave everything to the attorneys? Not necessarily. Here are some tips that might help you reach a settlement without going to court:

- *Never present your bottom line early in the negotiations.* It might sound childish, but it happens to be true. When negotiating, don't present your bottom line first; that could end up being the high figure, and it can drop from there.

- *Argue issues, not positions.* It might sound obvious, but it isn't always. For example, you and your spouse are discussing who will pay for your children's college education. Your spouse says the two girls will go to state schools. You say they'll go to the best school they get into. The two of you are arguing positions, not issues. The issue is the cost of college and how you'll finance it.

- *Make rules for your discussion.* If you and your spouse are meeting alone, write out a schedule of topics to be covered and stick to it. Agree that neither of you will interrupt the other. If you're meeting with your spouse and with the lawyers (commonly called a *four-way meeting*), you and your attorney should plan the meeting. You should have an agenda, preferably in writing, and you should know when to talk and when not to talk.

> ### You Can Do It!
>
> Focus on the problem, not on your feelings. Say you want to live in the family home until your youngest child graduates from college, but your husband wants to sell the house now. The issue is whether you can afford the house and whether your spouse needs the sale proceeds, but your husband's real concern might be that you'll remarry and have someone else move into "his" house. If that issue surfaces, it can be addressed by agreeing that if you remarry, the house would then be sold.

Before one four-way meeting, one husband's lawyer asked him not to talk to his wife. Within three minutes of the meeting's start, the husband was shouting at his wife, and she was yelling right back. The husband's lawyer was doodling, and the wife's lawyer was trying to calm her client. Considering that the combined hourly billing rate of the two lawyers probably exceeded $500 an hour, the husband (and wife, for that matter) were spending their money at a rapid rate.

- *Be flexible.* That doesn't mean cave in. It means be ready to compromise. Remember the example about the two girls and what college they'd attend? Suppose you don't want to pay anything for college, and your spouse wants you to pay half. What about paying one third? What about paying half only if your income is at a certain level by the time the girls go to college? What about agreeing to pay half but also stipulating that any loans or scholarships the girls receive offset your half?

As long as you stay locked into one position, it will be hard to settle your case. Be open to ideas. You might have to get some from your attorney, from your accountant, or from friends who have been divorced.

♦ *Be ready to trade.* Say that you really want the gold necklace your husband bought you on your third wedding anniversary, and he really wants the cookware. You want the cookware, too. Decide which one you want most, and, if the values are about equal, make the trade. It sounds obvious, but when emotions are running high, it might not be.

♦ *Leave heated issues for last.* This is a lawyer's trick. Resolve everything you can and save the heavy issues for last. Maybe you both want custody of your child. If you start off discussing that sore point, you'll get nowhere with any other issues. If you first sort out the house, the car, and the debts, you might make better progress on the last, toughest issue. After all, you've both spent so much time already, it would be a shame if you couldn't work it all out.

♦ *Have a judge or neutral third party, like a mediator, help resolve the issues you can't resolve.* Maybe you and your spouse have worked out everything except custody. A custody trial will still be cheaper than a trial on all the other issues, too. Don't throw in the towel on your settlement agreement just because you can't resolve everything.

♦ *If things get too emotional, step back.* Maybe you and your spouse have met with the best intentions, but before you know it, you're back to the old routine that never got you anywhere in your marriage. Break for a few minutes or a few days before trying to hammer out an agreement again.

♦ *Don't expect more than you had in the marriage.* Some spouses suddenly "forget" when getting divorced that they were married to the man who blew his paycheck every few weeks at the race track. When there's a missed support check, they're shocked. Maybe the two of you decided to put any extra money into your house over the years. Suddenly, your spouse is shocked that there are no savings.

Remember, getting divorced does not turn a frog into a prince. If you negotiate in good faith but lose track of who you are dealing with on the other side of the table, you could be in for disappointment.

◆ *Give up if you're getting nowhere.* Maybe you've met alone, maybe with lawyers, maybe with a priest or an accountant, and you've agreed on nothing. It might be time to move on to the next step, which could be a trial in front of a judge. Some spouses need to be told by a judge the way it's going to be.

In one case, the father would not voluntarily relinquish custody of the children (teenagers who wanted to live with their mother), no matter what. If a judge had told him he had to let them go, however, he would have complied.

As it turned out, the case did not go to the court. The lawyers finally worked out an agreement without using the word "custody." The children stayed with their mother during the week and with their father most weekends. The father could live with this arrangement because technically both parties still had custody.

Impediments to Settlement

Once you both feel you know what is and is not in the marital pot, the biggest impediment to settlement usually is *emotion*.

Maybe you're not ready to see the marriage end, so just when it seems like you're about to make a deal, you find a problem with the agreement. If the real problem is that you do not want the marriage to end (whether it's because you still want to be married or you don't want to give her the satisfaction of being divorced), then you should tell your lawyer to stop negotiating for a while. You need time to think things through, and there is no sense incurring legal fees by having lawyers draft and redraft the agreement when you know you're never going to sign it.

Silver Linings
As Freud once said, "Sometimes, a cigar is just a cigar." If your spouse isn't getting back to you about the agreement, saying he's too busy right now to look at it, maybe he is. One couple was on the verge of settling their case when tax season began. The husband was an accountant who relied heavily on returns for his income. He said he was just too busy to review the agreement; his wife was sure he was delaying. The truth was that the husband was too busy working to focus on the agreement, and negotiations had to wait until early May.

Maybe you're ready to be divorced—maybe it was your idea—but you're convinced your spouse would not agree to a deal unless he was hiding something. Despite all the financial disclosure, you're just not sure that you really know what assets your spouse has.

If this is the problem, tell your lawyer you want a representation in the agreement that your spouse has fully disclosed assets and debt, and if it later turns out your spouse lied, you have the right to reopen the deal.

Some people reject settlements because they don't understand the law, and they think they'll do better in court. For many spouses living in states where no-fault divorce is available, it is difficult to understand how a spouse can just walk out of the marriage without paying some kind of penalty. The "penalty" sought is usually an extra share of the marital assets. The law might provide, however, that no matter the reason for the divorce, assets are to be divided on a nearly 50/50 basis. An individual who refuses to accept this will never be able to settle on a 50/50 basis and might have to go through the expense of a trial just to hear a judge say the exact same thing.

Some people reject settlements because they feel the deal has been "shoved down their throats." Perhaps a lawyer was too pushy, and although the client didn't complain during the negotiations, she balks when it comes time to signing. Whatever the problem, discuss it with your lawyer. If yours is a case that needs to be decided by a judge because you just can't work out or sign a settlement agreement, stop the settlement process now before any more money is spent.

No Deal!

At what point is it worth throwing in the towel during settlement negotiations? Here are some criteria to consider:

- You think your spouse is hiding assets. You can have an expert locate them and testify to their existence in court. Remember, if you're sure that he's hiding assets but you can't prove it, a judge probably is not going to accept your position. Always consult with an attorney.

- The deal is too vague. For example, the proposal is that "visitation will be agreed upon later" or that "bank accounts will be divided according to the parties' wishes." Any proposal that's merely an agreement to agree is just putting off conflict, not resolving it. Reject it in favor of a specific proposal.

- The deal is unfair. Although that might seem obvious, it's not always easy to know when a deal is unfair. Here are some examples:

   You and your spouse ran up the credit card bills together, buying things for the family, but only one of you is going to be responsible for all the debt.

You filed "aggressive" joint tax returns, but now only one of you is expected to pay the debt.

You own two apartments, and your spouse wants both of them.

The test lawyers use for fairness is the law and the case law. You can use the "objective test": If you were not involved in this case, would you think the proposal was fair?

It's a Deal: Accepting the Package and Moving On

If the problem holding up the deal is your feeling that your spouse is hiding assets, but you can't prove it, you probably should take the deal.

If you're running out of money to pay a lawyer and the deal is reasonably fair, you probably should take it.

If neither one of you is completely happy—in fact, you're a little unhappy with the deal—you should probably take it. It's been said many times that the best deal is the one where both sides leave the table a little dissatisfied.

What Happens When the Settlement Is Reached?

When everyone agrees on the settlement, an attorney hired by one partner usually writes it up in a document called the *settlement agreement* or *stipulation of settlement*. Most of the agreement will have *boilerplate language*—language lawyers use all the time in agreements. For example, there's usually a provision that neither side will bother the other or that each side is responsible for his or her own debts. Lawyers can write the boilerplate provisions of the agreement very easily; the language is usually on a computer.

The heart of the agreement—usually custody, visitation, child support, or property distribution—can take a lawyer longer to draft. The agreement will be binding, just as though a judge had arrived at the decision after trial, so the lawyers need to make sure that there are no mistakes.

If your lawyer is the one who has drafted the agreement, he will review it with you and then send it to the other lawyer, who reviews it with your spouse. Finally, when the terms and language of the agreement are acceptable to everyone, you both sign on the dotted line. Usually, you need to sign five copies—one for the court, one for each lawyer, one for you, and one for your spouse. Some lawyers like clients to initial every page in addition to signing the agreement. That way, no one can later claim they didn't know what was written.

Silver Linings

Sometimes, when a divorce settlement is ready for signature, one or both parties will look for excuses not to sign. Experienced attorneys have seen this often. It represents a sudden, deep realization that the marriage has truly ended. It is not uncommon for one or both attorneys to encourage their clients to put pen to paper, have it done with, and go on with their lives.

This moment calls for reflection. It is a bittersweet moment—bitter because of the anger and hurt dragged out, perhaps to keep the relationship going at whatever level; sweet because a great weight has miraculously lifted from the shoulders of the embattled couple. Perhaps years of fighting and torturous nights are about to come to an end. Oh, there will be flashbacks. But, over time, those will fade into a daily routine that includes new projects and people.

So pick up the pen, and sign the agreement. It's okay to cry (or have a drink!).

The Cost of a Quick Divorce

Many couples we know have gotten their divorce for the cost of the court filing fees (usually under $300) and some photocopies. Others still needed a lawyer to work out the language of an agreement setting out their rights and responsibilities, tallying up costs of some $3,000 between the two of them.

In general, the less work the lawyers have to do, the cheaper your divorce will be.

Your Lawyer's Role

Even without a trial, if you have important issues to resolve, it's best to have a written agreement that you and your spouse can sign. The lawyer will draft that agreement, go over it with you, and send it to your spouse's lawyer who will review it and then go over it with your spouse. After the document is agreeable to everyone, one of the lawyers will probably also have to draft papers that can be submitted to a judge who will sign them and grant the divorce.

In some states, even when everything is agreed on, one of you might still have to go to court to testify. Your lawyer would conduct your examination, asking you legally required questions about the breakdown of your marriage, while you sit witness in front of a judge.

Do you really need a lawyer if you and your spouse have agreed on everything? In that instance, is there really anything for an attorney to do? Of course, you can get a quick divorce without a lawyer. However, if there's a chance you and your spouse will have outstanding issues, you're better off having legal counsel from the start.

The Default Divorce

Some spouses never answer the divorce papers they receive. They just don't care, or they figure they'll let you do all the work to get the divorce (maybe the way it was in the marriage). Do you have to wait until your spouse responds before you can move ahead?

Usually not. If you can prove that your spouse personally received the papers the law requires you to have served, you can probably get a divorce on default—your spouse's failure to respond. Although, by law, your spouse might have had 20 or 30 days to respond to the divorce papers before you are entitled to a default judgment, your judge might want you to wait three months before actually submitting the rest of the papers you need to be granted a divorce, just in case your spouse decides to respond after all.

There are some downsides to a default divorce:

◆ In some jurisdictions, your spouse can open the default within one year of its being granted if he or she can show "good cause" why it should be opened. That means your spouse can march into court and claim she never got the papers, or was sick at the time, or didn't understand them, and she wants a second chance. If the judge agrees that there is a reason to open the default, he will, and your divorce will in effect have to start all over again.

◆ People tend to follow agreements more than they follow orders. If you and your spouse negotiated an agreement, the chances are better that your spouse will abide by it than if a judge set down in an order what your spouse has to pay because he didn't come to court.

◆ You might actually do better if your spouse shows up in court. Maybe you can't prove how much money she earns, but if she were there, your lawyer could cross-examine her in such a way as to let the judge know that the tax return does not reflect all her income.

◆ The judge might refer certain issues to another judge, such as a special referee or master, thereby prolonging the amount of time it will take to get the case over with. Maybe the judge wants to give your spouse another chance to show up, so he refers the support hearing to another judge and tells you to notify your spouse about the new date. It's not fair, but courts tend to try to ensure that everyone has his day in court, even when the person who's getting the second chance is the defaulting party.

The scenarios described in this chapter provide some insight into what it takes to make a settlement happen. If you think you can settle and avoid litigation, it is in your best interest to make that settlement happen. Remember, the only winners in a protracted litigation are the lawyers! Judges in a trial will often try to give something to each party in the divorce, thereby imposing a form of settlement. Why not work out the issues yourselves? You and your spouse know better than anyone what's most important to each of you. If your marriage is at an end, orchestrate its conclusion in the least expensive, most expeditious way possible. Compromise where you feel comfortable—and weigh the cost of waging an all-out war. Push your pride and hard stance aside, but don't give up what's most important to you.

The Least You Need to Know

◆ Even if you qualify for a no-fault divorce, you might still need to resolve other issues, such as custody, visitation, and support.

◆ Never sign important papers without first consulting an attorney.

◆ In negotiations, be flexible; come up with new ideas. Argue issues rather than positions.

◆ Even with a quick divorce, you might still need a lawyer to draft documents.

◆ If you want to reject a deal, make sure that the basis for the rejection is rational, not purely emotional.

How to Find and Retain an Attorney

In This Chapter

- ◆ Choosing a lawyer who's right for you
- ◆ What to expect from your lawyer
- ◆ An introduction to fees
- ◆ Evaluating references
- ◆ How to interview a prospective lawyer

If you had a sizable wedding, you probably followed these traditions: You listened to various bands before choosing the music; you tasted food from different caterers before hiring a chef; and you studied portfolios before selecting a photographer. In an ironic twist of fate, getting divorced is easier in at least one way. You probably only need to find one person: a competent lawyer you like, trust, and can afford. And your spouse doesn't have to agree!

Why a Lawyer Might Be Essential

If you've been married a relatively short time and you don't have kids, if you don't have many assets or much debt, or if you and your spouse have worked everything out, you might be able to proceed without a lawyer. Court clerks are usually not allowed to give legal advice, but that doesn't mean they can't tell you where to file certain papers. And these days, with the new trend toward pro se divorce, legal forms are available for the taking on many state websites. If all else fails, legal form publishers sell "divorce kits" that you can use to do all the paperwork yourself.

Red Alert

Although divorce forms are now ubiquitous on the Internet, not all of them meet court standards. The court clerk in your county will be able to help you determine what forms you need, and perhaps even provide them and help you fill them out.

You Can Do It!

The American Academy of Matrimonial Lawyers in Chicago is a good source for names of qualified attorneys in your area. This organization sets high standards for membership. If you have allocated a sizable budget for your divorce case, this is the best place to start, although by all means not the only source for those of more modest means. You may reach them by phone at 312-263-6477 or via their website at www.aaml.org.

On the other hand, if you have children, if you have acquired assets (even if it's just a house and a pension or retirement plan), or if you and your spouse cannot agree on anything, you would be well-advised to seek legal counsel. Even if you agree on everything, getting a consultation is still money well-spent. It's perfectly acceptable to present a lawyer with the agreement you and your spouse have drafted and ask for comments. These days, with the new trend in "unbundled" and à la carte legal services, you may not need to break the bank to get all the protection you need.

One young father assumed that if his wife had custody of their young son, she would be free to move anywhere in the country. He was surprised, and relieved, to learn from his attorney that he could include a stipulation in his agreement that his wife not move more than 75 miles from her present location—provided he had not already moved himself. That was a provision he wanted, and got, in the agreement. For him, the attorney's fees spent were well worth it.

How to Choose the Best Lawyer for You

Even if your case seems pretty straightforward, go to someone who has handled matrimonial cases before. You don't need an attorney who works solely in that area, whose fees might be very high. But you do want someone who knows which papers have to be filed in which courthouse and who can take your case to trial if need be. Now is not the time to do your third cousin a favor by hiring her son, who was recently admitted to the bar.

Some very competent matrimonial lawyers will tell you from the outset that they do not go to court. They might be very good negotiators, but if your case doesn't settle, they will recommend another attorney, either in their firm or at another, to take over the case. For some people, that's fine. Others prefer to have an attorney who will go the distance. Be sure to ask.

When you call the lawyer, ask whether there is a fee for the initial consultation. Don't be shy. Some lawyers will see you for free; others will charge their usual hourly rate (which might be as much as $400 an hour in major metropolitan areas). The reasoning: they've already done work on your behalf (albeit during the consultation) by collecting the background information they need to begin. Others only bill you if they take your case. Still others bill by the task: so much for a finished separation agreement, so much for help in writing a motion, and so on.

Red Alert

Make sure you choose an attorney you can afford. Some lawyers want a large retainer, but their hourly rate is relatively low, or they have a junior attorney who can do some of the work at a lower hourly rate. If you want to hire a lawyer for only certain aspects of your divorce, you might prefer someone who specializes in unbundled services. If you have millions of dollars at stake, a legal powerhouse could be best for you. For more on attorney's fees, see Chapter 14I.

As you go about choosing an attorney, you might want to work other factors into the equation as well. How does the office look? You don't need skyline views, but if the office is dirty, or the magazines are months old, be wary. Will your legal papers be cared for the same way? On the other hand, some attorneys do share space with others, and upkeep of the office is not within their control.

Be sensitive, as well, to the amount of time you're kept in the waiting room. Your attorney's office shouldn't be Grand Central Station, after all. A small wait isn't always a bad sign, but if you are kept waiting more than 15 minutes, you might want to think twice about using that attorney. He or she should want to impress you most before you sign on. If you have to wait a long time before the initial consultation, what will it be like after you're a client?

Once you begin your meeting inside the lawyer's private office, are you constantly interrupted as the attorney takes calls? An emergency call is one thing, but a constant stream of interruptions is another sign that this lawyer might just be too busy—or too disinterested in your case.

Your First Meeting

When you're with an attorney for the first time, he or she will ask you for some background information about your situation. You should be told, briefly, how the laws work in your state and what that will mean for your own case. The lawyer can also tell you which court will handle your case. Is the court in your jurisdiction backlogged? Knowing this could determine your strategy in resolving your case—is it helpful to drag out the divorce or to end it quickly?

A lawyer who knows the judges and their individual biases and personalities will be ahead of the game. Unfortunately, a carefully weighted decision by a judge can be less common in some jurisdictions. Some for instance, may see all mothers as over-protective or all fathers as bill payers. Sometimes a decision can be made simply on the basis of whether the judge had a fight with his or her own spouse that day! A savvy attorney who has been around will be able to maneuver around a judge's personality or bias with more agility than someone who is new to the field or to the area.

Fees and Billing

During this first consultation, the lawyer should also explain his or her fees. Does she take a *retainer*—a lump-sum payment—up front? That practice is common. As the lawyer works on your case, she subtracts an amount equal to her hourly rate from the sum you have prepaid. For example, if you paid Attorney Greenfield $1,000 and her hourly rate is $100, you would have bought 10 hours of work in advance. Most will quote a flat rate for the retainer.

Other lawyers do not take a retainer and simply bill you every month as the case moves along. Some lawyers require that a cushion remain in the retainer until the case is concluded—for example, a few thousand dollars to cover the closing of a matter or to refund to you at the conclusion of the case. Whatever the arrangement, determine the details now. Remember, never sign on with a lawyer unless you have these financial details in writing. Be sure to read the fine print in your retainer agreement. More about fees in Chapter 14.

It's a Small, Small World

If your spouse has already hired an attorney, find out whether that individual has had any dealings with the lawyer you hope to hire. Remember, lawyers develop enemies and make friends. A lawyer will rarely come right out and say he hates your spouse's attorney and can't even call him or her, let alone negotiate, so you need to be crafty. Watch the attorney's reaction when you mention the lawyer's name. Ask whether they've had any cases against one another. Ask about the other lawyer's reputation.

You might even tell a white lie; say that you've heard the other attorney is impossible and ask whether there's any truth to it. A lawyer might be more willing to agree with an assessment that he or she thinks someone else has made.

> **Silver Linings**
>
> Hiring a lawyer who knows your spouse's lawyer and gets along with him or her puts you and your spouse in a position to resolve the case efficiently.

Good Referral Sources

Many people find a divorce lawyer through recommendation of a professional. Clergy, therapists, and marriage counselors might all be able to suggest divorce attorneys. Probably the most common way to get the name of a matrimonial attorney is through another attorney. You might already have a business lawyer, or maybe the lawyer who drew up your will is a friend and can recommend someone. Suppose you've gone to see one matrimonial lawyer, and you want the names of a few others. He or she will not be reluctant to give you some, especially if you explain that you can't afford the quoted fees.

Another source of referrals is friends who have been divorced. Sometimes they will recommend their ex-spouse's lawyer over their own, particularly if they thought they got the short end of the stick in the settlement. This, too, is a good way to get started.

Your local bar association might also have the names of attorneys who do matrimonial work, but that's a step away from using the Yellow Pages. Remember, lawyers can generally make it into the bar association list simply by joining the association, not by showing any particular level of expertise. Still, many of those lawyers will provide a consultation at a low fee or for free, and you might find one who meets your criteria. Some state bar associations have formal specialty certifications. If you can afford it, look for a certified family law or matrimonial specialist if your state has such certifications. If you are on a tighter budget, try to find a lawyer recommended by people you trust. (State bar associations are listed in Appendix C.)

Last but not least, the Yellow Pages can help. After all, you're only looking for an attorney with whom to have an initial consultation at this point. You're not actually hiring anyone blindly through any of these sources.

The Fox, the Shark, the Lamb, and the Peacemaker: A Look at Legal Styles

There are as many different legal styles as there are attorneys. Some attorneys are tough and aggressive and give you an immediate feeling of confidence or dislike, depending on your perspective. Others seem too nice or too soft-spoken, and you can't imagine them standing up to your spouse, let alone a judge.

Your attorney's legal style has to make you feel confident and comfortable. Of course, you want someone who will deftly help you negotiate and win power points in court. By the same token, if your lawyer is such a shark you're afraid to speak up and voice your concerns, all that aggression won't do you much good. In the end, it's a huge plus if you simply like your lawyer. Are you compatible? Can you be straightforward without feeling he or she is judgmental or condescending? Is your attorney genuinely concerned about you and the outcome of your case?

Some lawyers act one way when they are with clients, another when they're in front of a judge, and still another when they're with your spouse's lawyer. That's not always inconsistency; sometimes, it's just smarts. The best thing you can do is to watch prospective attorneys perform in court; this is difficult, of course, because legal schedules change at the drop of a hat.

Some lawyers are skilled negotiators, and others ace litigators. Some will take a case only if they are hired to handle everything. Others earn a living by selling a menu of services—one motion, settlement agreement, and counseling session at a time.

At the opposite end of the spectrum from sharks are the lawyers we refer to as "peacemakers." Specialists in collaborative law, these attorneys work together to provide clients with a structured, nonadversarial alternative to the adversarial system of dispute resolution. The collaborative movement in divorce law grew out of the realization that "some litigation, like nuclear war, is unwinnable," according to the Collaborative Law Center, based in Cincinnati. If you require that counsel attend to your rights with more vigilance than could ever happen in mediation, but at the same time you want to avoid conflict, a collaborative attorney could be for you. (Of course, a collaborative attorney can only sign on if your spouse hires a collaborative attorney. For a peacemaker to step in, you will both need to be on the same page this one last time.)

No matter what kind of lawyer you hire, you should request a client reference. Some attorneys might feel uncomfortable with the request because of confidentiality issues, but others might have clients who would be willing to talk.

CAUTION

Red Alert _____

Resist the temptation to hire a lawyer based on your notion of how that lawyer might relate to your spouse. You might think it's important for the lawyer to be able to stand up to your spouse. The truth is, the lawyer usually won't even speak to your spouse, only to his or her lawyer. Thus, the way your lawyer gets along with your spouse's lawyer is the issue. Don't worry about your spouse's opinion of your lawyer.

How to Interview a Lawyer

What exactly do you need to know before you hire a lawyer? Here are some questions to ask before you write a retainer check or sign on the dotted line.

Concerning general experience, ask these questions:

- How many matrimonial cases have you handled?

- How many of those cases went to trial? (An attorney who has done a lot of trials might not be a good negotiator. Keep that in mind, especially when the lawyer hasn't been in practice very long.)

- How many of these cases involved custody, support, business valuations, large financial settlements, or whatever issue feels like your major concern?

- Where did you go to law school? (Don't ask if the diploma is staring you in the face.)

- Are you experienced in unbundled divorce (or collaborative divorce, or whatever style of divorce you hope to enter)?

- Do you have the time to take on a new case now?

- Do you know my husband (or wife)?

- Do you know his or her attorney?

Ask about day-to-day operations:

◆ Will anyone (usually an associate) be assisting you on my case?

◆ What is his or her experience?

◆ Can I meet the associate now?

◆ What work would the associate do and what work would you do?

◆ Which one of you will negotiate the case? (If you want to be sure that the lawyer you are seeing is the negotiator, make that clear. You don't want an intern performing your quadruple bypass surgery, and you don't want an inexperienced associate you haven't met negotiating your divorce.)

◆ Who will try my case?

◆ Are you available to take phone calls?

◆ Is the associate available to take calls?

◆ What hours are you usually in the office?

◆ Do you have any time-consuming trials coming up?

◆ Will I get copies of all papers (letters, faxes, legal papers) in my case? (Be sure the answer is "yes.")

Make sure the fees are clear:

◆ What is your hourly billing rate?

◆ What is the associate's billing rate?

◆ If both you and the associate are working on my case at the same time, am I billed at your combined rates? (Some firms do that only if two attorneys are needed, such as at trial. Others do it routinely, and others only bill you at the higher attorney's rate.)

◆ Is your fee for trial different from your hourly rate? (Some attorneys charge a set fee for every day they are in court.)

◆ Do you charge a retainer, and how much is it?

◆ Will the billing arrangements be set out in writing? (Insist that they be.)

- What happens when the retainer is used up?

- Will you keep me informed each month as to how much of the retainer has been depleted?

- What happens if I get behind on the bills?

- Can you collect your fees from my spouse?

- How much am I billed for copies of all relevant documents? (If the fee is too high, you might want to make copies on your own.)

- What extra fees should I expect? (Your retainer will spell out your responsibility for "fees"—what the lawyer charges for his/her time versus "costs"—things like court filing fees, process server fees, excessive postage, messengers, stenographers, or similar out-of-pocket expenses.)

- Are those fees due in advance, and will I know in advance what they are?

- Am I billed for telephone calls?

- Do you have a minimum unit of time you bill me for? (Some lawyers will bill you for 5 or even 15 minutes when a call takes only 4 minutes.

Ask these questions about handling the case:

- Will I have input in decisions concerning strategy in my case?

- Will I be kept informed of all developments?

- What problems do you foresee arising in my case?

- What are your personal feelings about joint custody versus sole custody? Sometimes a lawyer has strong convictions one way or the other that could potentially affect the outcome of your case despite the fact that your wishes should prevail.

- Based on your experience, how much do you think my case will cost?

Before you make the final decision to sign on with a lawyer, be sure to fill out the following attorney checklist. It will guide you in your decision—and serve as a reminder about your agreement in the months to come.

Attorney Checklist

Name of attorney: _____

Address: _____

Size of firm: _____

Style of law practiced (e.g. traditional, unbundled, collaborative):

_____

Recommended by: _____

Date seen: _____

Consultation fee: _____

Office:

Is it an easy location for me to get to? _____

Was it relatively neat and clean? _____

Attorney:

Education: _____

Experience: _____

Was I kept waiting? _____

Were we interrupted? _____

Did I feel comfortable? _____

Did the attorney listen to me? _____

Fees:

Hourly billing rate: _____

Rates of others who might work on the case: _____

Retainer fee: _____

What happens when retainer is used up? _____

How often am I billed? _____

What happens if I can't pay? _____

Will attorney agree to collect from my spouse? _____

Who pays for disbursements and extra services? _____

Handling the case:

How long does the attorney think it will take to complete the case?

_____

Has the attorney handled cases like this before? _____

You're Hired!

After you have decided whom you want to represent you, a reputable lawyer will send you his or her written agreement concerning fees and will give you time to ask questions about the agreement before you sign it. If a lawyer asks you to sign an agreement in his or her office without giving you the chance to think it over, look for another lawyer. Sometimes it's worth showing the agreement to your business or personal lawyer, whom you trust. If and when you do return the written agreement, you usually have to include the retainer check required as your initial payment.

The Least You Need to Know

- Hire a competent attorney who makes you feel at ease, who you like, who's on your wavelength, and who your best instincts say you can trust.

- Hire an attorney competent in the kind of representation you seek. For instance, if you are purchasing services à la carte, make sure the attorney has provided unbundled representation or advice before. If you are seeking a peacemaker specializing in collaborative law, make sure you are not the first such case to sign on.

- Make sure you can afford the attorney's fees or are able to work out an arrangement for payment.

- Never pay a retainer fee without a guarantee that the unused portioned will be returned.

- Know whether an associate will be working on your case and determine the associate's billing rate. Find out whether you'll be billed for both the associate's time and the primary attorney's time when both are working on the case.

8

The Full-Service Attorney: What You Get in the Gold-Plated Divorce

In This Chapter

- ◆ How to decide whether you need or can afford full representation
- ◆ How to make sure your full-service lawyer is doing the right stuff
- ◆ Ethics questions
- ◆ When to find a new lawyer

Divorce settlements can be negotiated with the help of a mediator or even by you and your spouse, if the case is simple (no kids, no substantial assets, usually of short-term duration). If, on the other hand, your marriage is more complicated or there is conflict, you will need legal assistance. In many areas of the country you can decide how much legal help to buy, depending on your budget and your needs.

Is Full-Service Representation Right for You?

As you go about investigating your options and interviewing attorneys, the first thing you will need to decide is whether the traditional, full-service attorney is for you. It's important to state, up front, that virtually anyone might have a better outcome with a full-service attorney, provided they are able to pay the bill. Because full-service attorneys provide so much more, well, *service*, some bar associations, along with consumer advocates, have questioned whether selling services à la carte is even ethical. (As of this writing, the American Bar Association's Standard's Revision Task Force is deliberating this issue. They are weighing the financial needs of those seeking legal assistance against their responsibilities to the client.)

The conclusion arrived at by many experts who have examined the issue is this: although limited-scope legal assistance is by definition limited, it ends up being far more comprehensive in the long run for those of limited funds. According to the Conference of State Court Administrators, many middle-class clients run into trouble when they pay a hefty retainer to a full-service attorney. If the retainer runs out before the work is completed—the common scenario—the client will have to pay more for additional services. If the client has run out of funds, he will be forced to handle the rest of his divorce without any legal input at all. On the other hand, if the client had purchased legal services piecemeal—for the most complex tasks, only—he would wind up with more comprehensive legal representation for the duration of his divorce.

So while full representation is certainly in your best interest, that is only true if you can pay the hefty price. If you lack the tens of thousands of dollars required for such an investment, signing on with a full-service lawyer is risky, indeed.

"Some people pay lawyers an amount sufficient to buy the limited representation they need, but as a deposit for full-service representation," according to the American Bar Association. When the client cannot pay a later installment of the full-service fee, the lawyer can move to be relieved of counsel (the legal phrase for seeking permission to withdraw from a case). If the application is granted, it can leave the client and court frustrated, and it converts the former client into a *pro se* litigant.

If you have substantial property at stake, or if you are facing a custody war, it may be worth your while to go into debt to finance full-service legal representation for your divorce. If you are well-to-do, you should, by all means, sign on with a full-service lawyer or firm as your best means of protection. However, if you are a person of modest means with an interest in the law, and with no extraordinary issues at stake, you might do well to embrace the adage, "less is more."

> **Red Alert**
>
> An interest in and ability to navigate the law is key for the individual doing even part of the work him- or herself. Many people are simply incapable of dealing with the paperwork generated by divorce, let alone the sophisticated calculations, today derived from computer programs, needed to arrive at support payments or the tax ramifications of a property settlement. You need some proficiency in these areas, or you may find yourself lost, even with the best "unbundled" help.

Great Expectations

You have reviewed your personal circumstances and, after much soul searching, have decided that a full-service attorney is right for you. You have interviewed a number of attorneys, considered personal references, and finally, put down a hefty sum to retain the legal representation of your choice.

What should you expect? After you hire your matrimonial attorney, get ready to have a long, intense relationship with the person who will be your closest ally in your battle for "justice" against your spouse. You will be putting all your trust and faith into this person—once a stranger, but now piloting your case against the person who was once your lover.

This will no doubt be your first rebound relationship. Your divorce lawyer, and no one else, will be your most effective support during the separation and divorce process. Your relationship with your matrimonial attorney can be smooth or rocky, close or businesslike. You might come to think of your attorney as your confessor, therapist, Sir Galahad, or Amazon Woman.

> **Red Alert**
>
> Don't confuse your lawyer with your shrink and waste your precious dollars using your attorney to vent your anger, assuage your guilt, or comfort your feelings of loss. Instead, seek the help of a qualified psychotherapist.

But if you're going to make it through the divorce, you must banish these notions from your mind. Instead, it is to your advantage to learn (quickly) how to utilize your attorney in the most effective, cost-efficient way possible.

What Your Lawyer Should Be Doing and When

The practice of law is not a science, but it's not exactly an art either. There are certain things your attorney can and should be doing. For some guidelines, refer to the following list:

1. Your lawyer should have an overall plan for your case. This might simply mean that she plans to meet with your spouse's lawyer within the next month and settle the case, have documents drawn up within two weeks after that meeting, have them signed within two weeks after that, and then submit them to court.

   Maybe it means she's going to make an immediate request for support on your behalf and start demanding financial documents, with the goal of having your case ready for trial within six months.

   Maybe your lawyer can't say when things will happen because too much depends on what the other side wants; still, she should have a general idea of how the case will proceed from your side given any number of scenarios.

   One matrimonial lawyer tells us that clients often seek her out for a second opinion on their case. The most frequent complaint: their case has no direction, they see no end in sight, and it seems like they're always responding to their spouse's action with no overriding plan of their own. One such client eventually terminated his relationship with a lawyer—after five years of delay, during which he waited in limbo for decisions on child custody, child support payments, visitation schedules, and more. Often as not, delays were caused by his own attorney's exhausting schedule as her city's superstar divorce diva. She was on every talk show and in every newspaper, but somehow, in terms of this client, she was unable to do her job.

2. Early in your case, your lawyer should demand any and all financial documents in your spouse's possession so that you can learn what there is between you to divide up.

3. If you or your spouse has a pension or any kind of employee benefit, your lawyer should get a copy of the appropriate plan documents and account statements for the past few years. We know of more than one case where the lawyers agreed a pension would be divided up, only to discover that, under certain circumstances, the company had no obligation to pay the pension at all.

4. Your lawyer should assess whether any experts will be needed in your case. If your wife has a hat-making business she established during the marriage, you

might need a business appraiser to estimate the value of that business. Your lawyer should locate a well-respected forensic accountant or business appraiser now for possible later use.

Maybe custody will be an issue, and you'll need an expert to testify on your behalf.

In some jurisdictions, the judge will appoint an expert to report to the court, but you still might need someone to support your case. Your lawyer should start getting you the names of qualified people.

5. Your lawyer should, under almost all circumstances, tell your spouse's lawyer that you are willing to listen to any reasonable settlement proposal and to negotiate. Cases have been settled on the steps of the courthouse on the day of trial, so it's a good idea to leave the door open at all times.

6. Your lawyer should promptly respond to letters and phone calls and keep you informed of all such communication. Copies of letters should be sent to you within 24 hours of the lawyer's receipt. He or she should notify you about important phone calls—those concerning settlement proposals, for instance—as soon as possible. If the court hands down any decisions regarding your case, your lawyer should notify you at once.

   Your attorney should return your calls within 24 hours unless there's some reason why that's impossible—for instance, if she's in court or in the middle of a trial. On the other hand, you should only call when you have something to ask or something important to say. It's a good idea to write down questions and save them for a few days (unless they are urgent) so you can ask several at once. Some lawyers bill you a minimum of 15 minutes per call, so you might as well take up the time you'll be billed for anyway.

7. If your case is heading to trial, your attorney, with your input, should begin to interview and line up witnesses as needed. She should be sure to give your witnesses ample advance notice of the trial date.

8. If your case actually goes to trial, your lawyer should fully prepare you. If possible, you should visit the courthouse and even the courtroom in advance. Your lawyer should review the questions he himself plans to ask and alert you about what to expect during cross-examination.

   One attorney we know even tells her clients how to dress on the day they will be in court. ("Go for the schoolteacher look," she likes to say, "and leave the jewelry and fur at home.")

9. Throughout your case, your attorney should give you some sense of whether the law supports your position. No attorney worth her weight will guarantee you a victory, but a knowledgeable lawyer should be able to tell you whether there is a basis for your position and what is likely to happen if the case is tried.

10. If your case ends with a defeat at trial, or if there are any defeats along the way (say you lose a motion when the judge denies your request for something), your lawyer should be able to provide you with sound advice about whether to appeal or seek reconsideration at the trial level.

Crossing the Line

Observe the following attorney-client protocol:

◆ Although your lawyer might know more about you than your accountant, your shrink, or even your spouse, it's probably not a good idea to become drinking buddies. You want your lawyer to make objective decisions, not to cater to your demands because you've become best friends.

◆ In general, it's probably not a good idea for your lawyer to meet your kids. If the children are teenagers and their testimony is essential, then of course your attorney must meet them. But in other instances, they'll feel as though they're being made to take sides. Your attorney also runs the risk of being called as a witness in the case by virtue of his or her contact with the kids. (If your lawyer does become a witness, he or she will no longer be able to represent you.)

◆ Your attorney should not "come on" to you in any way whatsoever. (Agreeing to discuss your case on a Friday night at a fancy restaurant is not a good idea.) It doesn't matter if the attraction is mutual. If it's real, it can wait until your case is over. If your attorney does cross this line with you, report him or her to your state bar's ethics committee.

◆ Your attorney should not be in contact with your spouse if he or she has an attorney, unless his or her attorney has agreed to such contact.

◆ Your attorney should not have a business relationship of any kind with your spouse or his or her family. For example, if the attorney you want to use drew your will and your spouse's will, he or she should probably not be representing you in the divorce. (If your spouse consents, it might be okay, but the wiser course would be to find someone else.)

If the attorney had a prior business relationship as counsel for your jointly owned business, the attorney might be disqualified from representing either by you or your spouse. It is better to stipulate that a lawyer who has been representing you both in business activities should not act as a lawyer for one of you in a divorce.

What Your Attorney Needs to Know

Many clients aren't sure when they should contact their attorney about a potential problem—something that *might* be important to the case.

For instance, say your husband consistently brings the kids back a half hour late. Should you tell your lawyer? It depends. If she is hard at work on a motion about visitation, it's important that your attorney know about the problem right away. If a conference between the lawyers is not going to take place for another two weeks, it's probably better to save the call for later, when you have more questions to add.

The bottom line is this: if you're not sure whether something merits a call, call your attorney. When you're through speaking about the problem, ask whether you should call about this sort of issue in the future. Maybe your lawyer will simply ask you to keep a diary, which you can hand over for later use in your case. Maybe he'll want to be kept informed immediately, by phone.

How and When to Talk to Your Lawyer

With luck, you have hired a lawyer with whom you feel comfortable, and you can talk to him as you would a friend. Nevertheless, it's important to maintain the boundaries that should exist between any professional and client. Keep your conversation focused on the reason for the call. Chatting about what a bad person your spouse is might feel good at the time, but it won't feel so good when you get the bill for the venting session.

Avoid raising issues your lawyer has already addressed. If your lawyer starts saying such things as "We're going in circles," or "I think we've covered that," it's a gentle hint to move on to the next topic or say goodbye.

When on the phone with your lawyer, do avoid the tendency to speculate. No single activity on the phone probably wastes more of your legal fee dollars than speculating on why your spouse has done something, what he or she might do, what a judge might do, or what the other lawyer might do. The list is endless. Discussing the merits of your position is one thing; trying to figure out why something was done or what someone else will do is usually a waste of time.

If too much time has elapsed since you and your lawyer agreed on a plan of action (your lawyer was supposed to call your husband's lawyer last week and hasn't done it yet), then make the call. The squeaky wheel gets oiled, but be reasonable. If your lawyer said he or she would call you as soon as there is a decision in your case, don't call every day to check whether the decision has come.

How to Annoy a Lawyer

Unfortunately, you and your lawyer are probably in it for the long haul; some people have a longer relationship with their matrimonial attorneys than they had with their spouses.

Many attorneys (like many psychotherapists) will never let you know when they are annoyed with you. After all, they get paid to listen to you, and the more they listen, the more money they'll make. Indeed, for some, your endless complaints about your ex might help fill an otherwise empty time sheet. But let's assume you hear testiness in your lawyer's voice, or you think he or she is tired of your case. What do you do?

The best thing to do is to raise your concern. "You sound upset. Does it have to do with my case?" is one good opener. "Have I done something to annoy you?" is another. If you have, your attorney will appreciate the opportunity to let you know. Maybe your payment check bounced; perhaps you've been yelling at the secretary or keeping the attorney on the phone too long. Perhaps you told your spouse something your lawyer said to keep under wraps.

Apologize and make sure that the problem has not become so big that your lawyer feels she can no longer enthusiastically represent your case.

When to Fire Your Lawyer

One woman we know is in the fourth year of her divorce case—and on her third lawyer. Is she an exception? Not necessarily. Firing a lawyer is more common than you might think. Why does this happen? When is it warranted? And how do you pull it off?

Sometimes, lawyers are let go due to a straightforward personality clash. Characteristics you were willing to overlook when you hired your lawyer (a brash, aggressive personality or perhaps a cloying patronage) now bother you so much that you can't talk to him or her anymore. Maybe you feel that your lawyer has mishandled your case. You've gotten a second opinion and learned about strategies that could have saved you time and money. When you ask your lawyer about them, she just shrugs. Sometimes, it's just a feeling that your case needs fresh ideas. Your attorney seems tired of the whole thing and no longer has the enthusiasm she had when you first hired her. You might also feel that your lawyer is giving in too easily to the other side or that trust has been breached. You tell your lawyer something you do not want repeated to your spouse's lawyer, and your attorney goes right ahead and does just that.

Red Alert

The most common reason lawyers seek to fire clients is their failure to pay bills. Even if you've spent tens of thousands of dollars with a lawyer, if you are unable to meet a payment schedule, most lawyers will not want to continue representing you.

How do you fire your lawyer? The easiest way is to hire the replacement lawyer before you tell your present lawyer that you're making a change. Then, your new lawyer makes the call to your current lawyer and arranges to get your file, and you don't have to worry about the awkward moment of telling your lawyer it's over.

If you feel some personal statement or closure is in order, of course, you can send your attorney a short personal note. Depending on why you're "breaking up," you can simply send a thank-you note for past services or write a brief statement stating your beef. As with any close relationship, your lawyer might already be suspicious that you are unhappy with him or her, so your note or call might not be a total surprise.

Remember, most lawyers will expect to be paid in full before they release your file. Depending on where you live, your lawyer might be required to release your file even if you have yet to pay for all services—but the bill won't go away. If you have a problem paying the bill or a disagreement over the bill, discuss this with your present lawyer and work out an agreement. Or if agreement isn't possible, check out whether your state bar association has an arbitration protocol to resolve fee disputes between attorneys and clients. (Many states even offer free arbitration for this purpose.) Otherwise, have your new lawyer work things out for you.

The Least You Need to Know

- Before you hire a full-service attorney, make sure you can afford it.

- Your lawyer should have a game plan, be on top of your case, and keep you informed of all developments.

◆ Write out questions and call your lawyer with several at once, if possible, to save time. When in doubt about whether to let your lawyer know something has happened, call.

◆ Don't stick with your attorney if lines of communication have broken down.

◆ Find a new attorney before you fire your old one.

Chapter 9

Do-It-Yourself Divorce: Handling Your Case *Pro Se*

In This Chapter

- On your own behalf: an American tradition
- Is *pro se* for you?
- How the court can help you represent yourself
- The difference between legal information and legal advice

If methods of divorce are viewed along a spectrum, at one extreme are those employing full-service attorneys and at the other are those using no attorney at all. Despite the old adage that only a fool has himself for a client, increasingly more people are forgoing the expense of a lawyer and going "*pro se*," Latin for "on one's own behalf." A person who divorces *pro se* acts as his or her own attorney. In California, the process is referred to as *pro per*.

The *Pro Se* Legacy

Pro se representation has a long and honored history in the United States, according to Jona Goldschmidt, associate professor in the Department of

Criminal Justice at Loyola University in Chicago. "The Sixth Amendment does not provide merely that a defense shall be made for the accused; it grants to the accused personally the right to make his defense," Goldschmidt explains. "The Founders believed that self-representation was a basic right of free people." Thomas Paine, arguing in support of the 1776 Pennsylvania Declaration of Rights, said "either party … has a natural right to plead his own case; this right is consistent with safety, therefore, it is retained; but the parties may not be able … therefore the civil right of pleading by proxy, that is, by counsel, is an appendage to the natural right of self-representation …"

A Growing American Tradition

In line with Thomas Paine, Americans have been going to court on their own behalf since their system of jurisprudence began. The most common *pro se* litigant has historically been one who goes to small claims court, where suits are for $5,000 or less. But in recent years, with the explosion in legal costs and the burgeoning of legal information available over the Internet, divorces have increasingly been handled *pro se* as well.

In the State of Florida, for instance, 65 percent of divorce cases are filed *pro se*, according to the Office of the State Courts Administrator. At least one party is *pro se* in 85 percent of Florida divorces by the time a final judgment comes down, often because that individual has simply run out of cash. A survey showed that in Maricopa County, Arizona, where Phoenix is located, 88 percent of divorces had at least one *pro se* litigant, and both partners were *pro se* in 52 percent.

Sometimes people go *pro se* because they believe their divorce is intrinsically simple—perhaps they have been married for just a short time, or they have no assets or debts and no children, and they want to cleanly sever ties. Other times, people divorce *pro se* without that having been the original intent, often because the money has run out mid-way through the divorce process. Without the ability to pay an attorney, often these people are on their own.

Then there are those who never had the money for a lawyer in the first place. Instead of seeking legal solutions, they accept informal—and thus, unenforceable—agreements for things like child support and distribution of assets and debts. When these unbinding solutions fall apart, they find themselves among the great tide of Americans seeking divorce remedies *pro se*.

The Impact on the Court System

The nationwide glut of *pro se* divorce has brought chaos to family court: *pro se* litigants are often confused about which forms to sign. When they submit the right form, they may fill it out incorrectly. Some exploit the system in ways that attorneys would not, prolonging an action just to punish a spouse. The "Home Depot" approach to divorce has cut costs for many, but it also clogs a system never meant to serve amateurs. In short, *pro se* divorce has left a trail of turmoil in its wake, spewing a glut of extra work in family courts across the land.

In a typical *pro se* case, husband and wife—neither represented by counsel—might appear before a judge and start fighting. Often the divorcing spouses become aggressive and contentious, not just to each other, but to the judge, and they have little understanding of the law or their rights under it. Clueless about courtroom basics, including procedure, rules of evidence, legal reasoning, and even appropriate behavior and dress, *pro se* couples blunder through—introducing uncensored emotion and angst into a situation meant to be orderly and controlled. Their lack of knowledge leads to unreasonable expectations and impossible demands, all requiring a response from the judge.

The Difference Between Legal Information and Legal Advice

When the true magnitude of the *pro se* movement in the United States became clear, those working for the courts—clerks, judges, and others—were instructed they could provide the do-it-yourselfers with "information" but not advice. One reason is a 1977 court ruling that freed judges from the ethical responsibility of providing guidance. "The trial court is under no obligation to become an 'advocate' for or to assist and guide the *pro se* layman through the trial thicket," that pivotal ruling said.

On top of this, the judicial code of ethics specifically prohibits judges from dispensing advice or doing anything that would undermine their basic fairness and impartiality. Given such constraints, many judges refused to give the most basic feedback to litigants—the people involved often had legitimate complaints but they had no idea how to make a case in court, and no one stepped in to explain. Judges and clerks, for their part, were afraid to appear partial, and opted for passivity instead. In an effort to meet the letter of that law, some courts and judges were literally withholding information, sitting by as *pro se* litigants blundered through.

Help Is on the Way

Withholding help, courts and judges eventually realized, was not a workable plan. The reluctance to help *pro se* litigants navigate the court system was meant to encourage such individuals to play by the "rules" and seek legal help. But the strategy was ineffective and counterproductive. Without the ability to pay lawyers, and with *pro bono* attorneys in short supply, the *pro se* litigants could not be discouraged; they simply had nowhere else to turn—especially in family court. The attitude of discouragement turned out to be a barrier to justice, not to the *pro se* cases themselves.

In the last few years, many jurisdictions have stepped up to the plate. "We ought to make it clear that the two interests of being impartial and assisting *pro se* litigants are not mutually exclusive obligations," says Jona Goldschmidt. "At the end of the day, what we're talking about is minimal assistance, but assistance that is ultimately very necessary." In short, at the very least, court staff should be able to explain court processes and procedures to *pro se* litigants and tell them how to bring their problems before the court.

The new consensus: *pro se* litigants deserve to know the rules of the game—not only because it is their right, but also because their confusion has clogged the courts. Toward that end, jurisdictions across the United States have established outreach efforts to help the do-it-yourselfers, especially those going through *pro se* divorce.

> **CAUTION**
>
> ### Red Alert
>
> Even though the court clerk and judge are there to help you, there are limits. The line between legal information and legal advice still may not be crossed. Richard Zora, author of *The Self-Help Friendly Court: Designed from the Ground Up to Work for People without Lawyers* (NCSC, 2002), provides a clear example so that lay people may understand the difference between the two. "If you ask a question of two lawyers, and get two different answers, and neither lawyer is committing malpractice, that is legal advice," he explains. "But if there is only one right answer, that is legal information." Remember, it is your right to obtain legal information from the court. Neither the judge nor the clerk may provide you with legal advice.

In Ventura County, California, for instance, a large white Winnebago travels the highways and back roads, dispensing legal help to anyone who needs it on issues from divorce to civil suits. From the manicured streets of Leisure Village to the farming community of South Oxnard to the homeless population on Ventura Avenue, the Winnebago and its staff help residents fill out forms and understand the basics of the law.

In Vermont, *pro se* litigants can take courses offered by the court to aid them in the process. As with most other states, they can also download the forms they need, including "Complaint for Relief from Abuse," a "Petition to Modify Child Support," and many others. The most important one for the *pro se* individual could be the "Notice of Appearance," required before the person can show up in court and handle his or her case at all.

Tips for Do-It-Yourselfers

Vermont's tips to the *pro se* individual handling his or her own divorce are simple, but essential:

> Whenever you send anything to the court, you must send a copy to your spouse or the other parent, if it is a parentage case. If the other party has a lawyer, you must send the copy to the lawyer. Be sure to use your case's docket number on anything you send to the court.

> You must provide complete financial information when you are asked. If you try to hide income or property, the court will not trust you, and you could be prosecuted for a crime.

> The only time you may talk to the judge or magistrate is in a court hearing. The judge or magistrate are neutral and may not talk to parties about their case except in court. You may not try to talk to the judge or magistrate when the other party is not present.

> You must know the facts of your case and be able to present them to the judge or magistrate. The judge or magistrate will know little or nothing about you, your spouse, your children, or your concerns when the case begins. You need to know what is important to you and what information you want the judge to know. Do not waste your court time on matters that do not help the judge or magistrate to decide your case. Listen carefully to what is said. Make sure your presentation is relevant and to the point.

These are simple rules, but it is amazing how many *pro se* individuals are completely unaware of them.

Finally, many *pro se* litigants involved in divorce fail to realize that most divorce cases are resolved through settlement, not trial. Having come to court, they may rely on the judge to impose an external decision. Just because the couple has decided to divorce *pro se*, and no attorneys are involved, there is no reason for them to stop negotiating. It is often through negotiation that you arrive at a deal best for both of you. Do not let the excitement or immersion of representing yourself in court blind you to the possibility that you can walk away before trial and sign a deal of your own, if you so wish.

You Can Do It!

The State of Connecticut provides some basic instructions for *pro se* litigants:

You must file an "Appearance" form with the court clerk's office. It includes your name, address, telephone number, and signature. It tells the court that you are representing yourself. Filing it allows the court to contact you about all court events in your case.

You must follow the same court rules as lawyers, spelled out in the Connecticut Practice Book available in all courthouses.

Court clerks can give you information only. They cannot give you legal advice, such as telling you what you should do or what option makes the most sense in your particular case.

Courthouse law librarians can show you how to research a legal question or issue, or where to find a particular case or court form.

It is not our goal, in this chapter, to provide a manual for *pro se* divorce. Indeed, the instructions vary by state and personal situation to such a degree that everyone needs a manual of his or her own. Your best bet, if you are considering *pro se* divorce, is to get feedback of the most local variety possible. Contact your local family court to see what kind of help is available for free. Not every community dispatches a Winnebago to help litigants through, but most states offer some form of assistance in the "Home Depot" divorce.

Is *Pro Se* Divorce for You?

If you have been married just a short time, or if both you and your spouse have few or no assets and no children, *pro se* divorce could be your ticket. But those who go down this path, while potentially saving money, place themselves at risk.

"While self-representation is a right, it is also a heavy burden for persons exercising this right," Barrie Althoff, Washington State Bar Association Chief Disciplinary Counsel, recently wrote. "As our legal system tries to meet competing demands and needs of an increasingly complex society, the system itself becomes increasingly complex. Exercising the right to self-representation often becomes perilous to the self-represented person, a challenge to other participants in the system, and a strain on the system's limited resources. It is a right that most unrepresented persons would gladly give up if they could afford to retain legal counsel."

Indeed, the sheer legal logistics of the divorce effort can be tedious and enormously time-consuming, involving a large number of individual, detailed steps and requiring meticulous attention to detail. Some of the tasks you will have to attend to include drafting pleadings, including all accompanying forms and affidavits; filing the pleadings with the court; paying the court fees or applying for a waiver for indigent litigants; and fulfilling and documenting any mandatory requirements, such as attending a parenting class. Are you attentive to detail, comfortable with paperwork, persistent, and able to meet deadlines? Are you comfortable using a library, super organized, and able to read others' reactions and modify your actions? If not, despite your best intentions—and unless you have no other choice—*pro se* divorce may not be for you.

The bottom line: you may want to talk to a lawyer about your case before deciding to represent yourself.

The Least You Need to Know

- Despite the old adage that only a fool has himself for a client, increasingly more people are forgoing the expense of a lawyer and going *"pro se,"* Latin for "on one's own behalf."

- Jurisdictions across the United States have established outreach efforts to help those going through *pro se* divorce.

- The sheer legal logistics of the divorce effort can be tedious and enormously time-consuming.

- You may want to talk to a lawyer about your case before deciding to represent yourself.

Divorce à la Carte: Hiring a Lawyer for Specific Tasks

In This Chapter

◆ What to do if you can't afford a full-service attorney

◆ Hiring a lawyer to handle only what you can't do yourself

◆ Finding an *à la carte* attorney

◆ Understanding the role of the limited-scope attorney

If you have been married for more than a few years, if you have children, if you have received an inheritance, if you own a home or a business, or if you have a pension plan or other retirement/employment assets, then your divorce is going to involve some complexities. Under these circumstances and many others, specialized legal knowledge could benefit you enormously. In fact, it's probably required to make sure your rights are protected.

Like so many lower- and middle-income couples—those earning under $60,000 per year—what if you just don't have the money to pay a full-service attorney's hefty retainer fee? Should you risk representing yourself, as many now do? In the past, with most attorneys worried about the liability of handling cases piecemeal, hiring an attorney to handle your case might have been your only option. Fortunately, things have changed.

Americans of modest means are increasingly hiring attorneys as consultants and "piece-workers," paying for services that are especially complex and demanding of true expertise, but handling the rest themselves. The new style of divorce even has a special name—"unbundled divorce," meaning that legal services are dispensed individually—one motion, agreement, or issue at a time.

This option has become so popular, that the American Bar Association is developing, as of this writing, new professional standards to ensure that individuals who use lawyers for a part of their legal service are adequately protected. (For the latest American Bar Association standards, go to their website, www.abanet.org, and search for "unbundled legal services.")

A Fair Shake

It was Supreme Court Justice John Marshall Harlan who said, "It is to courts, or other quasi-judicial official bodies, that we ultimately look for the implementation of a regularized, orderly process of dispute settlement." But without the guarantee of fairness for all participants, the system of judges, courts, and lawyers, "the State's monopoly over techniques for binding conflict resolution could hardly be said to be acceptable."

There is no area of law more prone to inequality, more potentially unacceptable by Justice Harlan's definition, than domestic relations. Indeed, no matter what the crime, a criminal defendant is entitled to a state-appointed and state-funded attorney. But if a divorcing individual cannot afford an attorney, he or she is on his or her own. According to the American Bar Association, this includes "*most* low- and moderate-income families and individuals; that is, the *majority* of people in our nation!"

It is only in the last few years, with the increased acceptance of what the Bar Association refers to as "limited scope legal assistance," that fairness has been restored—at least to a degree. Limited scope assistance means the attorney will literally "unbundle" the full spectrum of services traditionally sold as a package and sell one service or task at a time.

> **Red Alert**
>
> Courts have held that lawyers who handle cases this way are not responsible to the client for malpractice in the same way they would be if they were handling the entire case. Thus, you get what you pay for: limited service, limited duty to the client.

The client and lawyer together can decide upon the service needed most, thus conferring some protection at a fraction of the cost. "By offering such assistance, private lawyers can make the legal services market work more efficiently," says the American Bar Association, in the process of converting "unmet legal needs into new practice opportunities."

In a sense, unbundled law is nothing new: Small business owners have long negotiated their own agreements and then asked lawyers for advice on a few points just prior to signing. Lawyers frequently draft documents reflecting agreements negotiated entirely by the principals with little input as to substance. And people scheduled for administrative hearings involving such issues as zoning or licensing matters often ask attorneys to help them prepare without attending themselves. Even in the area of family law, *pro se* clients frequently ask attorneys to review their settlement agreements before they sign on the dotted line.

But in the realm of divorce, law à la carte is relatively new. A decade ago, domestic relations lawyers were willing to work only in a full-service capacity. This was unfair to the lower- and middle-income Americans, who were priced out of the legal services they needed to protect their rights. By default, such individuals joined the ranks of those divorcing *pro se*. Yet with the legal system increasingly arcane and technical, it was often difficult for them to achieve the legal results they needed or deserved.

As *pro se* divorces continued to clog the courts through the 1990s, the status quo began to crumble under the weight of an urgent need. The watershed event, marking a change in the way courts and bar associations could choose to view partial representation, occurred in October 2000 in Baltimore, Maryland in the form of the First National Conference in Unbundled Legal Service. It was at the Baltimore conference that experts proposed national policies for unbundled legal services and made 26 recommendations suggesting, for instance, that the courts collaborate with bar associations and counsel to provide unbundled services to those who cannot afford full legal representation and that structures be put in place within the court system itself to identify individuals in need and refer them on.

Today, several years after the conference, the phenomenon of unbundled divorce is here to stay. Many judges and bar associations have

> **Red Alert**
>
> Some pundits have suggested that a little legal service can be more harmful than none at all. But in the vast majority of cases, the more legal help you have, the better. "An informed *pro se* litigant," says the American Bar Association, "is more capable than an uninformed one. A partially represented litigant is more capable than a wholly unrepresented litigant."

bowed to the popularity of what started as an underground movement in family law. Many legal ethicists have signed on as well, agreeing that, for divorcing couples who cannot afford full legal representation, the middle path—limited scope representation that confers attorney-client privilege—is the most viable choice and far more protective of their rights than going *pro se*. Even if you can't afford the same divorce lawyers as Brad Pitt and Jennifer Aniston, you can improve your chance of success if you obtain some legal help instead of going it totally alone. Slowly but surely, systems that enable you to divorce à la carte are being put in place.

How to Obtain Limited-Scope Legal Assistance for Your Divorce

If you are seeking true, unbundled legal representation for your divorce, your best bet may *not* be the storefront legal office that promises to take you through the process for anywhere from $99 to $399. At such offices, you'll often end up working with a paralegal who can fill out forms for you and file appropriate court documents, but who is not geared to offer specific, complex advice.

Likewise, websites offering inexpensive divorces are often staffed by paralegals filling out state divorce forms. If they give advice, it may be nothing more than a loss leader for continued services that end up being far more costly. One credible and helpful site we know offers a consultation session geared to your state for $34.95, without a specific time limit. For a yearly subscription fee of $89, you will be referred to attorneys in your area who, thereafter, charge $89 an hour. But remember, referral by your local Bar Association or self-help center is free.

In fact, although such options can yield appropriate legal feedback, we suggest you start your search for limited-scope legal representation offline, in the same place you would go for guidance as a litigant—the *pro se* assistance programs now available in jurisdictions across the United States. These centers, often state-sponsored and associated with the courts, can provide forms, videos, brochures, and general legal information, but you'll sometimes find attorneys working there and willing to provide advice. If the assistance program can't help you, they frequently can refer you to attorneys willing to help, one issue at a time.

If you aren't satisfied or if these attorneys charge too much, contact your local Bar Association to see if you can tap what's known as the "reduced fee panel," whose members charge for legal services based on income. Some won't handle divorce cases, but many do. If none of these venues helps you turn up your limited-scope attorney, you might check out the profiles approved by the group who coordinated the 2000 National Conference on Unbundled Legal Services, which you can find at www. unbundledlaw.org. You might also check out unbundled resources at the American Bar Association website, at www.abanet.org/legalservices/delivery/delunbund.html. (For inexpensive to free legal services, see www.abanet.org/legalservices/probono/ directory.html#).

As you search for a limited-scope divorce attorney, remember that this is a specialty, just like any other area of law. Sure, you *could* go to the highest-powered divorce firm in your city and request services à la carte, but that is unlikely to do you much good. Full-service divorce attorneys won't be seduced by the few hundred or couple thousand dollars you can part with to manage your marital woes. Even if they made an exception for you, they wouldn't be accustomed to delivering what you need. Likewise, storefront legal offices that function as "paralegal paper mills" are likely to consider your request to focus on an outside-the-box or individual issue a disruption to the work-flow. Instead, seek out an attorney who specializes in unbundled divorce—the kind of lawyer who handles family law as a solo practitioner, or as part of a small firm, who has recently decided to join the growing contingent of attorneys selling divorce services à la carte.

> **Silver Linings**
>
> Limited-scope legal assistance carries with it attorney-client privilege, but also limited attorney liability.

> **Red Alert**
>
> Buyer beware! Many websites that dispense legal services may provide initial legal advice on the cheap, but only as a loss leader for additional costly services. Many, ultimately, charge substantial fees.

The Limited-Scope Consult

Popular perception has it that an initial consultation with a divorce attorney is merely an opportunity to learn about fees and services. But Debbie Weecks, a limited-scope attorney from Sun City, Arizona, says there's no reason why the initial consultation can't "be several hours long with an express understanding that the attorney's role is limited to offering advice both procedurally and substantively based upon the information the client is able to provide."

The initial divorce consultation might be all you need to get through the rest of the divorce procedure on your own. "Interview and advice services may be the only ones a limited-service lawyer provides to a client," according to the American Bar Association. "The attorney-client relationship begins at the start of the interview and ends when it is over." In other words, the interview and advice (as opposed to mere information) comprise a discrete unit of legal work. While full-service attorneys often provide the initial consultation for free, as just the beginning of a long relationship, limited-scope lawyers virtually always charge at this point—it is often the first and last time the client will walk through the door.

You Can Do It!

If you are embarking upon divorce and haven't had legal input, this single session of legal advice can prove invaluable. Be sure to bring a checklist of any items or issues you'd like to cover to make sure no concern is overlooked.

The limitedservice lawyer could, for instance, give you preventive advice. Let's say you anticipate a custody battle and fear your spouse might run off with your child; in a single session with a knowledgeable attorney, you might learn how to file a motion requesting an emergency custody order and a requirement for your spouse to turn over his or her passport. Even if you have no money, you might be surprised how much emotional and financial risk you face when your marriage ends. A limited-scope attorney will keep you informed: Do you know how to protect your credit rating, not to mention your level of future debt, from a spouse on a spending spree? Are you aware that if you use your newly inherited money—no matter how small the amount—to pay household bills or if you combine it with marital monies in any way, it might become community property in some states?

Perhaps you are furious because your spouse is preventing you from seeing your daughter or son? A common assumption is that visitation is somehow tied to child support payments—no kid on Sunday, no money for your soon-to-be ex on Monday, regardless of what the judge ordered. The limited-scope attorney will quickly set you straight, letting you know in no uncertain terms that those issues are generally unrelated under the law, but by withholding payment, you risk not just child-support arrearages but criminal charges as well. On the other hand, if you continue to make the payments, you can correct the visitation situation *pro se*—with the attorney's behind-the-scenes advice.

In fact, if your rights are being violated in any way, the limited-service lawyer can tell you how to select and complete a simplified complaint form, request an order of default or evidentiary hearing, prepare and present the required testimony, and obtain a final order and judgment. Believe it or not, if your issues aren't outrageously tangled and messy, all of this can be accomplished in a single session, in the course of an afternoon. Depending on your city, you might be asked to pay the limited-scope attorney up to $250 an hour for his legal advice. This may sound like a lot, but the savings—not just in money but also heartache—could be immense.

Coaching, Ghostwriting, and Other Assistance

If your divorce is complex, you will benefit from additional meetings with your limited-scope attorney who can help you as a consultant, ghostwriter, and coach without ever talking to your spouse's attorney or spending a day in court.

The Domino Theory of Divorce

According to the American Bar Association, limited-service lawyers frequently prepare, or help clients to prepare, pleadings in divorce, child custody, child support, guardianship, and other domestic relations cases. "In many of these cases, filing the complaint triggers a default process—in effect, it tips the first domino in a row of legal dominos," the Bar Association says. "When the last domino falls, the default judgment is entered, and the case is over."

How might this work? In one common "domino" process, a husband and wife may have no substantial property—not even stock options or pension plans—and no children. If they want to sever ties amicably and inexpensively, one of them can be designated the initiating party, the so-called plaintiff or petitioner. The plaintiff will consult a limited-scope attorney, who may start by advising him on grounds for divorce. The most typical might be a no-fault petition based on irreconcilable differences, or a mutual separation without co-habitation for a fixed period of time, depending on your state law and the facts of your matter.

Then, at the appropriate juncture, the limited-scope attorney will help the plaintiff draft a complaint or petition requesting relief, in other words, a divorce or dissolution of marriage, depending on the language your state employs. The plaintiff will file the complaint and his spouse, by prior mutual agreement, simply will not respond. The plaintiff—with an attorney as a behind-the-scenes ghostwriter and coach—then files a motion for *default judgment* (a final judicial decision against a party who fails to file a required pleading or make an appearance in court). Again, the spouse does not contest. Finally, the limited-scope attorney advises his client to produce a witness who can appear at a default judgment hearing to substantiate that the divorce grounds are real. By prior arrangement, the opposing spouse, the "defendant" or "respondent," will not appear. After all the dominos have tumbled here, the judge enters a judgment of divorce and a divorce decree is issued.

The whole process has been swift and equitable—and for this particular couple, orders of magnitude less costly than full-service representation or even mediation. Alternatively, attempting this on their own—completely *pro se*—might have required months of false starts and might even have failed.

Couples involved in serious litigation involving custody disputes, child support, or abuse, on the other hand, would be best served by full representation; but even in these contentious situations, traditional legal help may simply be financially out of reach. In such instances, limited-scope attorneys can guide the way.

It might work like this: A victim of domestic violence, operating on instructions from her limited-scope lawyer, files a petition alleging abuse. After an *ex parte* hearing, in which she is representing herself, a judge may grant her an emergency protective order.

So what exactly has the limited-service lawyer done? He or she has helped the client fill out the petition, prepare supporting documents (*affidavits*, in legalspeak), and prepare for the hearing.

> **Divorce Dictionary** _____
>
> The Latin phrase **"ex parte"** literally means "*by, from,* or *for* one party." So, an *ex parte* hearing is a proceeding brought by one person in the absence of another.
>
> An **affidavit** is a statement of facts, which is sworn to (or affirmed) before an officer who has authority to administer an oath (for example, a notary public).

If the facts are in dispute, the attorney's role will be more pronounced. For one thing, the lawyer may accompany the client to an initial hearing, during which the other spouse may object. The result may be a second, adversarial hearing where both parties present evidence—and the limited-service attorney will want to appear there as well. In the aftermath of the hearing, the judge will often grant a longer-term protective order, frequently effective for six months or more. The American Bar Association says the order typically may enjoin the abuser from contact with the abused, ordering him to leave the family home. Temporary custody of children is then typically awarded to the abused, with a temporary visitation schedule for the noncustodial parent. Emergency family maintenance and attorney fees might also be awarded to the petitioner.

So what does all this have to do with divorce? For a small sum of money to purchase limited legal representation, the abused party in the aforementioned scenario has set a powerful legal precedent likely to carry over when she files for divorce. "The protective order can establish presumptions about how the similar divorce issues should be resolved," the Bar Association says. "These 'benchmarks' can substantially help the *pro se* party in the later divorce case."

In short, this is the domino theory of divorce at work, again.

How to Benefit from Unbundled Divorce

You will be most successful using unbundled services if you pick an attorney who specializes in the unbundled approach. According to Forrest Mosten, a pioneer in the unbundled movement, the most suitable lawyers want to "spend more time in direct contact with clients" and are "flexible with changing roles." Attorneys providing limited representation prefer "to teach clients skills and concepts" that will better their client's chances of winning—and maybe even improving their lives. If you want your divorce settled expeditiously, moreover, you should seek someone who appears at once proactive and nonadversarial. If the attorney can help you "prevent problems from ever ripening into conflict," Mosten explains, he or she is well-suited to the task.

Who is best suited for an unbundled divorce? Of course, the major qualification is financial: if you lack the money to pay for full-service representation, you may have no choice. Still, California attorney M. Sue Talia has some guidelines and tips.

If you choose limited representation, she says, you "must be prepared to live with the consequences of [your] decisions, even if they turn out differently than you hoped or expected." Talia says that the best candidates for this kind of legal help are able to emotionally detach from their situation. As with the most competent *pro se* litigants, they must be able to handle legal paperwork and juggle details, including financial details, in an organized and thorough way.

"In many situations, people who are less than ideal have no choice other than to accept limited representation and, therefore, to partially represent themselves," the American Bar Association says. In such instances, the litigants should try to assume only the simplest of the tasks and might seek further assistance from the self-help *pro se* programs in their state.

The Least You Need to Know

◆ These days, many lower- and middle-income couples choose to divorce *pro se*; but by doing so, they place themselves at risk. Most would come out ahead by hiring an attorney for the complex parts of their case.

◆ Look for unbundled divorce services through the same centers that dispense legal information to individuals divorcing *pro se*.

◆ If you cannot afford a full-service attorney and your legal funds are extremely limited, the best money you ever spend may be for a consultation with a limited scope attorney. You may have to pay by the hour, but you will walk away better understanding your needs and risks than if you never met with an attorney at all.

◆ Even if you are a *pro se* litigant, your limited-scope divorce attorney can help you draft documents and prepare your case every step of the way.

Chapter 11

Mediation, Arbitration, Collaboration

In This Chapter

- ◆ The advantages of mediation
- ◆ How to know when mediation is wrong for you
- ◆ How to choose a mediator
- ◆ The mediation process from beginning to end
- ◆ When to go into arbitration
- ◆ Why collaboration might be right for you

In the best of all possible worlds, couples facing divorce would work out agreements between themselves. That's often difficult, of course, because it's the very tendency to argue and diverge that leads to divorce in the first place. The most common solution is hiring attorneys—adversaries—who help the couple duke it out privately or in court. But for those who cherish the notion of an amicable parting, mediation is a popular and relatively inexpensive alternative.

Gentle Tactics

In *mediation*, you and your spouse settle the issues of your divorce with the help of a mediator, who could be a social worker or an attorney. Sometimes, a social worker and attorney pair up to help the divorcing couple. The mediator has multiple tasks, including the following:

Divorce Dictionary

Divorce **mediation** is a process whereby a neutral person—the mediator, who is usually a lawyer or social worker—works with the divorcing couple towards reaching a settlement agreement.

- Hearing the issues
- Understanding the personalities
- Explaining the divorce laws that form the necessary background to the mediation sessions
- Facilitating discussions
- Suggesting solutions to disputed issues
- Bringing the parties to a settlement agreement

A deft mediator will be able to handle two individuals who have been a couple, sleuth out the dynamics of their marital relationship, and cleverly bring them beyond their impasse towards a final resolution of all issues that must be resolved in order to compose a settlement agreement. This process takes more than one session. How long the process takes depends on how willing the parties are to compromise to finalize a settlement. If one person will not budge in his or her position, the mediator will have to use all his or her resources to break down the barriers to compromise. This may be futile in the end; but, if the couple is motivated to settle the case without litigation, eventually the mediator can help bring about compromise.

Say you want to keep the house and have primary custody of the children, but your spouse wants you to sell the house, split the sales proceeds, and have joint custody. There is a major challenge. The couple has a long way to go to reach an agreement. It's the mediator's job to find a practical solution that both parties can accept. At some point, the mediator will explain the laws of the state regarding these issues and how a court might likely rule. Then it is up to the parties to decide if they can live with the state's idea of a resolution or if they are willing to modify their respective positions to reach a solution they both prefer.

Once an agreement is reached, each spouse brings the agreement to his or her own attorney for review. If the lawyers find no questions or problems with the document, one of the attorneys drafts the requisite paperwork for approval by the parties. If everyone is in accord, the settlement agreement is then submitted to the court for the judge to sign. Once it is entered into the court's records, it is finalized.

Advantages of Mediation

For certain people, mediation is an appropriate way to reach an agreement. The best candidates are those who are willing to negotiate directly with their spouse to save money and heartache and get on with their lives. They are people who understand the value of avoiding expensive, heated litigation and are willing to give something up in order to settle quickly and as amicably as possible. Typically, they value the fact that, even in their darkest hour as a couple, they can sit down and talk face to face instead of interacting solely through their attorneys. Mediation usually takes place in a friendlier setting than legal meetings, although if there are hard feelings because of a betrayal, there can be considerable tension. But, more might be accomplished in a relaxed environment with the aid of a caring mediator.

As a process, mediation is also more flexible than the legal protocols that guide lawyers and courts. For example, you can set the pace of mediation sessions to correspond with your own emotional and logistical needs. After you enter the legal system, deadlines and delays come with the territory, imposed not just by individual judges, but also by the system's mandate to "move things along," or more likely, slowed by the huge backlog in the courts.

Finally, mediation might sometimes work better, even for the most calculating among us. Because mediators usually meet with both spouses at once, it's easier during these sessions to grasp just where the other is coming from. After all, you cannot read body language or facial expressions when your only communication comes from the whir of a lawyer's fax machine. This might be a plus for those who can "just tell" when their spouse is bluffing or when he or she won't budge.

When Mediation Works Best

Despite the advantages, mediation is not for everyone. The system works best when you and your spouse have mutually agreed you want a divorce, when each of you is fully informed of the other's assets and debts, and when, despite some disputes, you're both flexible and eager to work it out as amicably as you can.

Mediation also works best when you and your spouse are convinced of the mediator's impartiality. One lawyer tells us the most common reason clients give for having left mediation is the feeling that the mediator had begun to favor the other spouse.

Mediation also works best when there are no urgent needs that must be resolved with a judge's help. For example, if your spouse has cut off support and refuses to reinstate it, you can't afford the luxury of meeting once a week with a mediator to resolve the issue. You need a lawyer to race into court and ask a judge to order your spouse to resume supporting you now.

> **Silver Linings**
>
> Mediation is not binding. If you are not satisfied with the outcome of your mediation, you might have wasted some time and money, but you can start all over by going to court.

Finally, mediation works best when both individuals have had a relatively equal relationship. If one member of the couple has, historically, dominated the other, it may be more difficult for both to participate in the give-and-take of mediation.

When to Avoid Mediation

Take our "mediation-elimination" quiz. If you answer any of the following questions with a "no," mediation is not for you:

- Do we both want this divorce?
- Do I know what our assets and debts are?
- Are we communicating?
- Can we both be flexible?

> **Red Alert**
>
> If you do not know the value of assets in your marriage—pension or retirement plans, a business—or your spouse's income, mediation is probably not for you. The reason: The mediator lacks any authority to make one of you reveal assets to the other. An attorney lacks that authority, too, but he or she can go to a judge. The judge, in turn, can render a ruling requiring your spouse to reveal assets. The judge can penalize your spouse for refusing to cooperate, or worse, for lying. The mediator has no such power and does not give legal advice to either party.

Although wonderful in concept, mediation could be a disaster in certain situations. Even if you passed the "elimination quiz," take time to review the following list. As you consider your response to the questions, you might conclude that mediation is not for you:

◆ If you and your spouse are not talking, mediation sessions are not the time to start, and mediation is probably not for you. Remember, the mediator is not a marriage counselor but rather a conflict resolution specialist whose job it is to help the two of you address and resolve issues. If you're not even talking, there's not much the mediator can do.

◆ If you or your spouse harbor extreme feelings of anger, mediation probably won't work.

◆ If one of you does not want the divorce, mediation doesn't stand a chance.

◆ If you're trying mediation but you feel the mediator is siding with your spouse, you should stop the process. Maybe you're being paranoid, but it doesn't matter. When one of you has lost confidence, you should each retain a lawyer.

Red Alert

Many believe that mediation is not a fair process for women. The reason given is that some men are able to bully the women during the mediation process, and some mediators will not be strong enough to counter the bullying or apprise the woman of her rights under the law. If you are a woman (or a man who lived with a bully for a wife), and this scenario rings true, be sure the mediator is aware of your concerns. Alternatively, you might decide this process won't work for you.

◆ Mediators do not have "attorney-client" privilege in many states. That means that anything you tell the mediator can later come out in court. If you have secrets that impact your case, you should probably avoid mediation (or keep the secrets to yourself).

Mary Pauling found herself in that situation not long ago. She and her husband George decided to use mediation on the recommendation of friends—it worked for them. Each was in love with someone else, and there were no hard feelings. They had a four-year-old son, Evan, and they'd decided Mary would have custody. The only issue was the amount of support George would pay.

At the second session, before George arrived, Mary confided to the mediator that Evan was actually her boyfriend's son, not George's. The mediator felt obligated to share this information with George because it would have enormous impact on whether he even wanted to see Evan again, let alone provide for his support. Mary left before George arrived and hired a lawyer the next day, but that was a day too late. Had Mary gone to an attorney in the first place and made the same confession, the attorney could not have revealed anything without her consent.

◆ If your case is very simple, it might not pay to use a mediator because attorneys will have to review the agreement anyway, and you might be better off just starting out with those attorneys. Remember, mediation is useful when there are unresolved issues between you and your spouse. If there are no issues, you might as well go straight to lawyers to draft the agreement.

Choosing a Mediator

Unfortunately, there are no standards for mediators, and in most states, anyone can hang a shingle and call himself or herself a mediator. Your state or city might have an organization that admits mediators based on training and accumulated experience, and if so, look there for a list of references. Your local bar association might be able to give you the names of reputable mediators. Word of mouth is a good way to locate an appropriate professional as well.

The mediator should at least have a degree in social work, counseling, or psychology. It is helpful, but not imperative, that the mediator have a law degree as well. Even without a law degree, however, the mediator should be completely familiar with the divorce laws of your state.

How can you find out whether the mediator knows the law? Ask how long he has been doing mediation, how many cases he has handled, and how he keeps up with new developments in the law. The prospective mediator should be able to answer your questions without sounding defensive.

Find out what and how the mediator charges before you hire one. You and your spouse should agree on how the mediator's fees will be paid. Will you each pay half the fee at the end of each session, or will one of you pay all of it and be reimbursed when the case is over and the assets are divided? Will one of you foot the bill with no reimbursement? If you cannot work that out with the mediator's help, mediation might not be for you.

Finally, ask for references—and call those references. The mediator might not be willing to give you the names of clients (and should not do so without the clients' prior consent), but the mediator should be able to give you the names of attorneys familiar with his or her work. After all, the mediator should be sending couples to attorneys to review any agreement before it is signed. If the mediator doesn't know any attorneys or can't give you any names, interview someone else. Sometimes, it is useful to engage in a dual mediation process where there are two mediators, one a lawyer and one a psychologist. This raises the cost, but in the right case, it might be worth it.

Before choosing your mediator, fill out the candidate's credentials on the following checklist to decide whether a given mediator is for you:

Mediator Checklist

Mediator's name: _____

Address: _____

Date seen: _____

Mediator's education: _____

Mediator's experience: _____

Mediator's fees: _____

How fees will be paid: _____

Did I feel comfortable with the mediator? _____

Did the mediator seem to favor one of us over the other? _____

Was the mediator able to work out the payment of fees between us?

_____

Does the mediator have an overall plan for our case? _____

Will the mediator draft an agreement if we come to one? _____

Mediation as a Process

What goes on behind closed doors in mediation?

A mediator will often start the process by asking you to write out your goals—what you would like to come away with. You will be asked to anticipate such problem areas as custody or support. You might be asked to set forth your assets and liabilities in a sworn (notarized) statement, just as you would have done with an attorney. This gives everyone involved a clear idea of what you're dealing with and how far apart you really are.

The mediator will work with both of you to divide assets, allocate support, and resolve custody and visitation or any other disputes. The mediator should not advocate one side over the other but should help you both by noting where compromise might work or by coming up with new solutions.

If, at any point during the process, you don't like the way things are going, feel free to consult with an attorney. If you need to consult with your lawyer more than once or twice, however, you might be better off stopping the mediation and just using the attorney. After all, why pay for two professionals?

Red Alert

What if one of you really likes the mediator you're thinking of and the other doesn't? Don't be pressured. If you do not feel entirely comfortable, turn the mediator down. Besides, it's dangerous to start out with someone one of you likes better. As in the case of choosing an attorney, the mediator should be someone competent who you both like and feel relatively comfortable with.

In any event, after you resolve all the issues, the mediator will draft a written agreement and suggest that you have it reviewed by an attorney. Your attorney will want to make sure that all possible issues have been covered. For example, some people don't realize they're entitled to part of their spouse's pension or other employment benefits. Maybe the mediator overlooked this, or maybe you discussed it but you decided to waive any right to the pension or plan. Either way, your lawyer should point out your rights and suggest that you pursue them or waive them in writing. The agreement is then ready for signing by the parties and then brought before the judge for signing.

Can you go through the mediation process without ever using a lawyer? Possibly. But if you had enough issues to see a mediator, you're probably better off spending a little more on an attorney and making sure that everything is okay.

If you dislike the result of your mediation, *don't sign the agreement*. Say that you and your spouse have just spent four months and $2,000 on mediation, and as the process nears an end, you just don't feel comfortable. Perhaps you even feel the agreement is being "shoved down your throat." Maybe you began to think the mediator was siding with your spouse from the beginning, but you were afraid to say anything, or you feel as though your spouse is "pulling a fast one."

If there is some legitimate basis to your feeling, do not sign the agreement. Seek advice from an attorney. On the other hand, if the real problem is that you're just not ready to end the marriage, or you still hold the faint glimmer of hope that the marriage can be saved, you need to discuss these feelings with a therapist. The truth might be that you'll never be ready to sign an agreement, no matter how fair. If you are consciously or subconsciously subverting the negotiation process, don't take comfort in the thought that your spouse won't be able to get a divorce. You will simply be laying the groundwork for a litigated divorce. If you are in this situation, a consultation with a mental health professional might help you avoid the economic and emotional stress and time of going to court.

Silver Linings

The law is not the only consideration when trying to reach a settlement. If you can put any anger you might have aside, you might be able to appeal to your sense of fairness. The mediation process allows you to come to a settlement based on knowledge that only you and your spouse have about each other's temperaments and financial and emotional situations. If you can see past the breakup, both parties might come away from the process with less damage than simply relying on the laws of your state.

If You Think Your Spouse Is Lying

It might be your suspicion or your experience with your spouse that leads you to believe he or she is covering up the truth about finances or other matters. How is it possible to know, and, if it's true, how is it possible to continue using mediation as the vehicle to settle your case?

In a litigated divorce, the process of discovery is supposed to reveal the assets of both parties. This is a mandatory process that yields evidence admissible in court. During mediation, however, discovery is not required. The divorcing couple relies on mutual trust that the other will tell the truth and bring in all documents showing financial status.

How can you make sure that your spouse is telling the truth? If you are suspicious, hire a forensic accountant to review the financial papers and books of your spouse, especially if you are not a financial expert. Not only will a professional be able to notice a deficiency, but the very fact that an accountant is scrutinizing your spouse's affairs will help to keep him or her honest during the negotiations.

Reliving Old Patterns During Your Mediation

It may not be surprising to you to hear that the patterns of interaction that typified your marriage will characterize your behavior as a couple during mediation. It is the job of a skillful mediator to help the couple break the pattern that put one of the spouses in the driver's seat and give strength to the other spouse. Accomplishing this doesn't mean the mediator is siding with one party or the other; instead, it is the only way that a fair settlement can be established.

Rebecca did not want to mediate her divorce with Michael, but he insisted she not hire an attorney and give mediation a chance. She hesitated for a long time, but finally gave in, as was usually the case in their marriage. Once at the mediator's office, Michael took center stage in presenting the "facts" to back up why he wanted a divorce and how the settlement should look. Rebecca disagreed with Michael's version of the "facts" but was reticent to speak up.

The mediator was skillful in noticing the pattern of interaction between the two and encouraged Rebecca to speak her mind. This skillful mediator simply would not allow Michael to gain the upper hand or let a subject drop without a full hearing from both Rebecca and Michael on all issues during the negotiation sessions. As a result, the mediator was able to facilitate a fair settlement.

All About Arbitration

Arbitration is sometimes confused with mediation, but it's really quite different. In arbitration, an individual—the arbitrator—hears your case outside the court system and makes a decision that usually cannot be appealed. As in a court of law, you and your spouse would generally be represented by a lawyer, and depending on the arbitrator, he or she might even insist that the rules of evidence in your jurisdiction be followed by the book.

> **Divorce Dictionary**
>
> In **arbitration**, a case is decided by an official arbitrator who hears all evidence and makes a decision. Individuals are represented by attorneys. Unlike litigating in court, there are no appeals.

The arbitration itself usually takes place in an office around a conference table. In many ways, arbitration is like going to court, but unlike court, where you can appeal, the arbitrator's word is final.

Unlike lawyers, arbitrators do not make an effort to settle the case. They certainly do not do what mediators do—identify issues and then help you resolve them together. Instead, an arbitrator is more like a judge. You come to the table (with your lawyer), ready to present your side. The issues, whatever they might be, have already been determined by you and your lawyer. You must present the arbitrator with your position on those issues and argue your case as cogently as you can.

Given the restrictions, why would anyone ever choose to go into arbitration rather than to a judge? The reasons, for some, are compelling:

♦ Depending on where you live, it could take as long as a year to go before a judge, whereas an arbitrator might be readily available.

♦ You and your spouse might both feel that neither of you will appeal, no matter what the outcome. Maybe you have no more money or you simply can't withstand another round of litigation. Because you're not going to appeal, arbitration has no downside.

♦ Everything is private. Unlike a trial, in an arbitration proceeding, there is no public record of who said what or which records were put into evidence.

♦ Arbitration might be cheaper than a trial. In some jurisdictions, trials do not take place day after day until they are finished. Rather, the judge might schedule one day for your case in January, one day in March, two days in April, and so on. You get the picture. Each time your lawyer has to refresh himself about your case, it costs you. Arbitrators, on the other hand, usually meet day after day until your case is fully heard. Your lawyer only has to prepare once.

♦ Your case may have been in court (without being tried) for so long that you just want it over with, so you're more than willing to go to arbitration to save time.

After you and your spouse have agreed you want to have your case arbitrated, the lawyers usually pick the arbitrator. Often, arbitrators are retired judges or lawyers with an area of expertise, such as matrimonial law, and are thus quite competent. As with mediators, their fees must be paid by you and your spouse.

Collaborative Divorce

Finally, there's a new, peaceable method for cutting the ties, known by the name of collaborative divorce. If you need more protection than a mediator could possibly offer but still want your divorce to be as amicable as possible, a "collaborative lawyer" may be for you. According to the Collaborative Law Center of Cincinnati, OH, "Collaborative Law is representation without litigation. It provides clients

Red Alert

Nothing in the collaborative law agreement precludes parties from litigating if the process breaks down. But if they do so, they will have to move ahead with new attorneys.

and their lawyers with a new, formal and strictly nonadversarial approach to resolving legal disputes. It encourages mature, cooperative and noncombative behavior as the parties contract to eliminate litigation as an option. The goal of collaborative law is to offer lawyers and their clients a structured, nonadversarial alternative to an increasingly adversarial system of dispute resolution. By entering into a collaborative law participation agreement, lawyers and their clients limit the lawyer's role to that of negotiator, capable of representation toward settlement but not going to court.

What Sets Collaborative Law Apart

How is collaborative law different from mediation? Mediation involves the use of a neutral third party to facilitate the negotiation and settlement of a dispute. Parties can always walk out of mediation and decide to litigate instead. However, in collaborative law cases, lawyers and their clients will talk and negotiate without the assistance of a neutral third party, unless they find such an intervention would be useful. They are committed to continuing the dialogue until a satisfactory solution is reached, since litigation is not an option with these attorneys. Should the talks break down, the divorcing couple would be bound to find new counsel and start the process again. Even though litigation has been ruled out, clients remain protected in a way not possible in mediation. Whereas a mediator does not have attorney-client privilege, a collaborative lawyer never ceases to be the client's advocate, and privilege is maintained.

A Way to Stop the Madness

In an issue of *American Journal of Family Law*, Gregg Herman, a family law attorney, described one colleague's decision to enter the field of collaborative divorce. The attorney had represented clients in many contentious divorces and she found that often, even after the case had been settled or decided in court, the ex-husband and wife would find new things to fight about, and new hostilities would erupt. The children were the primary victims of this endless warfare. The attorney knew she could no longer be party to it when, after a particularly vicious battle, a 14-year-old girl committed suicide with her father's gun. The attorney was in court representing the devastated mother because the father had filed a motion for reimbursement of funeral expenses.

According to Herman, "All of the anger and hate which is intrinsic to family law litigation made her feel that her legal abilities were being abused. Rather than helping people, she felt that she was adding to their problems."

There had to be a better way. This lawyer and many others unwilling to perpetuate the madness found another model—"collaborative law," in which they help to solve problems instead of making them worse. Contractually bound to settle the case out of court, the attorneys will withdraw if the case goes to trial. The real intent is not to bail, of course, but to help their clients sustain amicable relationships long-term, especially when children are involved.

Is Collaborative Divorce for You?

Is collaborative divorce for you? Guidelines come from Pauline Tesler, a Mill Valley, California attorney and pioneering founder of the new model. "Selecting the dispute resolution process that best suits the couple's unique needs maximizes the likelihood of out-of-court settlement," Tesler states. "Choosing a process which is a bad fit can result in failed negotiations, anger, and a more adversarial divorce than might have been necessary."

According to Tesler, "mediation works best when both spouses share a basic trust in one another's honesty and are reasonably at peace with the fact of the divorce." Still, disparity—lopsided bargaining power or financial sophistication—can play havoc with the mediation process, with no guarantee that a neutral mediator will get it right.

In that instance, those hoping for an amicable divorce should consider collaborative law. Collaborative law "can help spouses arrive at creative settlements even when the problems are complex," Tesler says. "The settlement results can often be more creative than in other models, because neither lawyer succeeds in the job she or he was hired for unless both spouses' legitimate needs are met in the settlement."

The model may not be available everywhere. States that are particularly active in this area of law include California, Georgia, Connecticut, Minnesota, Texas, Wisconsin, and Ohio.

Red Alert

> If you want the best deal possible no matter what the cost or emotional pain for others, the collaborative divorce model is not for you.

The Least You Need to Know

◆ Mediation works best when both of you can communicate, when you know what assets and liabilities you have, and when you are both willing to be flexible and you want the process to work.

◆ Mediators should have a degree in social work, counseling, psychology, and possibly law. But even without a law degree, a mediator should be thoroughly familiar with the matrimonial laws of your state.

◆ Any agreement decided with a mediator should still be reviewed by an attorney.

◆ Do not sign an agreement with which you feel uncomfortable, but be sure that your discomfort is rooted in logic, not emotion.

◆ Consider arbitration if you and your spouse would not have appealed a trial judge's decision anyway, or if your case has dragged on due to a backlogged court. But, be sure you've gathered all the evidence you need for a fair hearing.

◆ If you want individual representation and the comfort of attorney-client privilege, but you also want your divorce to be amicable, consider hiring a collaborative lawyer—as long as your soon-to-be ex will hire one, too.

Chapter 12

Taking Your Case to Court

In This Chapter

- ◆ The judge: If you two can't decide, he or she will do it for you
- ◆ Understanding courtspeak: conferences, motions, and discovery
- ◆ The difference between family and civil court
- ◆ A word about military law
- ◆ Deciding to appeal: Is it worth it?

You and your spouse have tried for months, maybe even years, to settle your divorce on your own, but you've gotten nowhere. Your lawyer hasn't had any luck either. Finally, you've reached the end of the line: It's time to go to court.

Here Comes the Judge

Perhaps the most important person you'll deal with as you go to trial is the judge—just another human being, albeit one who has the power to make decisions for you and your spouse. In a small number of states, your case might be tried by a jury, but if not, a judge will decide the outcome. As the decider (*trier of fact*, in courtspeak), the judge listens, takes notes, sometimes asks questions, and when the case is over, makes a decision.

Because the judge is also the *referee*, he will set the schedule of the trial, make rulings when the lawyers disagree, and rap the gavel if the courtroom gets out of control. You might have one judge throughout the case or several different judges until trial, at which time you will have only one judge.

Behind Closed Doors: How Judges Resolve Issues

While those going through divorce await trial, they often find themselves unable to resolve even the most mundane issues on their own. When that happens, the judge on their case gets involved. For instance, John wanted to have his sons spend the last three weeks of the summer with him so that they could visit his sister (their aunt) and her family, who were in the United States for only a short time. Sara—the boys' mother—had already enrolled them in summer camp for those same weeks. Because John and Sara could not agree on a solution to this conflict, their lawyers were asked to intervene. Discussions between the lawyers also went nowhere.

Red Alert

If you attend a court matter, keep in mind that you will be in front of the judge who might eventually try your case. Do your best to make a good impression. Speak in a conversational tone and do not display emotion or make threats. Even if the current judge will not try your case, you stand a better chance of winning a request if the judge is happy with your demeanor.

Red Alert

In most states, you must file an application to put an issue before a judge for a ruling. The application has to be made through a "motion" or "order to show cause."

Finally, John's lawyer asked for a ruling from the judge. John brought a brochure from the summer camp, showing three sessions. He had contacted the camp and told the judge that the first and second sessions still had room for his sons. He explained that his sister, who lived in Spain, would only be in the United States for the last three weeks of the summer.

The judge immediately granted John his request. The cost to him? Less than $500 in legal fees. As an added bonus, he made a good impression on the judge (he had done his homework and had delivered his pitch calmly), whereas Sara seemed unreasonable and stressed. Not only would John get the boys when he wanted them, but he would also be walking into the upcoming trial with a reputation for reason, responsibility, and calmness.

Remember, if you have the same issue as John but lack an attorney, you are entitled to file an application with the court as a *pro se* to make the same request. If you do, be sure you have gotten as much legal guidance as possible beforehand—especially if your spouse has legal representation.

We suggest that if you have limited resources, you save them for a situation like this. If you are purchasing legal services a la carte, there is no better way to spend your limited resources than in pursuit of extra time with your children. And there is no question that such legal input will help you in the end.

How to Impress the Judge

Given the fact that your judge might be determining your fate and, if you have children, theirs too, making a good impression is vital. To make sure that you score points with this powerful figure, study the following helpful tips for appropriate behavior whenever you have occasion to be before your judge:

◆ Avoid gesticulating wildly with your hands. The judge might not remember the issues raised up until the trial, but if you had made a spectacle of yourself when before him, he might well remember that! Sometimes, it's hard to maintain control when you know your spouse is lying, but you have to do it.

◆ If your lawyer is present, it's best that you follow accepted courtroom protocol and not speak at all unless your lawyer instructs you to or the judge asks you a question directly. If you think your lawyer is missing an issue (or the boat), nudge her gently and ask if you can speak to her for a minute. You can also write a note and push it over to your lawyer.

◆ If you are a *pro se* litigant, be sure you have learned as much as possible about procedure and expectations before stepping into the court.

◆ Remember, don't overreact.

Going Through the Motions

Sometimes you cannot wait until the trial to resolve certain conflicts, and your attorney will have to make a request, usually in writing, for a court ruling on a matter within a period of days (a *motion*) or on an emergency basis (an *order to show cause*). If you want to obtain immediate, temporary support until the trial commences, temporary custody of the children, a visitation schedule, lawyer's

Divorce Dictionary

A **motion** is a request made of a judge while an action is pending or at trial. Motions can be made in writing for the court to consider, or orally, such as at trial. In matrimonial cases, motions are typically made for temporary support, temporary custody, visitation rights, or to enjoin someone from taking money or property. A "motion" may also be called an "order to show cause," if it's brought under emergency circumstances where the court must act quickly to resolve the issue.

fees, expert's fees, or any other temporary relief, these are the tools to use—although costly.

Filing a motion is like a tennis game, except paperwork—instead of a ball—flies back and forth. Say your spouse has stopped paying the mortgage on the marital residence. He has moved out, and he thinks you should pay for it because you're living there, but you don't want to use up your limited savings. It's been four months since he last paid the mortgage, and you're getting nasty letters from the bank. What do you do? Your lawyer will probably draft a motion asking the judge to immediately order your spouse to pay the back due mortgage and continue to make monthly payments. The motion will include your sworn statement, explaining that the mortgage has not been paid. Your lawyer will probably include the bank letters you've received as exhibits for the judge to see. Once your paperwork is completed, your lawyer sends a copy of the papers to your spouse's lawyer before giving the motion to the judge.

If you do not have an attorney, try to get help with the protocol for writing a motion from the court clerk. Many jurisdictions now provide plentiful help with such issues for *pro se* litigants in family court. There are even forms for common requests of the court. Some states make the forms available for download from their websites (see Appendix C).

Divorce Dictionary

A **cross-motion** is a counter request made of a judge in reaction to a motion made by the opposing party.

After you or your attorney files the motion, your spouse or spouse's attorney has the chance to answer. The answer will be in the form of a sworn, signed statement opposing your motion. Maybe your husband will say he gave you the money to pay the mortgage each month, but you spent it on a vacation. He might include canceled checks as exhibits. If he wants additional relief, such as an order directing you to pay the utilities on the house, he can ask for that as well. That's called a *cross-motion*.

If he has a lawyer, the lawyer will take care of it. If he does not have an attorney, he will be drafting the cross-motion himself, probably with the help of a court clerk.

You then have the chance to respond to both his response to your motion—maybe those checks were used for food—and his cross-motion. Some states will allow him to respond to your response to the counter-motion. All the paperwork eventually goes to the judge, who makes a decision. Expect the process to be limited to the movant's application, the cross-movant's response, and the movant's reply—anything more requires special permission from the court.

In some jurisdictions, even with all this paperwork, you or your attorneys still must appear in court to present oral arguments to the judge. This is just the type of legal ping-pong that runs the meter up on legal fees. You can well imagine that by the time all is said and done, the person paying a full-service attorney could have taken a trip to the U.S. Open instead of paying legal fees in his or her own tennis match.

The Discovery Zone

Before your case can go to trial, you will go through the process of *discovery*. Here, you and your spouse, generally working through your attorneys, exchange information that might be important to your case. In some jurisdictions, discovery is limited to financial and custody issues. In other places, the discovery can involve issues of physical and mental health, especially if these issues were part of the grounds for divorce.

How does discovery work? It's like a scavenger hunt. Your attorney will receive a list (usually long) from your spouse's attorney, setting out all the information that lawyer wants—bank statements, credit card slips, cancelled checks, loan applications, credit card applications, deeds, wills, names of anyone with whom you own property; the list is limited only by the lawyer's imagination and the local law.

What if you don't have the materials requested? Unfortunately, your spouse probably won't believe you. You could end up before a judge, with your spouse's lawyer claiming you're hiding information and your lawyer explaining that you no longer have it. A judge will then rule for or against you.

Discovery is not limited to the production of written materials. You could also be *deposed*— obligated to answer questions under oath in front

Divorce Dictionary

Discovery is the act of revealing information so that both parties are fully informed of facts before trial. Discovery can pertain to custody matters or finances or to one's physical or mental condition when those issues are relevant, such as when a spouse claims an inability to work due to an injury. Depending on the jurisdiction, other areas may be discoverable as well. Discovery methods include depositions, answering interrogatories, producing documents, and undergoing a physical.

Divorce Dictionary

A **deposition** involves answering questions under oath. In matrimonial matters, a deposition usually centers on a party's finances and is conducted in a lawyer's office or in the courthouse, but a judge will not be present. In some jurisdictions, the grounds for divorce may also be the subject of the deposition. A stenographer takes down everything that is said and later types it up for review by the parties and their attorneys. Once final, this deposition transcript can be used at trial to impeach your credibility or to prove a fact in the case.

of a stenographer, your spouse, and his lawyer. You could be served with extensive written questions, which you are obligated to answer truthfully.

Discovery could also involve a physical examination by a medical doctor (if, for example, the issue is your ability to work), a blood test (if the issue is paternity), and even a psychological examination (particularly if custody is at issue or you claim you need support because you have psychological problems).

Red Alert _____

While a *pro se* litigant is certainly entitled to step in and take deposition as well as conduct discovery, we do not advise it. In general, if you have enough money or property at stake to require these steps, you should dig in and hire an attorney to help you out. If there is enough at stake, it may well be worth a short-term loan.

A judge need not be involved in discovery if the lawyers agree on a schedule and stick to it and if they agree on what is to be disclosed. However, if one side doesn't agree on what is to be disclosed, then the decision will rest with the judge.

Trials and Tribulations: Your Day in Court

Judges generally try to help you resolve your case before the trial date, but that is often simply impossible. If, after months and even years of negotiations, conferences, and motions, you and your spouse or ex-spouse still have not reached an agreement, your last recourse is to have a trial. The trial gives the judge the opportunity to hear both parties' wish lists, substantiated by volumes of documents, possibly witnesses, and any other information the contenders think will persuade the judge in their favor.

After the judge ponders all this, she will make her decision. Because the judge has heard all the evidence and witnesses, a decision made by the judge at the trial's conclusion is taken very seriously by the powers that be. This decision should put an end to motions and conferences called for modifying temporary orders or changes in visitation schedules without a change in circumstance. Everyone has spent a lot of time, money, and effort at the trial, and asking for subsequent modification might not do you much good, unless there's been a substantial change in circumstances that would warrant modification after the fact.

Your trial will be very much like those you've seen on television and in movies. If you are the *plaintiff*, or petitioner—the spouse who started the action—your lawyer presents your case first. He will probably call you to the witness stand, where you will be sworn in and asked to take a seat. After your lawyer has finished asking you questions (*direct examination*), your spouse's lawyer has the opportunity to ask you questions (*cross-examination*). Your lawyer has the right to object to improper questions, so give her time to do that before answering. It's also a good idea to take a moment before you answer to collect your thoughts.

After the cross-examination, your lawyer can ask you questions again; maybe your spouse's lawyer interrupted you while you were trying to explain something. Your lawyer can now give you the chance to present your explanation (your *re-direct examination*).

After your re-direct examination, there can be a re-cross-examination. The questioning can go back and forth for as long as the judge will allow it. When there are no more questions for you, your lawyer can call a witness to the stand on your behalf, and the whole process starts all over again.

After you have presented all your witnesses (in divorce cases, it's often just you, your spouse, possibly your child's *guardian ad litem*, the court-appointed psychiatric evaluator, and expert witnesses such as an appraiser of real property or of a business), your side "rests." It is now your spouse's turn to present his witnesses. The same questioning occurs, only the roles are reversed. Your spouse's lawyer conducts the direct questioning, and your lawyer cross-examines the witness.

> **Red Alert**
>
> It is certainly possible for the *pro se* litigant to represent himself or herself at trial—but if there is enough at stake for you to get to this point, you might do best with a lawyer involved.

> **Divorce Dictionary**
>
> A *guardian ad litem* is a person, often a lawyer, but in some states a psychologist or social worker, selected by the judge and assigned to represent "the best interests" of the children. Some states do not have *guardians ad litem*.

After your spouse (in this case, the defendant) presents her witnesses, your lawyer can call witnesses to refute what's been said (called *rebuttal witnesses*). After you've called your rebuttal witnesses, your spouse can do the same.

It is the rare *pro se* litigant who has enough skill and experience to question an expert witness hired by the other side. When both sides have rested, the judge might allow each attorney (or if there are no attorneys, the spouses themselves) to make a short, closing speech. Alternatively, he might ask that memoranda be submitted to him by a certain deadline. Sometime later, he makes his decision, usually in writing.

If your trial was by jury, the jury decides the outcome after all the witnesses have testified, closing speeches have been made, and the judge has instructed the jurors about their responsibilities.

Some judges might give you a "bench" (oral) decision at the end of your motion or trial, as though you had a jury. (You or your lawyer should be able to find out, before the trial, if your judge makes bench decisions.)

Trials can be as short as half a day or as long as several months (although that would probably be unusual for a divorce trial). The length of a trial depends on the number of witnesses, how long each examination takes, and what motions are made during the course of the trial. The emotional and financial costs rapidly add up.

For further information, the American Bar Association's website has material on how the courts work at www.abanet.org/publiced/courts/home.html.

Judicial Bias

Do judges "play favorites" with lawyers? The answer is, probably not, but who knows? We like to think justice is blind, but there are some realities, too. In some jurisdictions, the same judges tend to hear matrimonial cases, and the same lawyers tend to appear before them. Does that mean they're all buddies, and you had better find the lawyer the judge likes best? No. Cases are decided on their merits. It does mean, however, that if you've hired a well-respected attorney, the judge has probably already observed him at work and trusts his or her integrity.

Do some judges favor mothers over fathers in custody disputes? The answer to that question is probably "yes." Even though custody determinations are supposed to be gender neutral, the reality for many fathers is that they go off to work while the mother stays home. Even if the mother does work, she is the one who probably did most of the childcare. It follows that the mother has spent more time with the children, the main criterion for custody. Many judges also work under the assumption that young children (seven and under) belong with their mothers, even though there is no law to support this premise. In fact, the "Tender Years Doctrine," which held that children belong with their mothers, has been stricken from the law since the mid-1980s.

Will a judge ever admit to a bias? No. But most lawyers will tell you that if you're a father seeking custody, you'll probably need a good reason why the mother should not have custody. Should you throw in the towel? Consult with an attorney first. If you have limited funds, this may be the time to spend some of it on legal advice or representation. On the other hand, many states now have some sort of joint custody (joint legal, or both legal and physical custody) preference. Even in states with a sole custody preference, parenting time has become more flexible and generous for the noncustodial parent (see Chapter 21).

What about other biases? Years on the bench, of course, can make one skeptical. Some judges have heard umpteen tales of the business that fails, miraculously, right before the divorce action, and a few years of seasoning means that they've seen the couple who's spent $100,000 a year while reporting income of $20,000 and even less. Does this mean you're doomed if your business really has taken a bad turn, or you had no idea what your spouse reported as income? No; but when you appear before a judge, you must be thoroughly prepared to prove your case.

Red Alert

Donna was more than a strict mother. She punished her children by hitting them—hard—for the least offense. That was one of the reasons Bill couldn't stand being in the marriage any longer. Bill was sensitive and could not tolerate the cold, abrasive, punishing mother that Donna was. He was asking for sole custody of the children.

While careful not to accuse Donna of physically abusing the children (his lawyers advised him that judges don't trust this often strategically used accusation in custody cases), Bill's lawyer asked Donna on the stand, "Isn't it true that you hit your children? Donna let slip out, "I haven't hit them for two years now."

While some judges adhere to the notion that hitting children is "parental style," this particular judge abhorred corporal punishment. Bill was awarded custody of his children.

Trial by Fire: When You're the Witness

As much as you might wish the witness seat would open up and swallow you, you will need to deal with the opposing attorney the best you can. (If your spouse is *pro se* and questions you himself, his lack of experience could be advantageous to your case.) What can you do when you're looking at a lawyer, but you feel as if you're peering into the mouth of a shark? Some pointers:

- Take your time before answering questions. Think before you speak, and give your lawyer time to object to the question. (This is a good time to have legal counsel by your side.)

- Do not let the lawyer get you riled. Control your emotions.

- If you feel faint, tell the judge you need a break.

◆ If there's water nearby, pour yourself a cup or ask the judge for some. Do not be shy about making these requests. Just be sure not to interrupt anyone else, unless it's an emergency.

◆ Keep shaky hands inside the witness box so the lawyer won't know what effect he's having on you.

◆ Remember to look at the judge and, if appropriate, at your lawyer, in addition to the lawyer who is questioning you.

◆ Don't be afraid to cry. If your emotions have clearly reached the boiling point. At this time, the judge will probably call a recess, and you'll have a chance to pull yourself together. If you're a man, you probably think you'd never do that, but there will be no adverse consequences should you become emotional during the trial.

CAUTION

Red Alert_____

Nothing irritates a court more than a manipulative litigant. Keep this in mind when the tears are about to flow.

Silver Linings

Although the issues being decided at your trial are extremely important and will affect you profoundly, this is not a criminal trial. No one is going to be sentenced to jail (unless this is a trial for contempt of court—a deliberate failure to make support payments, for example). Matrimonial judges might get annoyed at your bad behavior or obvious lies, but they are used to the deep feelings divorcing spouses have and are generally sympathetic and patient.

Traps You Can Avoid

A trial should be about the pursuit of truth and justice, not about who used what gimmick to "win." However, you can do things to help your case:

◆ Visit the courthouse before the day of trial, when a trial is in progress, if possible. You'll feel better knowing you're not stepping into uncharted territory.

◆ Tell your lawyer everything. If you have a secret bank account and you don't want to tell your lawyer (you're afraid she'll charge you more), keep in mind that your spouse might already know. It will be much worse for you if your lawyer hears about it for the first time while you're on the witness stand being cross-examined.

♦ Dress appropriately. Our picks: white, Peter Pan-collared blouse with a wide skirt for women; suit and tie for men. If you're a man claiming poverty, a sports jacket (or even a sweater, if you're claiming extreme poverty) with slacks and a business shirt can work as well.

♦ Leave expensive jewelry at home, unless you're trying to prove that your extravagant marital lifestyle included such trinkets.

♦ Be sure to bring all the documents needed. Pack them the night before. Bring paper, or ask your lawyer to bring an extra legal pad for you to take or write notes.

♦ Pause before answering any questions. Give yourself time to think and give your lawyer time to object.

♦ If you don't understand a question, tell the lawyer you do not understand and ask that it be repeated.

♦ If your trial involves a jury, look at the jurors when you answer questions, but do not stare at any one juror. You don't want to make any juror feel uncomfortable.

♦ Be aware that when your side is presenting its case, you're probably going to feel great during the direct examination by your lawyer and maybe even okay during the cross-examination, if your witness can hold his or her own. During the presentation of your spouse's case, you'll probably feel miserable.

♦ During the trial, get plenty of rest at night.

♦ When the trial is over, try to put it out of your mind, at least until there is a decision (if you didn't get one at the end of the trial). You might keep thinking about what you should have said differently. Try to forget it.

Ten Common Mistakes You Must Not Make

The following points might seem obvious in the calm of your living room reading this book, but under the stress of the trial, for your sake, they must be subjected to memory.

♦ Do not make faces, ever. If your wife lies like a rug, do not roll your eyes or shake your head (unless your attorney says it's okay). No matter how much you want to, a judge or jury might think you're being childish or that you're faking your reaction.

- Do not speak out in court. We know an attorney who represented the father during a custody hearing. While the lawyer was at the podium questioning the mother, her client began yelling at his wife to stop lying! When the case was over, the judge ordered the husband to attend an anger workshop. Needless to say, he did not win custody.

- Follow your attorney's instincts. This is a tough one if you've been very involved in planning the strategy of your case and now your lawyer wants to do something you think is wrong. When you're at trial, it's not a good time for the camp to be divided. If you feel very strongly, and there's a sound basis to your thinking, present your idea to your attorney. However, unless you are also an attorney, or you are very certain you are right (which might be based on your knowledge of your spouse), do not give your attorney ultimatums.

- Do not flirt with, excessively smile at, or in any way try to engage the judge or a juror.

- If your trial is by jury, never speak to a juror while the trial is in progress.

- Do not argue with your spouse's lawyer. If you're too angry to speak, wait or take a sip of water before continuing to testify.

- Avoid sarcasm.

- Avoid crossing your arms while you're on the witness stand.

- Don't doodle. The judge or jurors might notice, and it will look as though you just don't care.

- Don't talk to your spouse in court without good reason (scheduling the children, for example). Usually, there's just too much emotion for communication.

Family Court Versus Civil Court

Whether you go to family court is largely dependent on what state you live in and how far you have gotten in your case. In some states, you have to go to civil court if you want a divorce. In other states, all family-related matters may be handled in family court.

In general, family court might be a little more relaxed because many more people handle their own cases without a lawyer. The good news is that the courtrooms, whether by design or through lack of funding, might be much smaller than a "regular courtroom" and might feel less intimidating. The bad news is that while you wait for your case to be called, infants might be screaming all around you, and, depending on where you live, many cases might be ahead of yours. Civil court, on the other hand, tends to be quieter, less congested, and more professional.

Despite these outward differences, how the trial proceeds depends more on the judge than the courthouse. Some judges are very strict about the rules of evidence; others are more liberal. Some judges are very formal, requiring you to rise when they enter the courtroom. Others are more relaxed.

You're in the Army Now

If you're in the military, there are special considerations that are best handled by a military lawyer.

For starters, even serving the divorce papers has obstacles, since, if the serviceman or woman is overseas, there may be restrictions imposed by the hosting country, according to an article by Attorney Mark E. Sullivan (January/February 2005 edition of *GP Solo Magazine*).

Other issues pertaining to military personnel are also affected by being stationed overseas, such as getting them to a trial as well as determining the residence in order to know which state's laws prevail.

Child support is determined by a soldier's Basic Allowance for Housing, which in turn is based on geographic location, serviceman's rank, and whether or not she or he has dependants.

Medical expenses, custody, visitation, and financial issues also have their unique slant because of the special circumstances of being in the military.

We recommend contacting the American Bar Association's Military Committee or the ABA General Practice, Solo and Small Firm Section (phone: 312-988-5648).

Should You Appeal?

As with so much in life, the answer is, "It depends."

If the issue is critically important to you, *and* your lawyer thinks you have a reasonable shot at getting a reversal, *and* you can afford it, *and* you have the emotional fortitude to continue, you probably should appeal.

On the other hand, if the issue is critically important to you, *but* your lawyer says you have virtually no chance of winning, *and* you'd need to mortgage your share of the house, you probably shouldn't appeal. An appeal is expensive not only because your attorney has to do legal research and then write a brief, but also because you usually need to furnish the appellate court with copies of the entire "record below"—the evidence admitted in the case—as well as the transcript of the trial. Depending on how many days the trial lasted, that alone could cost thousands of dollars. Then, you usually need to supply the appeals court with several copies of the record below, the transcript, and the brief—adding hundreds of dollars more to your costs in photocopy fees. (Some jurisdictions have procedures whereby you can save money on the transcript or photocopying fees if you meet certain low-income requirements.)

To make matters worse, in some jurisdictions, the appellate courts are so backlogged that your appeal might not be decided for more than a year.

Can you do an appeal yourself? If you're a lawyer, maybe. However, it would be very hard for a layperson to do the legal research, and you would still be faced with combing your files to produce the record below (the evidence admitted in your case), the transcript, and photocopying costs.

When you consider whether to appeal, listen to your attorney and your head. As much as you might want to, this is not the time to vote with your heart.

The Least You Need to Know

- The judge is the final decision-maker if you and your spouse have not been able to come to an agreement.

- Motions tend to be expensive because lawyers have to put a lot of time into them. Settle whatever you can with your spouse to avoid having to make a motion.

- Always control your emotions in court. Never make faces in court.

- Pause before answering questions. Give your lawyer time to object and give yourself time to answer correctly.

- If you or your spouse is in the military, consult a lawyer who specializes in military divorce law.

- Consider the chances of success and the expense involved before you decide to appeal.

13

When Divorce Turns Vicious

In This Chapter

- ◆ Levels of conflict
- ◆ How to obtain an order of protection
- ◆ The limitations of court-ordered protection
- ◆ How to use the resources of the legal system to reduce conflict
- ◆ Stalking: why it happens and protective laws

There's high-conflict divorce, and there's *higher*-conflict divorce. We've covered high-conflict divorce in Chapter 12, which covers litigation—where such scenarios generally play out. When one spouse has been unfaithful and deceptive during the marriage, it is difficult for the "wronged" spouse to agree to an amicable divorce. This can lead to anger and resentment. Anger and resentment can turn to belligerence, which in turn angers the other spouse. Before you know it, neither party will cooperate with the other, and the divorcing couple is headed for protracted litigation.

Why protracted? Both people tend to dig in their heels on issues of importance to them. Add to that the huge backlog in the court system.

Before you know it, you're in for the long haul. Sometimes it's the system itself that finally wears you down until you both yell, "Uncle!"

Especially during the early years of a separation, fresh wounds from a betrayal or nonstop fighting during the marriage can generate such intense heat that neither person can be in the same room with the other. When children are an issue, things can get really nasty. (In Chapter 23, we discuss how harmful high-conflict situations are for the children and steps to mitigate the damaging effects on them.)

A custody battle can cause both parents to engage in extreme and hostile behavior never before seen by the other spouse. In some cases, a third party must be involved to help the children go from one parent to the next. Rude or aggressive behavior by one parent toward the other in front of the children is all too common in high-conflict divorce, and it is incumbent on both parents to walk away from situations where their "buttons" are being pushed.

Yet more conflict may arise when a spouse is completely unwilling to let go. Buckle your seat belt: when one spouse wants the divorce and the other opposes it, conflict can be extreme.

If you are the spouse who won't let go, our advice is simply to move on. By dragging out the proceedings, you are merely postponing the inevitable at enormous cost, not just emotionally, but also financially as you and your spouse dribble away your savings on legal fees.

If you are the partner who wants the divorce, step back and give your partner some time and space to get used to the idea. Pull back on significant legal action for a month or two.

> ## Red Alert
>
> If you have been abusing your spouse or children, you must stop and seek help. Often abusers have been victims themselves. A major effort is underway by the likes of famed Yankee manager, Joe Torre, and his Safe at Home Foundation to educate abusers and break the cycle of violence. Check it out at www.joetorre.net.

These high-conflict situations are bad enough, but it gets worse—much worse. One partner may have a genuine personality disorder or suffer mental illness. Now there's a dangerous situation—not just for the children, if there are any, but also for the other spouse.

Sometimes the battle is just a continuation of a long-standing abusive relationship. A spouse who has been battered for years finally has the courage to make a break. Other times, a rejected spouse goes beyond what would be normal anger and retribution into pathological behaviors that can lead to violence and even death.

We've included contact information for your state's domestic violence division and organizations in Appendixes D. The remainder of this chapter briefly touches on the issues involved with this extreme situation.

The Nightmare Begins

You've heard divorce horror stories, and you hoped you could avoid becoming one—but it looks as if your worst nightmare is coming true. Your spouse just won't leave you alone. He hangs out near your office and leers at you when you leave. She calls your new love interest on the phone in the middle of the night and mutters obscenities. He or she has threatened your physical safety and has even entered your apartment without your permission or against your will. Whatever harassment you might be experiencing, you will be able to deal with it most effectively after you have the legal system—and an attorney—on your side.

Harassment

Denise couldn't deal with Jack leaving her. He was her entire life, or so she imagined. She couldn't live without him, and she told him so—over and over, in every form of communication possible. She called him night and day, both at home and at work. She sent him faxes and e-mails, and even called his friends to tell them what a so-and-so he was, yet how much she needed him. Jack could not escape her attempts to get at him. He was sleepless. He was afraid to go anywhere he thought she might be—restaurants they had frequented, the supermarket, the cleaners, movie theaters, and more. He dreaded stepping out of his office building for fear she would be waiting for him. The same for his apartment building. In effect, he was under attack.

Clearly, he was dealing with a woman who had gone beyond the normal reaction of being rejected. What were his options?

> **CAUTION**
>
> **Red Alert** _____
>
> We don't mean to scare you, but if you have been accustomed to being abused, you must take the necessary steps immediately to get all the protection the law allows. If you think you are in imminent danger, contact the police and go to a local abuse shelter. As hard as it may seem, you must break with any old habits you have of accepting your spouse back into your life. Now is the time to free yourself so you can live a happier life.

Order of Protection

The first step toward protecting your rights and forcing your spouse to keep a distance is the *order of protection* (sometimes called a *restraining order*)—a document signed by a judge that prohibits your spouse from having contact with you or conducting himself or herself in a certain way in your presence. Judges don't always grant requests for orders of protection. You usually need to provide evidence to the judge showing that you have been or could be victimized by your spouse. If you have been beaten in the past, photographs of injuries, police reports, and hospital or doctor's reports concerning your injuries will help you present your case. Orders of protection can be issued for other offenses, such as harassment, stalking, interference with personal liberty, intimidation of a dependent, neglect, willful deprivation (e.g., State of Illinois, 19th circuit court).

Divorce Dictionary

An **order of protection**—which can only be filed against a current or former family member by blood or marriage, family or household members, or other like relationship depending on the state—is an order directing one spouse to refrain from abusing, harassing, or even contacting the other, among other restraints. Violation of an order of protection can result in arrest and imprisonment.

Typically, an order of protection may order your spouse to stay a certain distance from you, or it may prohibit your spouse from contacting, harassing, menacing, endangering, or in any way bothering you. In most states, you can obtain an order of protection yourself by going to court (often the family court or criminal court) even if you and your spouse have not yet filed for divorce. If you have filed for divorce, the court where you filed usually has the authority to issue an order of protection, and in many states, criminal court judges have that power as well.

You can also obtain injunctive orders against the use of property, against the changing of beneficiaries on insurance policies, and against the removal of the children from the jurisdiction. Although violations of these orders will not usually result in arrest and imprisonment, it is important to have these restraints in place as an incentive for spouses to refrain from such activities. These are typically called "temporary restraining orders" or more commonly "TROs."

Typically, you can get an *ex parte* temporary order of protection. *Ex parte* means that you (or you and your lawyer) have gone to court without first notifying your spouse. Based on what you present to the judge, she might give you an order enforceable only for a limited number of days or weeks. At the end of that time, you must return to court, and this time, your spouse will be present (or at least will have been notified in advance that he or she should be). The judge will listen to each of you and decide whether to issue another order of protection, usually good for a longer period of time.

> **Red Alert** _____
>
> The *ex parte* short-term order of protection that you or your attorney get from the court, without advance notice to your spouse, contains a date for a subsequent court appearance, usually within 10 days. You're obligated to make sure your spouse is served with a copy of the temporary restraining order. Under no circumstances should you give the order or a copy of the order to your spouse yourself. Instead, the sheriff's office will serve it, or you or your attorney can hire a process server to deliver the order to your spouse. When you return to court on the assigned date (the "return date"), you are required to present proof that your spouse has been personally served with the initial order. The proof is usually a sworn statement by the server. Your sworn statement will not be accepted as proof. Another reason why you should not serve your spouse with the papers is that he or she might react violently; it's best if you're not around.

Serving the Order

Who will serve the order of protection? At the courthouse, you can arrange for a police officer or sheriff to help. Alternatively, you may bring the order of protection with a photograph of your spouse to a licensed process server who makes a living by serving court papers. Process servers often have offices near the courthouse, or you can locate one in the Yellow Pages or, of course, on the Internet. Even if the local police will not serve the order of protection for you, you should still bring or send a copy to your local precinct so that the police have it on record.

The person who serves the order of protection must sign a sworn statement telling when and where he served the order and how he knew the person who received the order was your spouse. You or your attorney will then bring that sworn statement to court on the day you are scheduled to be in court, thus documenting to the judge that your spouse received notification of the court date.

The conflict, anger, and violence that can be a part of some extreme cases during and after divorce are cause for alarm and must be dealt with swiftly. If your spouse becomes violent, this is not a time to try to settle your case or work out your problems with a marriage counselor or mediator. Pull out all stops. This situation calls for the intervention of the authorities—your lawyer, the police, victim specialists, the district attorney's office, and the courts.

> **CAUTION** **Red Alert** _____
>
> If you suspect that you are being stalked, don't hesitate to get advice and help from local victim specialists to design a plan of action. Appendix C has most states' websites, including information on domestic abuse. You can also check your local phone book for phone numbers of victim or rape centers listed under *"Community Services Numbers"* or *"Emergency Assistance Numbers."* There are also victim assistance programs that are part of local prosecutors' offices or even some law enforcement agencies.
>
> For more information on stalking, contact the National Center for Victims of Crime, 2000 M Street NW, Suite 480, Washington, DC 20036. Phone: (202) 467-8700. Their web site is www.ncvc.org.

The Least You Need to Know

- High-conflict divorce can go beyond litigation to harassment or even violence.

- Call the police if your spouse is harassing you, even if you do not have an order of protection.

- Document whatever you can to help obtain an order of protection. Always file the order of protection with your local police and keep a copy with you at all times.

- If you or your children are in immediate danger, go to a local shelter.

- If violence is a pattern in your home, teach your children how to dial 911, and have a plan for where they can go to be safe.

- All 50 states now have laws against domestic violence. Use them.

Chapter 14

Paying the Bill

In This Chapter

- ◆ Understanding divorce lawyers' fees
- ◆ How you can save money on your legal fees
- ◆ Negotiating a retainer agreement
- ◆ Determining whether your attorney's charges are legitimate

Legal fees—the two most dreaded words in the English language. If you're going through a divorce and you get a staggering bill from your attorney, you might be hard-pressed to think of anything worse besides the breakup of your marriage itself. Why are lawyers so expensive, and how do they charge for services rendered? This chapter uncovers the mystery behind the fees associated with hiring a divorce attorney.

Why Legal Representation Is So Costly

All lawyers do is talk, right? And don't they say talk is cheap? Not when there's a Juris Doctorate after the person's name.

Lawyers charge a lot because they usually have high overhead: an office, a reception-ist, a secretary. Someone has to pay for it, and it won't be the lawyer. Lawyers have at least seven years of post–high school education (four years of college and three years of law school). For recent graduates, educational costs could be as high as $120,000 or more. The lawyer is recouping that investment.

Finally, lawyers charge what the traffic will bear. Put simply, moneyed clients are ready and willing to pay these high fees, and there are enough moneyed clients around to keep lawyers from having to worry about volume. As more attorneys enter the field, billing practices are beginning to change, and fees are coming down in some areas. But until that happens in more significant numbers, costs will remain high. Remember that you will need to pay your lawyer at the current market rate if you want her to work for you.

Silver Linings

Some competent attorneys are willing to work out a payment plan in advance. It is to the attorney's advantage to make it as painless as possible for you to keep up with the bills. Many attorneys never collect the fully billed amount. If you take responsibility by requesting a payment plan, the attorney is more likely to collect his fees and be agreeable.

How Matrimonial Lawyers Charge

Many lawyers charge an hourly rate and bill you for every hour worked. If Paula Smith's rate is $150 an hour, and she does 10 hours of work for you, you'll get a bill for $1,500. It can be pretty straightforward. If you are hiring your lawyer à la carte, you'll pay as you go.

Most full-service lawyers, on the other hand, want some payment up front. This fee is called a *retainer*. The amount will vary depending on where you live, your specific case, and the lawyer's hourly rate. In the New York City area, some matrimonial attorneys charge as much as a $10,500 to $20,000 retainer. In other states, some lawyers charge at least $25,000. (That's not the bad news; this might only get you started! You'll probably spend much more than this if you have a protracted case.)

After you pay the retainer, your lawyer subtracts her hourly rate from what you've paid for each hour worked until the case is over or until she depletes your retainer, whichever happens first. If your lawyer has used up your retainer, you'll start getting bills. Some lawyers will want a new retainer; others might simply bill you on a weekly or monthly basis.

Wait a minute, you might think. Doesn't the hourly billing rate encourage the lawyer to drag out my case to earn more money? Although this might seem easy, within the profession it is considered unethical for a lawyer to deliberately drag out ("churn," as lawyers say) a case. Another deterrent is that when a case drags on, lawyers can lose clients, or clients will not be able to afford to continue paying. It's possible that the lawyer won't collect everything he's owed. Whatever he doesn't get paid is written off and, in effect, reduces his hourly rate. On the other hand, if the lawyer finishes her work within the amount of time covered by the retainer, she gets her full hourly rate and comes out ahead.

Does that mean you don't have to pay your bill? No. However, it does mean if ethics don't stop a lawyer from dragging out a case, the practical realities of collection will.

In matrimonial law, it is very hard to predict how much time your lawyer will have to spend on your case. If you and your spouse have agreed on everything up front, the lawyer won't have to do much more than draft the legal documents, make sure you understand them, get them to the other lawyer, and then, eventually, submit them to the court. If you or your spouse are at war, a lot of time will be spent on your case, and you can end up spending an astronomical sum of money.

Before You Put Your Money Down

One of the most important things to understand as you enter a financial relationship with your matrimonial attorney is the retainer. If you do pay one, the first thing you will do is sign a *retainer agreement*. Remember, any agreement regarding your retainer must be in writing and should always provide for a refund if the fees are not used up.

The agreement should also stipulate what happens when the retainer is used up. Will you have to pay another lump sum, or will you be

> **Divorce Dictionary**
>
> A **retainer agreement** is a contract signed by an attorney and client setting forth the billing arrangement to be instituted between the lawyer and the client.

billed on a monthly or weekly basis? When it comes to your retainer, make sure that all the ground rules are spelled out first.

A reputable attorney will not only have no problem putting the retainer agreement in writing, but also will ask you to take the agreement home and study it before signing it. You should be invited to call and ask any questions you have. As eager as you might be to sign the retainer and write out a check, hold back until you read the agreement and thoroughly understand what it says.

The Fine Print

At a minimum, your retainer agreement should establish the amount of money you are paying up front and should stipulate hourly rates for the lawyer as well as others who might be assisting in your case, including paralegals and junior attorneys.

The agreement should also outline how you will pay for out-of-pocket expenses such as photocopying, process servers, stenographers, or court fees. Maybe those expenses will come out of your retainer, or maybe you'll have to pay them in addition to your retainer. Find out now.

A retainer agreement should explain how often you will be billed. Are you going to get a bill only when the retainer is used up, or will you be kept informed with a bill each month as the retainer dwindles?

CAUTION

Red Alert _____

Never sign any agreement in which you use your house as collateral.

What happens if you do not pay your bill? Does the lawyer have an automatic right to abandon your case? Does he or she have an obligation to work out a payment plan with you? Are you obligated to guarantee payment with collateral, such as your house? Watch out for any lawyer who demands security in the form of something you cannot afford to lose.

Usually, you will be asked to countersign the retainer and send it back to the lawyer with the retainer check.

Here's a sample retainer agreement. Keep in mind that each attorney's agreement will vary.

Elayne Kesselman, Esq.
Retainer Agreement

February 9, 2005

PERSONAL AND CONFIDENTIAL

John Doe
New York, New York
Re: Doe v. Doe

Dear Mr. Doe:

I appreciate your retaining me to represent you in connection with your matrimonial situation, and I write this letter in order to confirm our understanding regarding the financial arrangements between us with regard to that work.

As an initial retainer, you have agreed to pay, and I have agreed to accept, $1,500. Applied against this fee shall be my hourly billing rate. The rate presently applicable to my services is $150.00 per hour. Because of mounting costs, it may be necessary from time to time for the applicable time charges to be increased, and I will notify you of the same in advance of any such increase. You will be billed on or about the first day of each month for services rendered during the preceding month.

You will not be billed for any time spent discussing your bill.

I do not anticipate having anyone else work on your case, but should another attorney assist me in this matter, I will notify you of that in advance and of that attorney's billing rate.

You will also be charged separately for any out-of-pocket disbursements (such as court costs, messenger service, photocopier, long distance telephone calls, postage, service of papers, online computer-assisted research, and so on) that are incurred on your behalf. In addition, you may be asked to pay certain disbursements directly to the vendor or provider of services involved (such as appraisers, process servers, transcripts of depositions or court proceedings, and the like), and you agree to do so upon my request. I will advise you of any such costs in advance of incurring the same.

If your retainer is used up and work remains to be done on your case, you will be billed on a monthly basis, and you agree to pay the amount due for services rendered and disbursements incurred within thirty (30) days from receipt of the bill. In the event of your failure to make prompt and timely payment of a bill, and should we fail to agree on suitable alternative arrangements for such payment, I reserve the right to cease work upon your matter and, if I am in the midst of litigation, to seek permission from the court to withdraw from your case. Should a dispute arise between us concerning the payment of attorney's fees in the sum of $3,000 or greater, you may seek to have the dispute resolved through arbitration, which shall be binding upon you and me. I shall provide you with information concerning fee arbitration in the event of such a dispute or upon your request.

You will be provided with copies of all correspondence and documents relating to your case, and you shall be kept apprised of the status of your case. You have the right to cancel this agreement at any time. Services rendered through the date of such cancellation and not yet billed will be billed to you upon such cancellation, and payment shall be due within thirty (30) days of receipt of the final bill.

I look forward to working with you and ask, if the contents of this letter accurately reflect our understanding, that you please sign the enclosed copy and return it to me.

Very truly yours,

_____

Elayne Kesselman

EK:ek   CONSENTED AND AGREED TO:

Enc.   _____

                                   John Doe

Who Pays for What?

The assumption that the man has to pay all the legal bills is no longer true. Often, the spouse with the deeper pockets has to pay some or all the legal fees. In many cases, where the assets are going to be equally divided, the pockets are equally deep, and wives are shocked to learn that their share of the legal fees must come out of their share of the assets.

If a lawyer assures you that he will only collect what he can get from your spouse, have that put in writing. Most lawyers will not make that promise because they stand a chance of never getting paid. A reputable attorney will explain that payment will be due even if your spouse does not pay.

Sometimes, early in a case, a judge will order the wealthier spouse to pay temporary legal fees on behalf of the other spouse. By the time the case is over, however, both sides usually end up paying something.

You Can Do It!

For those of you who are of moderate income, consider that being reasonable in a divorce settlement could save you enormous sums in legal fees. How much in legal fees is it worth to get the sterling silver wedding present that cost $5,000? Is it worth $3,000 in legal fees? It could easily cost that. For your own sake, put your anger and hurt aside and save yourself some money and aggravation. (We like to advise heading for the racquetball court immediately after a divorce settlement meeting and putting a face on that ball!)

Twelve Tips for Keeping Fees Under Control

We can't emphasize enough the importance of being vigilant about how and when you spend your hard-earned money on legal fees. Self-restraint is the order of the day. Here are some tips from the trenches of divorce. You may say, "I don't have the patience for all this detail," but take it from us, you will save thousands of dollars if you follow these guidelines:

- Hire a lawyer whose billing rate is manageable for you or who is willing to create a payment plan you can live with. For example, the lawyer will agree to be paid at the rate of $300 a month for however long it takes you to pay the bill.

- Hire a lawyer who is willing to unbundle his services and charge you as you go—only for the specific issues involved.

◆ Ask to receive a detailed bill every month; the bill should describe services rendered and disbursements paid. Tell your lawyer you want this even if your retainer is not yet used up.

◆ Ask that, except in the case of emergencies, you be notified in advance of any major work to be done on your behalf. Typically, you and your lawyer have developed the plan of action, but it is possible your attorney might be ready to make a motion that you think unnecessary.

◆ Ask for an estimate of the disbursements in advance. You don't have to be told about every postage stamp being billed to you, but your lawyer should tell you about messenger services (whose fees can run from $50) or stenographers (deposition or trial transcripts can cost thousands of dollars).

◆ Keep a record of the time you spend with your attorney on the phone and in person. When you get your bill, check it against your personal records.

We know of one instance in which two attorneys representing opposing sides in a divorce case met to reach a settlement. After the meeting, they went out to dinner together. One of the lawyers had the audacity to charge his client for the time spent at dinner and for the dinner itself! Needless to say, the outraged client agreed to pay only for the time spent on his case. Then, he changed attorneys.

Red Alert _____

Can the divorcing couple use the same lawyer? It's possible, but it's not a good idea, no matter how friendly the divorce may be. Later, one of you might claim you didn't understand what you signed or that the lawyer or the deal was really one-sided. When claims of unfairness arise, judges usually don't like situations where there was only one lawyer. If your case is simple, both spouses might represent themselves in negotiating a basic settlement; then they might hire a single attorney to draft it.

◆ Before you sign the retainer agreement, ask whether you will be charged a minimum for phone calls and what that charge will be. Some lawyers charge a 15-minute minimum under the theory that your call has taken them away from other work and they need time to "get back into it." Others will charge a minimum of five minutes. Still others will only charge the actual time spent on the phone. If there is a 15-minute minimum, save your questions for one longer call rather than several short calls.

◆ If you've gone to a firm with many attorneys, ask whether a good attorney with a lower billing rate will be able to do some of the work on your case. However, make it clear that for certain work—negotiations, for instance, or the actual trial—you want the attorney you hired.

◆ If more than one attorney will be working on your case, find out before you sign the retainer how double services will be billed. If two attorneys are discussing your case, are you going to be billed at their total hourly rate or only at the higher attorney's rate?

◆ Find out what you will be billed for photocopying and photocopy whatever you can yourself. Some firms charge as much as 25¢ a page. Time permitting, you could get copying done yourself for 4¢ per page overnight.

◆ Ask your attorney to use faxes, delivery services, and express or overnight mail only when necessary.

◆ Organize materials your attorney wants in the way she needs them to be organized. For example, if your attorney sends you a list of 20 documents demanded by your spouse's counsel, organize the records by year and category in separate folders. Your lawyer might want to change what you've done a little, but the cost will be far less than it would have been had you brought in a shopping bag full of receipts.

◆ Don't engage your attorney in aimless phone calls. For example, don't start bad-mouthing your spouse, your spouse's attorney, the system, or the judge. Do not make small talk or discuss anything irrelevant to your case. You might feel better after venting, but you won't when you get your bill.

How to Tell Whether Your Lawyer's Charges Are Legitimate

It's often hard to tell whether the amount of time your lawyer spent working for you was "legitimate." After all, you weren't there, and you're not a lawyer, so how are you supposed to know whether the charges are correct?

Although you can't keep track of every microsecond, you can keep an eye on things. First, always ask your lawyer to discuss the amount of time and cost that will be incurred for a project your lawyer has in mind before he begins that project. Maybe your lawyer wants to make a motion asking the judge to order your spouse not to call the kids during dinner. The motion might cost a thousand dollars. You could ask the lawyer whether he can call your spouse's lawyer first or send a letter about the problem. In fact, many states require the attorneys to certify that they attempted to resolve the issues with their adversaries before filing motions with the court.

Check your bills carefully. Sometimes law offices, like any business, can make a human error and charge for work not done on your behalf. If a lawyer tells you he has to be in court on your case and might have to sit there for three hours before the judge calls your case, ask whether he can do anyone else's work while he's there and not charge you for the waiting time. Some lawyers do just that and then "double bill"—bill you and the other person. An honest attorney won't do that, but it doesn't hurt to ask.

What if you're just not sure whether you're being ripped off? You probably need to reevaluate your relationship with your lawyer. If you think he or she is deliberately cheating you, why would you want that individual involved in your case?

Getting Your Money's Worth

Hourly rates depend on a lawyer's experience and education as well as the market itself. In a major urban setting such as Los Angeles, lawyers often charge $300 to $400 an hour. In smaller cities, equally competent lawyers might only charge $150 an hour because no one will pay more.

If you hire an attorney from a major law firm, chances are that the rates will be higher than those of a solo practitioner or a small law firm. The larger firm has more overhead and has to add that to the bill. However, if the attorney at the larger firm is more competent than the attorney at the small firm, it might be worth the higher fees because he can cut the case shorter by virtue of his experience. This is not to say that small firms and solo practitioners are, on the whole, less experienced. It depends on the attorney.

The truth is, you should not judge an attorney by his or her hourly rate because that rate might be arbitrary. It's not as though the legal community got together and bestowed a high hourly rate on the best attorney, a little bit lower rate on the second best, and so on. It's more an ego and business decision, loosely translated as, "What can I get away with?"

For some, the hourly rate will always be considered an indication of talent and quality. A well-known lawyer might be just the one, you're thinking, to bully your spouse into settling. Maybe so, particularly if your spouse is a businessperson who is impressed by names, but it's a ploy that rarely pays off. In fact, if you hire a well-known lawyer, they are usually quite busy and your case might get lost in the shuffle. The attorney's ability, integrity, and attention to your case—not his or her fee—is most important.

The Least You Need to Know

◆ Make sure you can afford your attorney, and work out a suitable payment plan before you hire her.

◆ Put your fee arrangement in writing. Unearned retainer fees should be refundable to you.

◆ Ask your attorney to let you know in advance the cost of anticipated legal work or third-party expenses, such as process servers, delivery services, or stenographers.

◆ Keep a record of time spent with your attorney.

◆ Do not be impressed by hourly rates. High rates can indicate a lawyer who's too busy to call you back.

Chapter 15

Closing the Book on Your Case

In This Chapter

- ◆ When the divorce decree goes into effect
- ◆ When you can collect pension, Social Security, and other benefits
- ◆ How remarriage can affect the divorce decree
- ◆ When a spouse does not comply with the decree
- ◆ When it's really over

It's finally over, or at least you think it is. You've been to court and had a trial, or you've signed a convoluted (or simple) settlement agreement. You're done, right?

Probably not. Depending on where you live, your lawyer (or your spouse's lawyer) most likely must draft a document known as the *judgment of divorce* or *decree of divorce*. If your case has been decided by a judge after trial, the judgment of divorce usually refers to everything the judge wrote in his decision. If you and your spouse settled your case, the judgment of divorce might include provisions on custody, child support, division of property, visitation schedule, or other issues; it might also simply refer to your settlement agreement with the assertion that all its provisions are deemed to be included.

If you and your spouse simply bought a "divorce kit," a collection of printed forms necessary to obtain a divorce, it probably includes a judgment of divorce. You'll need to fill in the relevant information and then submit the judgment to the proper court.

When the Judgment Is Final

After the judge signs the judgment of divorce and any record is made of that signing, the divorce is usually effective. (In some jurisdictions, recording in a record book the date on which the judge signed the judgment of divorce is called *entering the judgment*.) In some states, the judgment of divorce might be deemed effective even before it is entered. Either way—whether the judgment has to be entered or merely signed—for better or worse, you're single again.

You can usually get a copy of the judgment of divorce from the court or from your lawyer. It's a good idea to get a certified copy of the judgment of divorce (a photocopy with a stamp from a court official stating that the document has been compared with the original and is the same). There is usually a fee for this service. Also, depending on where you live, you might need identification to be allowed to look at your divorce file, so be sure to bring some identification to the courthouse.

After the Judgment Has Been Entered

When your lawyer (or your spouse's lawyer) has the judgment of divorce, he'll send it to your spouse's lawyer (or vice versa). This isn't just a courtesy to let him know you're divorced; it starts the clock running during which an appeal can be filed. If you and your spouse settled your case, in some states, there can't be an appeal, but your lawyer will send the copy anyway. If a judge tried your case, either one of you could appeal, but the clock doesn't start running until the actual judgment or decree is signed. Some states are more lenient and stop the clock from running till the date that the court clerk serves the judgment on the parties or their counsel, or when one lawyer sends the judgment of divorce to the other, with notification of when it was entered.

Divorce Dictionary

A **judgment of divorce** is a written document that states that a husband and wife are divorced. In some states, this may be called a **decree of dissolution**. Typically, lawyers draft the judgment of divorce for the judge to review and sign.

But no matter where you get your divorce, it is very important to determine when the clock starts ticking and when it stops, because once that time is up, you cannot ask the court to extend it or relieve you from your default if you did not file your notice of appeal on time.

If you and your spouse handled the case yourselves, make sure that you both get a copy of the judgment of divorce. If you're no longer talking, have a friend mail your spouse a copy of the judgment with notification of when it was entered and ask the friend to sign a notarized statement that he has mailed it. This is your proof that you had the judgment sent to your spouse.

Your Benefits

Your settlement agreement or decision by the judge should include getting the part of your spouse's Social Security, retirement, survivor, or disability benefits that you are entitled to.

When will you receive your benefits? Usually, you receive them when your ex-spouse does or at the earliest possible time he could have received them. For example, some retirement plans allow employees to take out money when they turn 55, even if they are still working. The plan might allow ex-spouses who have been awarded part of the plan to do the same. Every plan is different.

You probably won't get these benefits right after the divorce. To get your part of your spouse's Social Security, survivor, or disability benefits, the Social Security administration will usually need a certified copy of your judgment of divorce and any agreement in order to process your claim. In the case of pension benefits, your lawyer (or your spouse's lawyer) will usually have to draft an order (either a qualified domestic relations order, referred to as a "QDRO," pronounced "Q-dro" or "Quadro," or a court order acceptable for processing, known as a "COAP," depending on the kind of plan you're dealing with) at the same time he drafts your judgment of divorce. The order (QDRO or COAP) explains when you'll get your pension benefits. The judge then signs it, while your case is fresh in everyone's mind, and your lawyer sends a copy to your spouse's pension-plan administrator. Notify the plan administrator if you move, and as the time draws nearer for you to receive your benefit, contact the plan administrator (the address should be in the order) to find out what information it needs to process your claim.

Changing Your Last Name

In some jurisdictions, the judgment of divorce will include a paragraph giving a wife the right to resume her maiden (or birth), or other, name. Government offices usually require that you show them a certified copy of the judgment of divorce before they'll issue documents in your maiden, or other, name.

For the most part, however, you can simply start using the name you now want to be called. For some, it's the maiden name. For others, it might be the name from a prior marriage. Many women who have children retain their ex-husband's family name until their children are out of school. Although divorce is common now, they'd rather not flag their status, and some find it easier, from a practical point of view, to have the same last name as their school-aged child.

Modifying the Divorce Decree

Modification of a divorce decree is complicated, and you will need your attorney's involvement. In some states, it's easier to get a decree modified if you had a trial and a judge decided your case than if you and your spouse settled.

When Bobby Kingston was 4 years old, his parents divorced and signed an agreement including all financial issues as they related to Bobby until he turned 21. Unfortunately, no mention was made of who would pay for Bobby's college. When Bobby turned 17, his mother, Irene, tried to get Bobby's father, Joe, to help pay for college. Joe refused to pay. Irene hired an attorney, who made a motion asking the judge to order Joe to pay for college. The judge refused, saying Irene had the chance to ask Joe to pay college tuition when she signed the agreement 13 years earlier. The judge protected the settlement agreement.

If, on the other hand, a judge had decided the case between Bobby's parents after a trial, Irene would have had a good chance of getting the tuition paid by Joe. Because the trial took place when Bobby was only 4 years old, the judge would probably not have made a decision on college tuition. After all, what if the child doesn't want to go to college? Because tuition might not have been considered by a judge when Bobby was 4, Irene's request would seem reasonable to a judge 13 years later.

Red Alert

A growing number of states don't distinguish between tried cases and settled ones when it comes to subsequent modification. Rationale: Courts prefer not to punish less aggressive litigants (i.e. those willing to settle) by denying relief at a later date when the facts warrant it.

What if you notice a mistake in your divorce decree right after you get it? It will probably be easy to modify if the mistake is clerical, such as an incorrect date. It will be harder to modify if there is a dispute between you and your spouse over what is correct.

For example, it is not a clerical error if your lawyer forgot to include in the judgment of divorce your wish to be with your children on Mother's Day. Your lawyer can try to have the decree modified. Judges will usually agree to a modification if both sides agree to it.

How Remarriage Alters Things

If your case was settled, your agreement probably took into account the possibility of remarriage. For example, if your ex is paying you maintenance and the agreement says that stops if you remarry, you can be sure your ex will comply with that part of the agreement! If your ex's lawyer forgot to put in that provision, your ex might have to go to court to be allowed to stop paying maintenance, and he might not win.

On the other hand, the law in your state might affect what happens if you remarry. For example, the law might provide that support automatically stops on remarriage. Your ex does not have to go to court to have this change made; the law has made it for him.

Can you keep your remarriage a secret? Of course you can, but that's not a good idea. Most agreements require you to notify your ex-spouse (or your lawyer, who will notify his lawyer) about a change that affects the deal. If you don't have an agreement and you're collecting maintenance, the law probably provides that it stop on remarriage. Eventually, you would have to give back the money you kept. If for some reason your case went back to a judge, your actions would work against you.

When Your Second Marriage Ends

What if you get divorced from your second spouse? Does your first spouse have to resume paying you? Not usually. The same applies to any benefit you gave up when you remarried. A second divorce does not bring your first spouse back into the picture, so be sure that you want to give up your entitlements before you tie the knot a second time.

Remarriage after a divorce has the most impact on the person who was the breadwinner in the first marriage. If you're the breadwinner, suddenly you're contributing to two households, not just to your former household and your own expenses. Your new spouse might resent the money that's going to your ex or your children. Also common is that your new spouse might resent the time you spend with your children or the time they spend with the two of you. These are issues to consider before remarriage.

Henry married Eleanor two years after his divorce. Henry, a real estate broker, earned enough to live comfortably on his own while giving child support to his two children. Eleanor was a nurse. Her income plus Henry's enabled them to live in a small, two-bedroom apartment in Chicago. When Eleanor and Henry had their first child, money got tight. Eleanor, who early in her marriage was very understanding of Henry supporting his kids from his first marriage, suddenly began resenting Henry for continuing the child support. She began to feel that the support money belonged to their own child. This put a tremendous strain on their relationship.

> **CAUTION**
> ## Red Alert
> When negotiating your settlement agreement, if you are the spouse who might pay alimony, consider adding a clause to the agreement stating that you no longer have to pay alimony if your ex-spouse remarries or dies[md]the latter event is important for tax purposes. As always, see a tax professional before agreeing to the terms of a divorce settlement.

What If You Lose Your Job?

If your case was settled and not tried and you lose your job, *you might still be obligated to pay whatever you were paying while you were employed*, depending on the laws of your state. Why? You (or your lawyer) had the opportunity to include in your agreement a provision calling for reduction of maintenance or child support should you lose your job.

Might a judge give you a reduction anyway? Possibly, but it would be easier if your case had been decided at trial, where the judge would address only what was before him, not what may or may not happen. In some jurisdictions, unforeseeable events might provide a basis for changing an agreement. Also, in some jurisdictions, if your children's economic needs are not being met, a judge might be more likely to review and possibly change the agreement. It is essential that the paying spouse go to court immediately for the modification. Generally, spousal support continues to accrue unless you obtain an order modifying it and child support definitely does.

When Your Ex Does Not Comply

Enforcement of the decree is difficult, if not impossible, without the help of a lawyer. Some lawyers specialize in collections, and others won't touch it. Before you incur the cost of trying to chase your spouse to collect money, ask yourself:

◆ Does my ex-spouse have the money or income for me to collect? If the answer is "no," you might be wasting your time and money trying to collect what he owes you.

◆ Are there any other assets that the judge will allow me to collect? A car, home, boat? If so, how much will it cost me to collect against those assets, and how long will it take? Again, it simply might not be worth it.

◆ Has my ex-spouse put assets in someone else's name? If so, you might run into serious collection problems. Or, if you can prove your ex did this, sue the third party and try to recover the assets from him or her.

◆ If you're dealing with the collection of child support or spousal support, try having your state support enforcement agency work with you to collect from your ex. (Read on!)

Silver Linings

If you are having problems collecting the child support ordered by court or put into your settlement agreement, it is a crime, and you do have recourse.

Your ex-spouse's wages can be garnished.

You can contact your state's child support enforcement agency.

The child support enforcement division for your state is listed in Appendix C. You can also contact the Federal Office of Child Support Enforcement online at www.acf.dhhs. gov/programs/cse/index.html or the National Child Support Enforcement Association at www.ncsea.org.

What if money isn't the issue? The problem is that your ex-spouse has custody of the children but refuses to send you their school reports.

If you still have a lawyer, you can ask that she call your ex's lawyer about the problem. Sometimes a phone call is all it takes. If lawyers are no longer in the picture (or never were), you might want to write a letter to your ex. It might not do any good, but at least you'll be making a record of the problem should you later decide to pursue the issue in court. (First, make a copy of the letter. Unless your agreement requires you to do so, you don't have to send it by certified mail. Some people don't pick up certified letters.)

Of course, some problems with compliance must be handled by a judge. A woman lived in Missouri, but her daughter flew to New York every summer to visit her father, in accordance with the parties' separation agreement. At the end of one summer, the father refused to send the daughter home. He claimed his daughter's stepfather spanked her. The judge ruled that the child should not be spanked by anyone except a parent, but that she should be returned to her mother in Missouri.

Bidding Your Lawyer Adieu

Once the divorce is final, and the time for appeals has expired, your lawyer is no longer your lawyer. Technically, the case is over, and any new problems that might arise can be addressed by any lawyer you hire to work for you. Will lawyers help if there are problems after the divorce decree is final? That depends. Some will assist and bill you for the work. Others will tell you they can no longer handle your case. They might be too busy, or they might not like your ex-spouse's lawyer, or they simply do not want to be involved anymore. Still others might take a call or two from you without asking for payment.

In some jurisdictions, a lawyer must take formal steps to withdraw from your representation after the case is completed. Family law matters are often ongoing because of support payments or later division of assets, so someone must be "of record" to receive service of process in the event that there is a reason later to go to court. When your lawyer withdraws, the person of record is you, by default, and your address must be on file with the court.

Breaking Up Is Hard to Do

For those who tapped the full-service option, the months or years of dependency on a lawyer are at an end. Indeed, once the judgment of divorce is final, some people feel lost. Others feel angry that the lawyer who won them a big award and earned thousands of dollars on their case is not willing to help them collect it.

It might be hard for you to accept that lawyers are simply in the business of providing legal services. Don't take it personally if your lawyer says goodbye. It is time for you to move on to your own, independent life.

The Least You Need to Know

◆ Be sure that your spouse has received a copy of the final judgment of divorce with the date of its entry. Have a friend mail a copy if need be, and then sign a notarized statement that she mailed it. Include the date of mailing and the address where it was sent.

◆ Entitlement to Social Security, pension plan, and retirement benefits should all be addressed at trial or during negotiations. Don't wait until after the judgment of divorce is final to discuss your ability to collect against your spouse's benefits because, unless your ex is willing to agree to give you what you want, it will be too late to get it from a judge.

◆ In some states, it is more difficult to modify a judgment of divorce that was the result of negotiations than it is to modify one that was the result of a trial.

◆ Before you hire a lawyer to collect unpaid moneys, ask yourself whether you have a reasonable chance of collecting, how much it will cost you to collect, and, if you have children, whether re-engaging in battle might unravel their now-stable lives.

◆ Your lawyer is technically off your case once the judgment of divorce is final.

Part 3

The Economics of Divorce

When we're young and idealistic, it's difficult to understand how mere money—or lack of it—could cause conflict in a marriage, let alone destroy it. As we go through life, however, the importance of money looms large. Even in the best of marriages, a lack of money can cause tension as working parents burn the candle at both ends attending to their relationship, their children, and the bills. If money causes such dissension in marriage, it's only natural that during divorce it may become the white-fanged monster that destroys any remaining civility.

In Part 3, we help you navigate the financial minefields that can turn even the friendliest of divorces into *The War of the Roses*. We explain how to negotiate effectively and protect your interests; how to land on your feet despite the financial hit; and how to mitigate financial fallout such as bankruptcy or credit card debt.

Chapter 16

Dividing It Up

In This Chapter

- ◆ Simple, low-conflict techniques for dividing your assets as fairly as possible
- ◆ How to look out for your interests when dividing money, property, and debt
- ◆ The difference between community property and equitable distribution: how your state will tend to view your claims
- ◆ What to do if your spouse files for bankruptcy or transfers assets
- ◆ How to divide the cash, the house, and the family business

An unhappy wife hired two movers the weekend her husband was out of town. They hauled away all the furniture and put it in storage. It's not the fairest way to divide the spoils of a marriage, and it's not the most cost-effective, either. She had to pay big bucks to the movers and her lawyer, who faced the unenviable task of explaining to a judge what her imprudent client had done. The woman's actions also placed a significant emotional impediment in the way of settlement.

The Art and Science of Division

If you can't just take the money and run, how should you go about fairly splitting the accumulated possessions of your life together?

Depending on what you have, the job can be easy. You can go around the house and simply take turns choosing what you want. Whoever chooses first during the first round will choose second during the second round and so on. This worked for a friend of ours—until her husband went up to the attic and selected an antique lamp she'd forgotten about. But she swallowed her protest and went on with the process, and she's glad she did. This game of round-robin might sound childish, but if it works for you, go for it! It's better than paying your lawyers hundreds of dollars an hour to do the same thing.

Many people divide furnishings and other items in the home, including collectibles, by listing everything and then taking turns choosing from the list. The key is establishing ground rules. If sets (sterling, bedroom, dining room) are not to be broken up, for instance, then you might decide to allow each person to choose three items per turn, not one. Write each person's name after chosen items. Then, when it's time for one or both of you to move out, each one receives the items allocated on the list. (For more complex issues, see Chapter 17.)

Variations in State Law

What do you need to know and do? First, you must familiarize yourself with your state's law. (See Appendix C for information on accessing your state's divorce laws.)

The laws governing the division of property vary depending on where you live. Lawyers use legislation (the state's statutes or codes), court rules, and case law (decisions from cases decided by judges) as a guide to what would happen in your case should you end up in front of a judge. Based on these laws, your lawyer should have a pretty good idea of where the chips would fall if your case went to court. If your lawyer (full-service or limited) is doing the job, he or she will use that knowledge to work out a fair distribution of what you've acquired. If you are purchasing your legal services à la carte, this is one area where a consultation will pay off.

Courts divide property (and debt) according to whether a state adheres to the *community property* scheme or the *equitable distribution* scheme. The community property scheme assumes that a married couple owns all assets and debts equally, except for separate property, and is divided accordingly upon divorce. Under the equitable distribution scheme property and debt is supposed to be divided "fairly" upon divorce. Most states follow the equitable distribution scheme.

Things get tricky when couples move from one type of state to the other. A competent certified public accountant can help you determine how your property will be categorized if you and your spouse have moved either from a community-property state to a common-law state or the other way around.

Community Property States

Arizona, California, Idaho, Louisiana, Nevada, New Mexico, Texas, Wisconsin, and Washington are known as *community property states*. (In Alaska, since 1998, married couples have been given the option of adopting community property rules by signing an agreement to that effect.)

There is no federal definition of community property. Instead, each community property state has its own definition, which is provided in their statutes. In general, community property is determined by what is *not* separate property, which is property acquired before the marriage, by gift, or bequest.

Although community property—the idea that property acquired during the marriage belongs to both spouses equally—is based on the theory that marriage is a partnership, each state has its own unique twist. Focus on your own state's laws.

When distributing assets in the wake of a divorce, community property states presume that husband and wife jointly own all money earned by either party from the beginning of the marriage until the end of "the community," generally determined by the date someone physically moves out of the marital residence—with an intent to end the marriage—or when the couple signs an agreement stating their intention to end "the community" of their marriage. (The rules concerning when a marriage or "the community" ends varies widely, so check your state's laws.). In addition, property bought with community money during the marriage is owned equally by both the wife and husband, no matter who purchased it. What is true for money and property, however, is also true for debt; from credit card bills to loans, any debt assumed before the date of marital separation is the responsibility of both spouses in equal measure.

Equitable Distribution (Common Law) States

States that are not community property states are called *common-law states*. These states adhere to the equitable distribution scheme. In these states the court considers a range of factors when dividing property, such as the length of your marriage, amount and sources of income, liabilities, the contribution to the marriage of each spouse, the nature of the property, the responsibilities each of you had in the marriage, whether you have children and who they are going to live with, your health, your education, your noneconomic contribution to the marriage, vocational skills, employability, and your estate, among other things. In a long marriage, the likelihood of a 50-50 division of assets is much greater than in a brief one.

Re-Learning Long Division

"Four. I don't think I can eat eight."

—Yogi Berra (when asked if he wanted his pizza cut into four or eight slices)

After you've determined the ground rules in your state under which your property will be divided, it's time to take a full accounting of your assets.

Unfortunately, for most people married more than a couple of years, complexity rules. The game of round-robin, described earlier, is a lovely exercise in forgiveness, but most of us own more than furniture, china, and knick-knacks. There's a pension, a savings account, an account for the kids' college tuition, some bonds still left over from the wedding, and some paintings that aren't worth much now, but you never know.

How do you work it out? The first step is, again, a detailed list of all your assets.

Taking Inventory

Your master list must include all the assets you have accumulated during the course of your marriage. Include the date the asset was acquired. (If you can't remember but you know it was acquired during the marriage, that's good enough.) Make sure to note the cost (if you can recall) and what you think it's worth now. Also, note to whom it belongs—you, your spouse, or both. Remember, in community property states even if one spouse bought it, if it was bought during the marriage, it belongs to both of you.

Even-Steven: Furniture, Cars, and the Small Stuff, and the Cash

According to financial planner Carol Ann Wilson, furniture and personal belongings are valued at "garage sale" value in divorce. So it's up to you and your spouse to pick through your possessions and divide them up according to who is more attached to which item, making trades as you go along.

In the wake of divorce, many people like to start from scratch and leave the furniture behind. Our friend Lisa, for instance, didn't take a single sheet or towel from the family home following her divorce. Her sudden liberation signaled, for her, a chance to reinvent herself. All her new possessions, in the context of her new life, became symbols of her personal growth as well as her release from marital pain.

For others, the possessions accumulated during a lifetime represent luxury or comfort; association with a former spouse presents no problem at all. For those who end things amicably, dividing the furniture and cars should present little problem. Just set values for your belongings, and then divide them according to value. If one item, such as the car, is worth more than all the furniture, the spouse who keeps the car will have to pay the difference out of the cash that you will be dividing. Personal assets, such as tools used to repair the house or for gardening, should remain with the spouse who used them the most—or the one who "keeps" the home or garden.

Who Gets the House?

If you have children, the spouse who has primary custody usually remains in the house with the children, unless you and your spouse can't afford it. If there are no children, you and your spouse can also work together to decide what to do with the house. The easiest solution is to sell the house and divide the proceeds. However, one of you may be more attached to the house than the other. In this case, you will, of course, need to have it appraised. You might each hire a real estate appraiser to value the house and then take the average of the two values. If you both trust and like the same person, you might decide to save money and hire one person.

Your current equity in your house is usually stated on your monthly mortgage bill. Or, you can calculate the equity by subtracting the mortgage from its assessed value. What's left, the equity, is what you will negotiate with your spouse if one of you decides to keep the house.

If you are considering selling the house, review the following considerations before placing your home on the market:

♦ Will your spouse or you be able to find comparable or sufficient housing at a lower monthly cost? Remember, mortgage payments are often tax-deductible, rent usually is not. You might be better off paying a higher monthly mortgage than a slightly lower rent. However, when insurance and taxes are figured in, renting might be cheaper.

◆ Are you selling at a loss because of the divorce? If you hold onto the house a year or two longer, will you fare better?

◆ Does the house require significant work? Will a renovation make it more marketable, and if so, do you have the funds to pay for the work? If not, you might decide to hold onto the house for now—even if you rent it to someone else—and sell it later.

◆ Will a move be so disruptive to the children that holding on to the house is important, even in the face of financial sacrifice?

◆ Consult a tax professional to help you determine what the best option is for you.

When You Keep the House

Suppose that you've decided to hold on to the house until your youngest child turns 19 and has been out on his own for a year. Assuming you and your spouse are working this out (rather than letting a judge decide for you), you can make whatever arrangements you both agree to, but here are some suggestions:

◆ The spouse who pays the mortgage from the time of the divorce until the house is sold should probably get a credit from the net sale proceeds (gross proceeds less outstanding mortgage, broker's fees, and so on) to the extent the principal of the mortgage was reduced while he or she lived there and paid the mortgage (with his or her own income or assets). But do adjust for any mortgage deduction for tax purposes. However, if the remaining spouse is paying the mortgage with support from the other spouse, it might be fairer to simply agree to divide the net proceeds with no credit to the remaining spouse for his or her mortgage payments.

◆ Credit any spouse who has paid for improvements to the house following divorce and prior to sale so that such cash outlays are recognized in division of the sale price.

◆ Consider agreeing that if the remaining spouse remarries or has a significant other move into the house, the sale provisions that were going to go into effect when the youngest child turned 19 (or 21, whatever you have agreed) will instead apply after the move-in or remarriage. For some, having a stranger move into "his" or "her" house is too much to bear.

◆ Decide now how you're going to handle the sale of the house when the time comes. How will you choose the list price and sale price?

Now is the time to consider such strategies as dropping the price by a certain percentage if the house is not sold within a certain number of months from when it is first listed.

> ### Red Alert
>
> According to the Internal Revenue Service (Publication 936) "If a divorce or separation agreement requires you or your spouse or former spouse to pay home mortgage interest on a home owned by both of you, the payment of interest may be alimony. See the discussion of Payments for jointly-owned home under Alimony in Publication 504, Divorced or Separated Individuals."

Even if the sale of the house seems far in the future, you might take the time now to devise a "first option," which comes into play if the house, still jointly-owned, is put on the market and an acceptable offer made. In that instance, either spouse has the right to match the offer and buy out the other spouse, thus maintaining the house.

Finally, anyone who's bought or sold real estate understands that the tax issues can be substantial. If you plan to keep the house "in the family" after the split, you should consult a tax attorney or accountant about the ramifications of keeping your interest in the home and leaving your name on the deed, even though you yourself will be living elsewhere. The last thing you want to discover, 20 years down the road, is that you're liable for capital gains taxes you never dreamed of.

Speaking of capital gains (if any), now is the time to decide who will pay the tax on the profits from the sale of your house. Will you split the tax fifty-fifty? In the same proportion as the proceeds of the sale? Remember, you might get a larger share of the net proceeds if you made the mortgage payments. You might then have to bear a larger share of the taxes as well. Again, consult an accountant before finalizing the deal with your spouse.

When negotiating over the house, remember to give credit where credit is due. If the person who keeps the car has not paid the other spouse for half the value of the car at the time of the split, it's reasonable to post that sum as a credit against the car keeper's share of the house or deduct it from the cash assets.

Make sure to put everything in writing. Ask a lawyer how to make the agreement legally binding. (Do you need witnesses? Should your signatures be notarized? Find out now, or be sorry later.)

Silver Linings

Remember, if you can agree to agree with your spouse, you can create ground rules that work for both of you. Perhaps you want to agree to a credit equal to only a percentage of the amount of the mortgage paid off. After all, whoever stayed in the house had the benefit of its use. Maybe you want to wait until the youngest child turns 21 before selling the house. Whatever the two of you agree on is okay, but to maximize the money in your pockets when the home is sold, make sure you get tax advice before you sign any binding document.

CAUTION

Red Alert

If your spouse won't cooperate with the appraiser, you may need to go to court. Since this issue is probably too complicated for you to handle on your own, now is the time to get an attorney.

Dividing the Family Business

One of the potentially most contentious tasks facing the divorcing couple is dividing a family business. The first step in avoiding conflict is determining the value of the business through a reputable business appraiser. That step is expensive, but it's probably well worth it. After that, the business should be treated like any other asset.

Leave No Stone Unturned

When dividing the spoils of a life spent together, make sure you account for all the financial elements, including retirement and employee benefits, taxes, and debt. Here are some tips:

- **Pensions and other retirement plans.** In some states, pensions and other retirement accounts can be divided between you and your spouse, even though only one of you earned it. (Remember, marriage is viewed as a partnership in most states.) Check with an attorney. Pensions are often divided 50-50 from the date of your marriage until the date you separated, started a divorce action, or actually became divorced.

- **Tax liability.** Be sure to decide in advance how you will handle any audits of jointly filed tax returns. If a deficiency is found, will the spouse whose income was underreported or who took too many deductions shoulder the tax debt? If it's impossible to figure out or prove who's to blame, do you each pay half the debt? Although the spouse who didn't work might be appalled at such an idea, the truth is if you both enjoyed the money when it was earned, then you were also both responsible for paying Uncle Sam. On the other hand, if you had no idea what your ex was up to, tax wise, you might not be liable under the theory you were an innocent spouse. But if you've received a "deficiency" notice from the IRS about a joint income tax return, you will need the assistance of a tax lawyer to help you out.

◆ **Debt.** Debt is a joint burden. Judges will divide debt just as they divide assets. Although the lion's share of the debt might go to the spouse with the significantly larger income, an individual who has managed to avoid paying bills during the marriage might be saddled with large loan payments after divorce, providing that individual has the income or assets to make the payments.

CAUTION

Red Alert _____

Consider paying off all the credit card debt with available cash. This will both decrease the amount of dollars owed and secure the credit history of both parties. A late payment by either party on a jointly held card will be reported on both parties' credit reports.

If your spouse is accumulating unreasonable credit card debt, both of your credit ratings will take a hit. In this case, cancel the joint card and get your own as soon as possible.

It's essential that you subtract debt from savings before you divide stocks, bonds, or cash. If the debt is larger than the savings, or you don't want to deplete savings to pay off the debt, you still need to divide the debt. You can divide it any way that seems fair. If one of you overspent against the wishes of the other (maybe that's part of the reason you're divorcing), it might be fair for the spender to pay the debt, unless he or she spent the money for the family, in which case a 50-50 division of debt might be more fair.

To protect your interests and arrive at a fair solution, make a list of your debt, when it was incurred, who incurred it, and why. Write down the monthly payment due, and then figure out who should and can pay it. If all else fails, ask for legal advice. It will cost you money, but it might save you money, too.

Devious Ways a Divorcing Spouse Might Hide Assets

If someone has been planning a divorce for a while, and if that person is so constituted, he or she might devise numerous strategies for hiding money or other assets from a spouse and children. With the right legal help, however, wronged spouses can often come away with much of what is rightfully theirs.

Bankruptcy

To avoid payment to an ex, some people will go so far as to file for personal bankruptcy in the middle of their case. The bankruptcy law (as of October, 2005) is based on income and requires the filer to submit to credit counseling before applying for bankruptcy, among other obligations. If this problem comes up, consult an attorney, since the issue is quite complex.

Illegal Transfers: How to Catch Your Spouse in the Act

Another devious way the moneyed spouse might try to reduce the amount of assets declared during a divorce action is to transfer assets to a friend or family member. The spouse will then claim that he or she no longer has these assets. The lawyer for the recipient spouse has to then prove the transfer was made to deprive that spouse. If the transfer is about to happen, the recipient's lawyer can go to court to try to block the transfer. To substantiate this claim, the lawyer has to prove to the judge why he thinks the property is about to be transferred and what property or money is involved.

Marion Dupont came from a wealthy family, from which she inherited several properties after she married Andrew Billings. After three years of marriage, Marion met a man with "more intelligence and energy than Andrew could ever hope to have." After she broke the news to Andrew and filed for divorce, she began transferring the titles of her property to her sister. Andrew was clever enough to suspect Marion would do something sneaky, so he hired a private investigator. The PI did his homework and was able to provide proof that Marion was in the process of transferring the titles. Andrew's lawyer then brought this to the attention of their judge and was able to block the transfer.

Although the property would not likely be distributed to the husband because it was inherited, this asset might affect the determination of total equitable distribution for Marion, in some states, because it showed her total net worth. In general, it's better not to transfer assets just before divorce simply because judges don't like it.

Gathering Your Financial Information: A Worksheet Approach

With the help of financial analyst Ted Beecher, we've developed a series of worksheets to help you move toward financial settlement and cut the best deal you can. In the end, whether you plan to settle or litigate, you will need to document your assets and your debts. The sooner you compile these documents, the better off you'll be.

In addition, the very act of compiling your financial information will help you work through the process: You will find out what your true financial position is, get a sense of what you can really ask for, and start thinking about what kind of counter-proposal you are likely to get from your spouse.

Just as important, by filling out these worksheets, you will come face to face with the likely gap between your position and that of your spouse. Thus prepared, you will be better able to support your position in settlement negotiations or in court. It's this simple: The more prepared you are, the more likely you will be to come out ahead.

The information these worksheets ask for is the sort of information you will need to present in any court-ordered financial affidavit. By organizing this material in advance, you will save time and legal fees.

Getting Started: A Basic List to Get the Ball Rolling

This first list is intended to give you a sense of your overall financial situation. Start by listing the assets below, alongside their net value:

| | | Net Value | | |
	Joint Property	Husband's Separate Property	Wife's Separate Property	Net Value
House	_____	_____	_____	_____
Business	_____	_____	_____	_____
Car	_____	_____	_____	_____
Savings	_____	_____	_____	_____
Checking	_____	_____	_____	_____
Pension	_____	_____	_____	_____
IRA	_____	_____	_____	_____
CD	_____	_____	_____	_____
Furniture	_____	_____	_____	_____
Jewelry	_____	_____	_____	_____
Other	_____	_____	_____	_____
Total:	_____	_____	_____	_____

After you've made your basic list, gather the details, if relevant, requested below:

Residence

Current market value (FMV) _____

Current mortgage amount _____

Monthly payments, including utilities and rent or maintenance) _____

What did you pay for the house? _____

Will the house be sold now or later? _____

If the house is not sold, who will live in it? _____

Asset Checklist

Annuities _____

Checking accounts, bank accounts, certificates of deposit, savings accounts, and so on _____

Stocks, bonds, mutual funds, limited partnerships _____

Real estate (in addition to the primary residence, other rentals, vacation properties, and timeshares) _____

IRAs, 401(k), 403(b), pension, deferred compensation, etc._____

Unpaid bonuses and noncash compensation such as company car and paid lunches _____

Defined benefit plan (you will need details for later) _____

Life insurance cash value _____

Personal possessions _____

Antiques and collectibles _____

Debts (credit cards, loans, personal debt, and so on) _____

Make sure you have gathered sample paycheck stubs and tax returns for the last three years as well.

Financial Affidavit

Finally, it is in your best interest to assemble a financial affidavit before documents become scattered in a spouse's reorganization or move. Some of the information here may pertain to support and not division of assets or debt. Either way, it will be to your advantage to have all this information filed in a single, safe place as soon as you possibly can. Courts typically require most of the following information before they will hear your case. Remember, if there is a policy, you need the policy number and related documents. If there is an account, you need a copy of the most recent statement.

Job title: _____

Primary employer: _____

Hours per week: _____

Payroll: _____

Monthly gross income: _____

Monthly payroll deductions: _____

Exemptions claimed: _____

Federal income tax: _____

Social Security: _____

Medicare: _____

State income tax: _____

Health insurance premium: _____

Dental insurance premium: _____

Retirement contributions (401[k] and so on): _____

Total deductions: _____

Net monthly income: _____

Other sources of income: _____

Deductions from income, including legitimate business expenses: _____

Net monthly income from other sources: _____

Net monthly income from all sources: _____

Net monthly income of children: _____

Income reported on last federal tax return: _____

Monthly income of other party: _____

Real estate, including location, market value, outstanding mortgage, net equity, and a list of all furniture:

_____

_____

_____

_____

Motor vehicles, including year and make, market value, outstanding loans, and net equity:

_____

_____

_____

_____

Bank accounts, including name of bank and current balance:

_____

_____

_____

_____

Stocks, bonds, and mutual funds. (Attach broker statements.) Include stock or bond name, shares or par, and the market value for each position or holding:

_____

_____

_____

_____

Life insurance. List the company name, the policy number, the owner's name, the insured's name, the beneficiary's name, the face value, and the cash surrender value:

_____

_____

_____

_____

Pension, profit sharing, and retirement plans. For each plan, list the plan name, the participant, and the value:

_____

_____

_____

_____

Monthly expenses for ___ adult(s): _____

⠀⠀⠀⠀⠀⠀⠀⠀⠀⠀⠀⠀⠀___ child(ren): _____

Housing: _____

Rent: _____

First mortgage: _____

Second mortgage: _____

Homeowner's fee: _____

Total: _____

Utilities: _____

Gas and electric: _____

Telephone: _____

Water and sewer: _____

Trash collection: _____

Cable TV: _____

Total: _____

Food: _____

Grocery items: _____

Restaurant: _____

Total: _____

Medical (after insurance): _____

Doctor: _____

Dentist: _____

Prescriptions: _____

Therapy: _____

Total: _____

Automobile insurance: _____

Life insurance: _____

Health insurance: _____

Dental insurance: _____

Homeowner's insurance: _____

Total: _____

Transportation: _____

Vehicle 1: _____

    Payment: _____

    Fuel: _____

    Repair and maintenance: _____

    Insurance: _____

    Parking: _____

Total: _____

Vehicle 2: _____

    Payment: _____

Fuel: _____

Repair and maintenance: _____

Insurance: _____

Parking: _____

Total: _____

Clothing: _____

Laundry: _____

Childcare: _____

Childcare related: _____

Education: _____

For children: _____

   School: _____

   Lunches: _____

   Sports: _____

For spouse: _____

   Tuition: _____

   Books and fees: _____

Recreation: _____

Entertainment: _____

Hobbies: _____

Membership in clubs: _____

Miscellaneous: _____

Gifts: _____

Hair care/nail: _____

Books/newspapers: _____

Donations: _____

Settlement Software

After you have recorded important financial information, what should you do with it? Clearly, dividing your debts and assets and predicting the outcome of that deal into the future is a task more complex than most of us can handle. To help you—and your accountant—crunch the numbers, there are a number of family law software programs on the market.

One of them, called Divorce Plan, was created by Boulder, Colorado financial planner Carol Ann Wilson, who found that clients came to her months or years after a divorce settlement had played out, complaining of inequity in the arrangement. To better predict long-term outcome of a deal,

Divorce Plan's calculations include property division along with income, expenses, assets, alimony, child support, college expenses, investments, retirement pay, social security, taxes on maintenance, and recent tax law changes. The program incorporates assumed inflation and pay raises. It generates financial status, cash flow, net worth of each spouse, settlement scenarios over a lifetime and provides this information in graph form as well.

In addition to software that delivers a comprehensive financial settlement, online calculators are available that cover the various financial aspects of divorce. First, check your state's website (see Appendix C). Many states provide free divorce calculators specific to your own state. If your state doesn't have a calculator, there are many others available on the Internet.

The most comprehensive suite of divorce calculators we've found for laypeople can be accessed online, through Family Law Software, Inc. and its website, Split-Up.com (www.split-up.com/calc/calculators.htm.) Among the calculators on the site are a tax calculator to help you determine your and your spouse's income after alimony, support, and taxes; a property division calculator; an "alimony buyout" calculator that shows the difference between a one-time buyout payment and a series of payments; and a home sale calculator that estimates how much money each party will keep after the sale. For a fee, the more ambitious can purchase the Split-Up software, which enables you to play out different scenarios, calculate child support, calculate the value of specific pension plans, and more.

Of course, if you have significant assets your best bet is consulting a certified financial planner or perhaps even financial advisor specializing in divorce. There are so many quirks, loopholes, and pitfalls for each state that it takes an experienced pro to navigate them all.

The Least You Need to Know

◆ When dividing assets, strive to share fairly with your spouse.

◆ If left up to a judge, debt will be allocated based not only on who incurred it, but also on what it was incurred for and who has what income.

◆ Before selling your house, be sure that is the wisest financial course of action, particularly considering the tax implications.

◆ If one of you is going to have continued use of the house, be sure to spell out the time frame by which such use will stop, and decide up front a mechanism for selling the house.

◆ Consult with an accountant or financial advisor about the tax consequences of moving out of your house but keeping your name on the deed.

Chapter 17

Coping With Complexities: Inheritance, Wills, and Other Estate Issues

In This Chapter

- ◆ What happens to property you owned before you got married?

- ◆ Inheritance during a marriage: Do you get to keep it all?

- ◆ When one spouse dies before the divorce is final

- ◆ The role of the will in divorce

Donna and Jonathan, both divorced, met on a cruise to Alaska in 1990 and less than a year later tied the knot. It was a second marriage for each. Both in their mid-forties, they had children from first marriages but expected none this time around. By 1996, their relationship was in shambles, and after attempting to reconcile later that year, they realized their marriage had come to an end. It was in 1997 that Jonathan filed for divorce, alleging that Donna had been involved in numerous affairs and was unusually cruel.

As it turned out, Jonathan, an entrepreneur, had accumulated significant personal wealth a few years before meeting Donna. With so much money at stake, each hired a full-service attorney. Because Jonathan wanted to give Donna as little of his personal wealth as possible, the case inched toward trial. In the equitable distribution state of New York, Donna knew the bulk of the assets were Jonathan's separate property, but she felt she could do better in court than through negotiation, given the offers made by Jonathan's attorney.

But in a shock to everyone—not just Jonathan's children but Donna herself—Jonathan was killed in a car accident the week before the trial was to begin. In line with the law, the divorce action was halted at once and Donna, still Jonathan's wife, became executor of his will. A relatively young man, Jonathan hadn't bothered to change his will prior to the divorce action; after all, once the divorce was finalized, the will would be null and void.

But with Jonathan now dead and the will unchanged, Jonathan's intent to keep the bulk of his money and leave his estate to his children from his first marriage could not be fulfilled. The will had bequeathed to Donna far more than she could ever have hoped for in court, even under the most favorable of circumstances.

Furious, Jonathan's children sought legal advice, but were told to back off. They could not successfully contest the enormous inheritance to Donna because they simply had no grounds.

Inherited Money and Personal Property: Who Gets What?

Whether you reside in an equitable distribution state or a community property state, the rules and guidelines are not always clear-cut. Depending on your state of residence and your situation, you may need tax and estate experts to guide you through.

For instance, what about property you had before you got married? In theory, in most states, it's not considered marital property providing it's been kept in your name alone, but there are many loopholes and complications. What if the property has increased in value during the marriage? What if you have taken a mortgage on it and, with your spouse, paid the mortgage off? What if the property has been renovated? You need to talk to your attorney. Depending on where you live and what was done to increase the value of the property, part or even all of the property might be subject to distribution.

Likewise, property inherited during a marriage is said to belong to the heir, alone, as long as it hasn't been sold and the proceeds pooled in a joint account. Yet, once a property is sold, it's difficult to prove that money has remained untangled and aloof, unless it's placed into an individual account.

On the surface, things could not be clearer than the "community property" state of Texas, where all property is divided into two categories: separate property or community property. Under Texas law, separate property includes anything the individual owned prior to the marriage, anything he inherited during marriage, and any payment accrued in a lawsuit, as the result of personal injury, except any recovery for loss of earning capacity during marriage.

Community property in Texas is everything acquired during the marriage aside from separate property. It doesn't matter if just one spouse holds the title to a car or is named on a credit card; if it was obtained during the marriage, the asset or debt belongs to both.

In a Texas divorce, the court can only divide the community property and does not have the power to divide separate property. But it isn't that simple. You have to prove the property is truly separate by tracing it with documents to the moment it was acquired to the present time. If separate assets somehow become commingled over time, it will be considered community property no matter how you acquired it. For instance, if inherited cash has been deposited into a joint account or any account with money that might be considered community property (for example, salary), the "separate money" becomes subject to the joint management of the spouses, unless they sign an agreement to the contrary.

Despite some of the loopholes, in Texas, ownership of one spouse's separate property cannot, in general, be awarded to the other spouse.

This is not true in Connecticut, which is not merely an equitable distribution state—but what is called an "all-property equitable distribution state." Connecticut law spells out the situation clearly: "At the time of entering a decree annulling or dissolving a marriage or for legal separation … the Superior Court may assign to either the husband or wife all or any part of the estate of the other." In Connecticut, it would be possible for a spouse to receive at dissolution a large percentage of an inheritance that the other party received a few days before the marriage dissolution action was filed, even though that party made no contribution to the acquisition, preservation, or appreciation of that inherited property.

If you're about to divorce a spouse who's just inherited a windfall, it might be in your best interest to move the family to Connecticut—or one of the other "all-property" states, including Alaska, Hawaii, Indiana, Iowa, Kansas, Massachusetts, Michigan, Montana, New Hampshire, North Dakota, Oregon, South Dakota, Vermont, and Wyoming. On the other hand, if *you* are the heir, beware that Connecticut law might force you to share your birthright with your soon-to-be-ex. In this case, you might want to move to New York.

When a Spouse Dies Before Divorce Is Final

In most instances, of course, the distribution of property is protected by wills. But when it comes to divorce, confusion about wills and inheritance abounds. The widespread lack of knowledge leaves many divorcing people in the lurch—and because they haven't attended to the technicalities, they could unwittingly leave hard-earned assets to a soon-to-be-former spouse, with children from a prior marriage out of luck.

Writing in *The CPA Journal*, Louis Skroka, a Minneola, New York attorney specializing in complex divorce and related matrimonial matters, describes the problems that can result when one spouse dies before the divorce has been finalized in New York State: "Without insight and planning, unanticipated consequences will almost certainly result if one of the spouses dies unexpectedly during the transition period. It is crucial to take necessary precautions in order to prevent the problems that may occur," Skroka says.

The reality, in a nutshell, is that "a marriage endures until a judge executes a final judgment of divorce, regardless of the length of separation, lack of communication, or bitterness of allegations," Skroka says. Thus, when a spouse dies in the midst of a divorce, the parties are still legally married and the divorce action automatically stops. The court loses jurisdiction to decide the marital status of these individuals, and also the right to decide property issues arising out of that status. As a result, the decedent's estate plan and prior will prevails. The law states that the surviving spouse is entitled to whatever bequests are described in the will and whatever accounts or assets for which she is the named beneficiary.

"As soon as a divorce decree is signed, the provisions of a will leaving property to the now-divorced spouse become null and void, and the will is construed as if the divorced spouse predeceased the survivor," Skroka explains. "But until a judge's signature is affixed to the final decree, the marriage lasts, and so does the effectiveness of the will," along with any trusts and beneficiary assignments on things like life insurance policies and bank accounts.

If the deceased spouse's estate plan was generous to the soon-to-be ex, and if it was left unchanged with the expectation that divorce itself would take care of it, the surviving partner would come into a windfall. The children from a prior marriage—the intended beneficiaries—would have few grounds on which to protest the will. On the other hand, if the will was changed to disinherit the surviving spouse prior to divorce, that individual could mount a legal fight and might well prevail. "A spouse, including a nearly divorced one, is protected by law from being disinherited," Skroka says. "A surviving spouse may 'elect' against the estate and receive the 'elective share,' which is the greater of one-third of the net estate or $50,000." In addition, the spouse is entitled to other assets not even part of the probate of the will: pension plan, profit-sharing accounts, and the like.

In short, the surviving spouse, whether as a beneficiary or an "elector," stands to inherit far more than might have been the case had he or she been subject to the equitable distribution of the divorce. There is just one caveat: At least in New York, the surviving spouse cannot become an "elector" in the estate if he or she has abandoned or otherwise failed to care for the deceased spouse, despite an ability to do so. What does this mean? The law defines abandonment as leaving the marital home without any intention of returning and without the consent of the other spouse. In one pivotal case in New York State, says Skroka, "the husband was found to have lost his right to an elective share [of the estate] when he moved out of the marital residence several years before the wife's death and never paid any rent despite the fact that she was evicted."

Given all the twists and turns in the law and all the nuances, anyone dealing with significant property or wealth would do well to consult a knowledgeable attorney as soon as possible. Do not do anything until your situation has been analyzed under a legal microscope.

"When an individual wants to disinherit a spouse, a new will should be prepared and all beneficiary accounts should be changed to eliminate the spouse," Skroka says. "To maximize the chances of prevailing in an elective share contest (in New York, at least), the individual should develop a case for abandonment or lack of support against the other spouse, and include such claims in any action for divorce or separation. Often, such specific planning is not done."

As for the spouse to be disinherited, the advice is opposite. Indeed, despite the fact that you may want to leave your partner as soon as possible, the best course of action may be to take up residence in a separate wing of the mansion instead of moving to a

Penthouse of your own. While it may sound aggressive and cold, if your soon-to-be-ex is in a coma, a bedside vigil is the best strategic move you can make. Most of us don't have to worry about who gets the mansion in the Hamptons and who gets the townhouse in New York. Still, even for those of more modest means, the same laws apply. An inheritance of $10,000 will be subject to the same guidelines as one of $10 million.

The Least You Need to Know

- Property that you brought into the marriage is considered yours going out; but your spouse may be eligible for a portion of any increase in its value.

- Inherited property is viewed differently from one state to the next. Be sure to check the laws governing your particular situation.

- If a spouse dies before the divorce is final, the estate is distributed as it would have been had the marriage stayed intact.

- A disinherited spouse can contest a new will. It's best to spell out in the will why you're doing what you're doing.

- When drafting your marital settlement agreement, insert explicit mutual waivers relinquishing rights to receive anything from the other's IRAs, insurance policies, and employment plans in the future, except for those rights outlined in your agreement.

- Make sure you change beneficiary designation on qualified retirement benefits like pensions and 401(k)s, 403(b)s, and the like, as well as life insurance policies, as soon as the law permits.

Chapter 18

Spousal Support

In This Chapter

- What is maintenance and when is it appropriate?
- The rules governing spousal maintenance
- How to get the best deal for yourself
- When altered life circumstances affect what you receive or what you pay

Long after the ink is dry on your judgment of divorce, you might still be writing checks to your ex. Whether your state calls the payments alimony, spousal support, or maintenance, you call it punishment. Is there any end in sight?

Maybe the payments haven't begun. You're not divorced yet, but you want some idea of what this breakup is going to cost you. Or perhaps you need to know how much money you can expect to receive so you can start to rebuild your life.

The Who, When, and How Much of Maintenance

Whatever your situation, you must first understand the maintenance basics—what *maintenance* (or *alimony*) is exactly, when it is appropriate, and how the general rules applying to maintenance will determine what happens to you.

In a nutshell, maintenance is financial support that one spouse provides to the other in the event of divorce or legal separation. Maintenance is determined, in large measure, by the laws of the state where you live. Some basic rules, however, are virtually universal:

Divorce Dictionary

Maintenance, or **alimony,** refers to payments made by one spouse to the other to assist with the support of the recipient spouse. Payments usually terminate upon the death of either spouse or a date decided by a judge or agreed upon by the husband and wife. They may also terminate upon remarriage or cohabitation of the supported spouse. Payments received are usually taxable for the recipient spouse and tax-deductible for the paying spouse.

- A wife can pay her husband alimony and vice versa. Gone are the days when only husbands paid wives support.

- In many instances, these payments are time-limited, but in longer-term marriages, they can continue for life.

- Although you can negotiate otherwise, the payments are usually tax-deductible to the person who pays them and considered taxable income by the recipient. Stated another way, what you receive might be reduced by virtue of taxes, whereas your payments might cost you less when the tax deduction is figured in. Have a tax professional or lawyer explain the requirements of the Internal Revenue Code's section 71.

Safety Net for the Homemaker

It's understandable that maintenance can be a key cause of resentment following divorce, especially when it must be paid for years. Except for the very wealthy, helping to support not just one household, but two, is an extraordinary burden. For the one receiving the payments, meanwhile, the reality of a restricted lifestyle and dependency on an ex-spouse can be onerous, indeed.

Take the case of Patty and John. When they married, both were teachers. Three years later, when Vivian was born, Patty stopped working. Patty and John decided she would go back to work in four years, but then, they had two more children, and four years became eight years. When all three children were finally in school, Patty no longer wanted to go back to work. During the school year, John took some coaching positions to make ends meet while Patty took care of the kids. In the summer, John did construction work while Patty took the kids to the beach. John resented Patty's refusal to work, but went along with it.

Now, Patty and John are getting divorced. Patty would like to work, but there are no jobs in her immediate area. Besides, she hasn't taught in more than eight years. She needs to take some refresher courses. John is panicking. He could barely pay the bills when he was supporting one household. Now, he'll have to support two. It just doesn't seem fair that he's done all the work, and now he'll have to do even more.

Patty is upset, meanwhile, because the family cannot afford to keep the house. Of course, if she had known they were going to divorce, she would have kept working. She's angry about the position she's in.

Could this nightmare happen to you? Remember, just because you are divorcing does not mean you can ignore decisions you and your spouse made about how you wanted to live your married life. You might be able to eventually alter the course of those decisions, but in the beginning of a divorce, they are the realities you have to live with.

Rules of Thumb

The basic rule is simple. The breadwinner spouse pays, and the nonbreadwinner cashes the checks. If you both worked or both have the ability to work and can easily get jobs, the chances are good that neither of you have to pay the other. If one spouse earns vastly more than the other, a certain amount of maintenance may be required as well.

In one case we've followed, a couple—a teacher and a police detective—were divorcing. Their salaries and benefits were comparable, and neither had to pay spousal support to the other.

Child support, which we cover in the next chapter, is a different matter. The teacher-husband had custody of the parties' two children, and he was entitled to support from his wife, the detective, who earned somewhat more. Most states have a system whereby child support is determined by guidelines based on a percentage of the parents' income and the number of children, the children's needs, or a combination of the two. Check with your lawyer or your state's website. We've listed the link to each state's child support guidelines, if they are available online, in Appendix C.

What's Fair? Coming Up with a Number

How do you know how much maintenance to pay or to demand? There are well-established parameters. In general, courts look at the following factors to determine the size of the support check. It follows, of course, that lawyers who try to settle a case out of court need to look at these factors (or you and your spouse must consider them if you're trying to do it yourselves):

◆ **Your income.** Is there sufficient money to enable both of you to enjoy the same lifestyle, or are you both going to have to cut back?

◆ **The length of the marriage.** The longer the marriage, the stronger the claim for support.

◆ **Your ages.** Younger people are thought to be better able to find work. Older people nearing retirement might be unable to pay support for a long period of time.

Social Security might be an issue if either of you is close to retirement age. In a marriage of more than 10 years, if the non-working spouse does not remarry, at retirement age, he or she will be able to receive benefits based on the ex's Social Security record.

◆ **Your health.** Is one of you ill and unable to work? That could affect how much will be paid and for how long it will be paid.

◆ **Job sacrifices you made during the marriage.** Did you give up a good position because your spouse had to relocate for her job? Maybe you never used your degree because you worked as a bookkeeper in your husband's business. Whether your sacrifice was obvious or subtle, it could affect the duration of your support award.

◆ **Education and job skills.** The easier you can find work, the shorter the duration of your support.

◆ **Who the children are going to live with.** If they're going to live with you and that shortens the time you can spend working each day, you might be entitled to more maintenance than if the children were living with your spouse or if you had no children.

◆ **Independent income sources.** Maybe you have a trust or other source of income. You never touched it during the marriage because you planned to leave it all to your children. Now, its existence could affect the amount of support you'll receive or have to pay.

- **Distribution of other assets.** If you and your spouse accumulated a lot during the marriage that will be split, you might not be entitled to any maintenance. Let's say your wife built up her medical practice while you were married, and now she has to pay you half its value of $350,000. Depending on where you live, the receipt of that lump sum could reduce additional support payments.

- **Marital fault.** In some jurisdictions, the reason for the breakup of your marriage could affect the duration and amount of support.

- **The tax implications of the payment.** If you have to pay taxes on what you receive, you might need a larger amount than if you do not have to pay taxes on the payment.

- **The past standard of living, assuming that it was based on fully reported income.** In many states, the idea of maintaining the same lifestyle is part of the alimony statute and is a goal, although it may not be reached.

Judges and lawyers look at these factors to determine how much maintenance one of you should pay the other. The single most important factor is, of course, how much money there is to go around.

You Can't Always Get What You Want, but You'll Get What You Need

We've all heard the notion, bandied about on TV and in the movies, that maintenance should enable the receiving spouse to continue to live "in the style to which he or she has become accustomed." Well, in a perfect world, it'd work out that way. But the reality in many cases is that the income used to support one household simply isn't enough to support two, at least at the same level as before.

So, in the world of alimony, although the "style to which you have become accustomed" is the ideal, it often cannot be maintained. (And sad to say, in too many cases, luxurious lifestyles are fueled by a failure to pay appropriate taxes or "loans from the family store." Such dirty little secrets often come to light during a divorce action, limiting the available funds for everyone.)

It is, in short, impossible to state any rule about how much you should expect to pay or receive. Unless you are wealthy, you should expect to cut back a bit, create and stick to a realistic budget, and consider going to work or working more.

You Can Do It! _____

Here's a word to the wise: take that job. Don't turn down a job for fear it will lower your maintenance settlement. If it's a good job with the possibility of advancement, you'll be better off taking it than depending on maintenance payments that are likely to fall short of your needs. In fact, a judge might just look at your lack of employment and, instead of increasing payments to you, simply declare you "under-employed"—that is to say, earning less money than you're capable of, and *imputing* or attributing the dollar difference to you anyway!.

Getting the Best Deal

When negotiating for maintenance, be sure to look at the big picture. For instance, Ann Parsons didn't want to sell her house under any circumstances. Her lawyer told her that if her case were decided by a judge, the judge would order the house sold and would order her husband to pay her support. Ann's husband had a checkered job history, although he was well paid when he did work. Ann decided that rather than take any support, she would keep the house and get a job to pay the bills.

You Can Do It! _____

When negotiating, start by asking for more than you either need or expect to get. Then, during negotiations, be willing to give up what you don't mind losing.

It wouldn't have been the right deal for everyone, but for Ann, it was. She decided what she really wanted was the house and looked at the big picture. She couldn't rely on her husband to pay her support, and the house would give her income when and if she was ever ready to sell it.

All situations are different, of course, and negotiating the terms of maintenance will vary from one couple to the next. However, as you go about cutting your own deal, make sure to follow these general guidelines:

◆ The deft negotiator will first figure out what he or she really wants and will cast a cold eye on the reality of the situation. Do you want to stay home with the kids or go back to work? Do you want the house or your share of the cash from its sale? Will your spouse be responsible enough to meet his or her obligations? Don't hold out for promises you know your spouse probably will not live up to.

◆ If you decide you want support above all else, you must determine your expenses, including recurring expenses and one-time costs due to the divorce. Will you have to move and have cable, telephone, and electricity installed? Or are you staying put, but you need some replacement furniture?

Make a detailed list of these one-time and recurring expenses. Then, make a list of all income and savings. Look at your checks and credit card bills from the previous 12 months and get an average of your monthly expenses. You should, by the way, come to terms with the fact that you might need to use some of the savings for your one-time expenses.

After you determine the monthly expenses, calculate your shortfall. Is the shortfall a sum you can realistically expect to receive from your spouse? If so, great. (Remember, you might have to pay taxes on the money, so subtract that from your spouse's payments.)

If you know your spouse can't pay that much, look at your list again. Is there any place where you can compromise? Is there any way you can add to your income?

♦ You don't have to be Donald Trump to know that, when making a deal, you never present your bottom-line figure right away. Maybe you've played enough mind games with your spouse to last a lifetime, but you *must* play one more to get a fair shake. Start high (or low if you're the one who has to pay), and gradually move down (or up).

♦ If you're going to pay, avoid a deal that requires you to reveal your income every year. Of course, if you do have to reveal your income, make sure it's a mutual obligation, so you can see what your ex is making, too!

♦ Make sure that the duration of the alimony has a limited timeframe, if you are paying.

♦ Make sure you can afford to pay or accept what you're about to agree to. However guilty, angry, or in love with someone else you might be, do not agree to something you cannot afford.

♦ Consider using a lawyer to negotiate alimony. Even if you and your spouse have worked out everything, this area is usually so fraught with emotion that it is not a bad idea to let someone else handle it. If you have allocated limited funds for unbundled legal services, consider spending some of them here.

You Can Do It!

If possible, arrange spousal support through mediation or settlement, not litigation. This will provide both parties with the most flexibility in getting what they deem most important from the arrangement.

A Word of Warning

Make sure that spousal support payments are not crafted to end when a child comes of age. In general, the Internal Revenue Service will view such payments as disguised child support and might disallow the tax deduction for them. That is because the recipient spouse does not have to count that money as income (though the paying spouse doesn't get to deduct the payment from his or her taxable income). Although this might be good for the recipient (who now won't be taxed on the support), it is bad for the paying partner (who will now be unable to deduct the payments from his or her income), and it can wreak havoc on a deal.

In addition, reworking an agreement after it's been in place for a while can present a sticky problem because the IRS might go back to recharacterize what is taxable and what is not taxable. Presumably, the receiving spouse has been paying the taxes. You would now have to amend your returns and seek a refund. It is better to draft your agreement correctly the first time.

When Circumstances Change

We all know that life is a roller-coaster. One moment, you're flying high, on top of the world; the next, your world has been shattered to a thousand bits. Economies can crumble; companies can fold; real estate values can soar or plummet based on world events or the fates.

The roller-coaster is one reason why it might be best, in some states, to see a judge when negotiating spousal support. In a few states, if a judge decides your case, you will have an easier time changing a support award than if you and your spouse sign off on the payment in a separate agreement.

Why is that? According to the law in these states, when you sign an agreement, judges will assume that you thought of all the possible things that might happen in the future and that you accounted for them in the agreement. For example, if you were to pay support at the rate of $300 a week for five years, the agreement could have provided that if you lost your job, you would no longer have to make payments. If you didn't provide for that and you do lose your job, you can ask a judge to allow you to stop making the payments—but the judge might point out that you had your chance to include that in the agreement and now it's just too late.

When a judge decides your case after a trial, on the other hand, he or she does not account for future possibilities. The decision is based solely upon what the judge has heard in court. Therefore, if you or your spouse lose a job some years down the road, you'll have an easier time, in these states, convincing the judge to make a change than if you had signed an agreement.

Bottom line? Try to account for all possibilities when you sign an agreement, and always consult with an attorney.

Silver Linings

Despite the security of those monthly support checks, it may be the best thing for the receiving spouse when the period of spousal support is over and the maintenance ends. At that point, both partners are economically independent and, with the umbilical cord cut, can go their own ways. Such separation affords a true sense of closure—often not possible, even after divorce, when financial strings persist. Of course, with a long-term marriage, this may not be possible.

The Least You Need to Know

◆ Spousal support (also called maintenance or alimony) is based on a number of factors, whereas child support is usually based on a fixed percentage of your income, the children's needs, or a combination of the two.

◆ Spousal support is usually included in the receiving spouse's income for tax purposes and is tax-deductible from the paying spouse's income.

◆ When negotiating, never reveal your bottom line in the beginning. Figure out what you really want before you start.

◆ In some states, it is easier to change support that a judge ordered than it is to change an amount you agreed to pay or accept in a negotiated settlement, so be sure that you think of all possibilities before you sign an agreement. Better still, consult an attorney.

Chapter **19**

Child Support

In This Chapter

- Understanding child support
- Figuring out what's fair
- Dealing with deadbeat parents
- Paying for your child's insurance and healthcare

Let's face it. Raising kids is expensive. Medical expenses alone can account for a huge portion of the budget. Add to that clothes, food, a big-enough house or apartment to accommodate the kids, child care, toys for the little ones, computer games for the bigger ones, activities and lessons … the list goes on and on. Married couples combine their resources to cover these costs, but the expenses don't end just because you're separated or divorced.

When parents live apart, and custody resides with one parent, the parent who lives with the children the *least*, the noncustodial parent, pays his or her share of the children's expenses to the parent who lives with the children the *most*, the custodial parent. This payment is called *child support*. The parent with whom the child primarily resides is presumed to pay his or her share of the expenses directly to the child.

In almost all cases, the amount paid is based on the relative incomes of the parents and the needs of the child and presumes that the lifestyle of the child should be the same as if the family had remained intact.

If the parents have *joint physical custody*, where the child spends about 30 to 50 percent of her time at both homes (virtually equal), child support usually is adjusted.

A Closer Look at State Child Support Guidelines

According to the American Bar Association, "the starting point for determining child support usually is the state's guideline or a formula that considers the income of the parents, the number of children, and some other factors. The formulas are based on studies of how much families ordinarily spend for raising children," the American Bar Association says. "Numbers are plugged into the formula, yielding an amount of support each child should get."

Most states have the guidelines on their website. Some even have a child support calculator, which lets you punch in your income and other factors, and then calculates what you can expect to pay. Some commercial websites have calculators as well, but these are not as reliable because they might not be current on the states' guidelines.

If your income is either very low (under $13,000, for example), or very high (for example, over $80,000), additional rules usually take effect, depending on the state.

Income can be defined in the very broadest way—to include not only wages, but also assets, such as stocks or a pension, government benefits, or regular, annual gifts from family members—or it can be defined in a narrow way, limited only to earned income.

For the purpose of calculating income for the paying parent (to determine the amount of child support to be paid), the law usually provides for deductions to be taken from the income, and those deductions vary from state to state as well. Federal, state, and local taxes, mandatory retirement contributions, union dues, and health insurance, as well as payments already being made on behalf of other children and spouses from prior relationships are among the common deductions.

Unless you live in one of the few states that uses gross income as a basis for setting child support amounts, your net income (what's left after the allowed deductions) becomes the money from which you pay your child support obligation. Different states use different methods to allocate child support payments between parents. Most use percentages, and the percentage usually increases with each additional child you have.

In the majority of states, parents receiving public assistance can exclude that income from the calculation. For these parents, there might be special guidelines for child support.

On the other end of the income scale, some states place a ceiling on the income used to calculate child support, such as a combined parental income of $80,000. All income above $80,000 might be subject to a different percentage from the first $80,000 of income. Or a cap might apply to the amount of income above the $80,000 for the purposes of calculating child support.

In addition to child support, parents are often required to maintain health insurance for the children and sometimes life insurance to guarantee the child support in the event of a parent's death. In most states, parents are also required to pay for child care, minus any child-care expense tax credit the other (typically, custodial) parent might receive.

Child Support in Sole Custody Arrangements

Let's look at an example of how child support is determined in New York. Unless the parents agree otherwise, the state assumes a child will live primarily with one of his parents, as opposed to both parents sharing physical custody after the divorce. (More on state presumptions regarding custody in Chapter 21). We will use New York State's child support guidelines as an example.

The State of New York's child support guidelines state:

- ◆ "The gross income of each parent is determined and the incomes are combined;

- ◆ the combined parental income is multiplied by the appropriate child support percentage—17 percent for one child, 25 percent for two children, 29 percent for three children, 31 percent for four children, and not less than 35 percent for five or more children;

- ◆ this figure is the basic child support obligation, which is then divided between the parents on a pro-rata basis, according to the amount of their respective incomes;

- ◆ additional amounts to be paid for child care, medical care not covered by health insurance, and educational expenses are determined by the court and added to the basic child support obligation; and,

- ◆ the noncustodial parent is ordered to pay his/her share to the custodial parent— sometimes called the 'parent of primary residence.'"

The amount of child support calculated in accordance with the (New York) guidelines is presumed to be the correct amount. "Either parent can offer evidence that this amount is not correct, and the court has the authority to decide whether the guidelines amount is unjust or inappropriate," the guidelines state. "If the court orders a different amount than the basic support obligation according to the guidelines, the court must set forth its reasons for doing so in writing. Either party can object to the findings of the court."

You Can Do It!

Many states now make payment of child support easy by allowing you to pay right on their websites!

Red Alert

Federal law requires states to review their child support guidelines and make any necessary revisions every four years, so be sure to check your state's website for the latest information before thinking about your situation.

Here's an example of how such calculations might work in the state of Anywhere, USA:

Mark's income as a bank manager is $90,000. Nancy's income as a paralegal is $50,000. Their combined income is $140,000. For the purposes of child support, their child is entitled to 20 percent of the combined parental income, up to $70,000 in their state. The child support is to be paid in the ratio of the parents' incomes to their combined income. Because the combined income is double the amount used for the purposes of the base calculation—$140,000—the law in their state allows the judge to decide how to use the extra $70,000 of income. The judge decides to cap the income to be considered for support at $110,000. He then calculates that 20 percent of $110,000 is $22,000—the total amount of child support. Nancy has to pay 36 percent of this amount, or $7,920, and Mark has to pay 64 percent, or $14,080.

Child Support in Shared Custody Arrangements

Many states have laws that presume it's best if parents have joint or shared *legal* custody of their children after a divorce, unless there's some reason not to (again, more on custody in Chapter 21). But what happens if the parents share joint physical, as well as legal, custody? More to the point: how does child support work if each parent has physical custody an equal amount of time, as is often the case in a joint physical custody arrangement?

"When parents have joint physical custody, shared custody, or split custody of a child, the determination of child support is complicated and may not fit the formula," according to Michigan's 2004 Child Support Formula Manual.

Michigan's formula is indeed complicated, and it is indeed a formula! Are you ready? Take the number of overnights the children will annually spend with Parent A squared times Parent B's base support obligation and subtract the number of overnights the children will annually spend with Parent B squared times Parent A's base support obligation and divide the whole thing by the number of overnights the children will annually spend with Parent A squared plus the number of overnights the children will annually spend with Parent B squared. That will give you your *base support*.

The good news is that this formula is only valid if the "noncustodial" parent has a minimum of 128 overnights.

Michigan also has an abatement formula for parents who are not using the preceding formula, when a noncustodial parent spends a long period of time with the child. The abatement is 50 percent of the daily expenses as prorated by the child support award.

According to the American Bar Association, 28 states include a shared parenting time offset in their child support guidelines. (For a chart of general child support criteria in every state, see the American Bar Association website at www.abanet.org/family/ familylaw/Chart3_ChildSupportGuidelines.pdf.)

As we repeat again and again, every state is different. Each state has its own very unique child support guidelines; so you must investigate the guidelines in *your* state to know where you stand.

Direct vs. Indirect Child Support: Which Is Right for You?

Child support comes in two flavors—direct and indirect. Child support is when one parent pays support to the other parent directly on a regular basis—every week, every other week, or every month. Indirect child support, on the other hand, involves payments made to third parties for expenses such as school tuition, camp, lessons, after-school activities, and healthcare costs.

Whether you are the custodial parent or are involved in a joint custodial arrangement, if your ex has been ordered to pay child support, you might wonder whether you're better off receiving a larger amount of direct support and paying the third parties yourself or letting your former spouse make those payments and getting less direct support. Conceptually, it is nearly always better to receive sufficient funds directly. It's about more than money; it is a question of control. When you write the check to the school or camp yourself, the decision-making is in your hands. Yet the subject warrants a bit more thought.

If you are the parent receiving funds, choosing to receive direct or indirect support has its pros and cons:

Pros	Cons
If your former spouse pays the third party directly and those expenses increase he or she will pay the increase.	If what you receive includes amounts to be paid to the third parties, and the costs of those third-party expenses rise, you might have to bear the increase.
Some former spouses will be more reliable if they are paying third-party expenses directly because they feel more involved in their children's lives.	Some spouses will be less reliable if they are obligated to pay the third-party expenses. You will have to chase your former spouse for payment while the third parties are hounding *you*.

If you are the parent making the payments, choosing to pay direct or indirect support has its pros and cons as well:

Pros	Cons
If you're obligated to figure third-party expenses into your direct payments, your former spouse will probably bear the cost of the increase.	If you pay the third parties, you'll bear the cost of any increases.
You might feel more in control and more directly involved with your children if you pay third-party expenses.	If you give your former spouse money to pay third parties and he or she doesn't make the payments, the third parties might chase *you*.

How do you decide whether direct or indirect support is right for you? If a judge decides your case after a trial, you'll have no choice; whatever the judge decides goes. If you're settling your case, on the other hand, you can compromise. If your former spouse is the noncustodial parent (or a custody partner with greater income) and is reliable, you're probably better off having him or her pay the expenses directly to the third party to avoid responsibility for increases in big-ticket items, such as school tuition. If your former spouse is unreliable or disagrees with you about signing up your child for an activity, you're better off receiving more child support and paying these extra costs yourself. The point of child support is to enable the child to enjoy the lifestyle of the wealthier parent. If that has a benefit to the ex, so be it.

One of the most frequent questions lawyers get from their noncustodial clients is "Why can't I pay child support directly to my child?" (So what if the child is two years old!) "Why can't I set up an account so I know the money is being used for the kids?" The real question being asked is, "Isn't my spouse the one benefiting from the child support?"

The truth is, your ex *is* benefiting, to a degree. If your former spouse pays the rent with child support, of course, he or she is also benefiting. The same goes for the phone, electricity, cable TV, and even food. Let's face it, your ex isn't going to buy steak for the kids and hamburger for himself or herself.

Silver Linings

If you are the parent paying child support, you can negotiate a smaller amount of maintenance, also known as *spousal support*, in return for a larger child support payment. Bear in mind that your child support obligation, depending on the ages of your children, can last for many more years than maintenance. Alternatively, if your children are teens when you divorce, child support may end while alimony can go on and on. Remember, too, that there's no tax deduction for child support, whereas maintenance is usually tax-deductible. (See Chapter 18 for details on spousal support.)

What's Fair?

If you and your spouse believe you can reach a settlement, how do you determine what's in your child's best interest but also fair to both of you? It's not easy, but you can do it.

To Settle or Not to Settle? That Is the Question

Now that most states have formulas for determining child support, there is little mystery about the outcome if you were to have a judge decide. If you are the custodial parent and your spouse isn't willing to meet the state's guidelines during negotiation, why should you settle? Most of the time, of course, you shouldn't. But there are exceptions. The following are some important reasons for agreeing to less child support than the state's guidelines might otherwise allow:

◆ **There's more certainty that you can collect the support.** Most parents will pay what they can afford and especially what they have agreed to pay. In contrast, when they fall hopelessly behind or a judge orders them to pay more than they can afford, they often default, and, if your ex lacks a job or assets, it can be a lot harder to collect.

◆ **Add-ons.** If you agree to a child support figure that is less than the formula, you might be able to get your spouse to add on other items. Maybe the law of your state doesn't obligate a parent to pay for after-school activities, camp, or even college. You might be willing to accept less child support than the formula provides if your spouse will pick up some of these items.

◆ **Exception to the formula.** Remember, hardship provisions to the law usually make the formula inapplicable. If your spouse demonstrates to a judge that hardships exist, the judge might not apply the formula. If that situation is a possibility for you, negotiation might be in your best interest.

Likewise, if you are the noncustodial parent, negotiating child support might be best for you because …

◆ Your spouse might agree to less than the guidelines allow.

◆ You have more say over what your financial needs are and can tailor the agreement to your situation.

◆ You can modify the agreement to state that if your income decreases by a certain amount, your child support payments can be reduced accordingly.

Red Alert

In most jurisdictions, you cannot just agree to change child support informally, with your ex. Instead, you must go to court to obtain an order modifying the amount of support. Otherwise, your support obligation continues to accrue and is enforceable under the law.

Duration of Child Support

Child support should terminate at the age your child is considered emancipated under your state's laws. In some states, that means age 18; in others, age 21, or beyond.

Other events can terminate child support as well—the child's entry into the military, assumption of full-time employment, or marriage before the age of emancipation. If the child moves in with the non-custodial parent on a permanent basis, child support also should stop. (You might want to negotiate a sum the former custodial parent will have to pay you in that case.)

If you and your spouse agree, child support can extend beyond the age of emancipation. For example, if in your state the emancipation age is 18, but you want your spouse to continue to pay child support until your child graduates from college, you could try to negotiate a provision stipulating that child support continue for as long as the child is a full-time undergraduate student, but in no event beyond the age of 21 or 22, whenever the child graduates in due course.

Red Alert _____

If your child support agreement includes a mechanism to increase child support without returning to court, consider a similar mechanism to decrease child support in the event of a financial setback, such as a job loss or a reduction in income of, for example, 25 percent or greater. If you are the parent paying child support, you might want a provision that reduces it by, say, a third or half when the children are in camp or away at college, particularly if you are also contributing to camp or college. Why not a 100 percent reduction? Because your former spouse still has to maintain the home for your child after camp or during college vacations (assuming that your state is one of the few in which the age of emancipation is 21). But beware, you'll have to formalize each decrease by way of court order, or your "official" child support obligation will remain as it was per the last court decree.

What Should the Child Support Figure Be?

How do you go about determining exactly how much child support *you* should pay or receive if you are negotiating an agreement that deviates from your state's guidelines? Keep in mind that the state is unlikely to allow you to give (or receive, depending on your position) less than what is provided in the guidelines, unless you persuade the court it's appropriate to deviate from those guidelines in your case.

To ascertain a fair amount of child support without using your state's formula, it is best to figure out a monthly budget for the children. Household expenses, such as mortgage or rent, food, and utilities can be allocated one half to the children and one half to the parent, or they can be allocated one part each among all the children in the household and the parent. Clothing costs for the year should be added up and divided by 12, as should camp, extracurricular activities, birthday party gifts, and similar items that are paid only once or twice a year.

After you and your spouse have worked out a budget, you can determine the total contribution for each of you. You should agree on a mechanism for calculating future cost-of-living increases for this payment. You can base your formula on the cost-of-living increase as determined by your state's department of agriculture or other indices, or if you prefer, you can base it on increases in your incomes. Because most people prefer not to reveal their income each year, it's common to base such payment increases on outside, objective criteria.

Don't Miss a Beat: Taking All Your Expenses into Account

If your child is a toddler, it's difficult to think about what college will cost or who will pay for it years down the road. If a judge is going to try your case and you have young children, you'll probably have to return to court when the child is a junior or senior in high school to have the judge address the issue of who will pay for college. If you want to settle all the issues now, however, a provision that often works is this: you and your spouse simply agree now to pay half of what it would cost to send your child to the most appropriate school in your state's college system. Any excess amounts (say your child gets into Harvard) will be paid by the parent or parents who can afford it. This way, both parents have a minimum obligation.

What about the First Communion, Bar Mitzvah, the Sweet Sixteen party, the first car? If you negotiate an agreement, anything goes. If your case goes to court, judges may or may not address those types of expenses.

If you want to be ready for anything, you'll want to figure some of the following expenses into your agreement now:

- Babysitter and day care
- Birthday parties
- Camp
- First Communion
- Bar/Bat Mitzvah
- Sweet Sixteen party
- Application fees for colleges
- Travel costs to visit prospective colleges
- SAT, achievement test fees, and tutoring costs

- ◆ Other tutors as needed

- ◆ Orthodontia

- ◆ Psychotherapy

- ◆ After-school activities

- ◆ Sports activities, uniforms, equipment, and fees

- ◆ Boy Scouts or Girl Scouts

- ◆ Car, driving lessons

- ◆ Wedding

Wait a minute, you might be thinking. If all those items are extras, what am I paying child support for? Answer: food, shelter, clothing, telephone, utilities, and so on. Of course, depending on the amount of child support you are paying, your spouse may use some of the support for these extras.

Be careful, though. Anything you sign might come back to haunt you. Harvey, for instance, felt so guilty about leaving his wife, Jessie, that he agreed in writing to pay for each of their four daughters' weddings at the Waldorf-Astoria or someplace comparable. The daughters were only teenagers at the time. Unfortunately, Harvey's business took a turn for the worse. Although he could not afford the expensive weddings, he was obligated to pay for them. He went into debt to do so.

If you have a breakdown in negotiations, you can fall back on your state's child support guidelines, which really should be the floor for any child support award. Remember, that's the base level, and anything beyond is extra. Don't be afraid to seek help from your lawyers or a mediator.

When a Parent Is in Default

Being financially responsible for your children is so important that it is now considered a crime to stop paying child support.

In 1992, the federal government passed the Child Support Recovery Act. This law punishes people who willfully fail to pay a past-due support obligation to a child who resides in another state. A judge can fine and imprison (for up to six months) first-time offenders. Repeat offenders can be fined and imprisoned for up to two years.

The U.S. Department of Justice Prosecutive Guidelines (1997) for this law states the parent owing child support must be a person …

- ◆ Having the ability to pay,
- ◆ Did willfully fail to pay,
- ◆ A known past due (child) support obligation,
- ◆ Which has remained unpaid for longer than one year

  OR is an amount greater than $5,000,

- ◆ For a child who resides in another state.

This law has rapidly gained popularity as the crackdown against "deadbeat" parents has grown.

In 1998, the Deadbeat Parent's Punishment Act came into play as well. In that law, anyone who owes $5,000 for more than one year or $10,000 for more than two years is subject to legal consequences. Punishment may include prison time of up to two years, and mandatory restitution is required.

Each state has its own enforcement procedures, so it's best to consult with an attorney about how to enforce your award. (The state websites listed in Appendix C have links to the child enforcement division for your state.)

A common method of ensuring regular child support payments is garnishing some of the wages that the defaulting parent earns. Garnishment means that the child support will go directly from your ex-spouse's employer to you, or to the state collection agency, and then to you. Although there are federal limits on amounts that can be garnished, they are generous when it comes to child support. Ask for more information from your state's child support collection agency.

When You Think You're Paying Too Much

If you and your ex-spouse are on friendly terms and you have been laid off from your job or have had a reduction in your pay, the first person to talk to is your former spouse. If you're lucky, she or he will be willing to reduce the amount of child support for a period of time until you get back on your feet. Or, your ex might agree to make a trade, such as less child support now but more later. And remember, get your agreement in writing and send it to the judge to sign and make legal.

If talking to your ex is not realistic, or if a judge decided your case, you can appeal his decision, provided you do so within your state's time deadlines. Consult with an attorney who is knowledgeable about how the appeals courts have ruled in such cases. In some jurisdictions, the higher court tends to defer to the lower court in child support matters, on the theory that the lower court judge had the opportunity to observe you and your spouse in court and may have reached a decision based on what he or she saw. Stated more directly, if the judge thought you were lying about your income, the appeals court might be inclined to go along with that judge's decision.

You can also return to court after a period of time—at least a year—if the situation has changed or if you were unable to prove something at trial that you can now substantiate. Peter testified that he could not afford the full percentage of child support because he suspected he was going to lose his job. The judge would not consider the

possibility of Peter losing his job as sufficient to warrant his paying a lower percentage of child support. Six months later, Peter did, in fact, lose his job. He went back to court and was able to get a reduction in his child support obligation after a period of time had passed and he was unable to find other employment after looking in good faith.

> **CAUTION**
>
> **Red Alert**
>
> Even if your ex-spouse remarries into wealth, most courts will not require the stepparent to shoulder the expenses for someone else's child.

When You're Not Receiving Enough

What if the child support you are receiving no longer pays for your growing child's food, let alone clothing, shelter, and after-school activities?

If you're not having your payments made through the state payment agency (which should help you seek an increase), see an attorney. Your ability to have the payments increased depends in large part on the circumstances. In general, if you can show a judge that your children's economic needs are not being met, you probably have a good chance of getting an increase.

Insurance and Healthcare for Your Children

If a judge is trying your case, health insurance will be one of the items he or she will direct you or your spouse to maintain. If you are negotiating a settlement, here are some things to consider:

- ◆ If you have health insurance through your employer, keep your children covered. If neither you nor your spouse has health insurance through an employer, agree to allocate the cost of the premiums between you.

- ◆ Be sure to allocate financial responsibility for uninsured healthcare costs. Allocation can be in the same proportion that your individual incomes bear to your total income. If one of you is not working, then the other should pay all these costs.

- ◆ Get a Qualified Medical Child Support Order, which requires employer-sponsored group health plans to extend health care coverage to the children of a parent/employee who is divorced, separated, or never married when ordered to do so by state authorities.

If you and your spouse are negotiating, you should both agree to provide life insurance for the benefit of your children (assuming child support otherwise ceases upon the paying spouse's death). The parent who is paying child support should provide enough each year to cover his or her support obligation, which means that every year the amount of life insurance coverage needed lessens incrementally as the children get older. (Remember, child support usually ends when the child turns 18 or 21.) The amount of life insurance should include the paying parent's share of college as well, if you have agreed to include college expenses.

The parent who is not paying child support should also maintain life insurance coverage to help with college, if he or she can afford to do so and if he or she is obligated to pay a share of college expenses.

Who should the beneficiary of the life insurance be? This is an emotionally charged issue, but it doesn't have to be.

Here are a few solutions. If your children are young, name your former spouse as beneficiary and hope he or she will use the money to care for your child. If the children are older, you can make them the beneficiaries, but you still have to hope that the children are taken care of. You can, of course, name a relative, but we don't recommend that. Your ex-spouse may justifiably express doubt as to whether the relative will ever use the money for the children at all. Alternatively, a custodial trust can be set up to continue paying child support.

The Least You Need to Know

◆ Try to include all important points in your agreement. In some states, it is easier to modify child support a judge ordered you to pay.

◆ Child support payments are not tax-deductible for the paying spouse, but are tax-free for the receiving spouse.

◆ Each state has its own guidelines for how much child support should be paid, and each has exceptions to those rules. Check your state's child support guidelines, now easily available for most states on the Internet (see Appendix C). If you are still not sure, consult with an attorney before entering into a deal where you might be paying too much or receiving too little.

◆ Don't forget the items that add to the expense of raising children—parties, gifts, activities—when you negotiate child support.

Chapter 20

Managing Your Money Solo

In This Chapter

- ◆ Taking a look at the big picture: your financial profile then and now
- ◆ Reestablishing yourself financially
- ◆ Selling your house, business, stocks, or other holdings to make ends meet
- ◆ Creating a budget you can live with

If you have been married for a short time, divorce might have only a minor impact on your finances. Before you married, you may have lived on your own, worked, and supported yourself just fine. If this is the case, you are one of the fortunate ones. It will be relatively easy for you to get back on your feet—financially, at least.

If you've been married for years, however, the lifestyle changes brought on by your new circumstances—and your new finances—can be more profound. You'll find yourself far ahead of the game if you know what to expect. In this chapter, we present a guide to money management for the newly divorced.

Expect Your Financial Situation to Change

There was a time—it might seem like centuries ago—when you casually went out to eat, vacationed at the Jersey shore, and thought nothing of buying your child the latest computer or toy. Now, you count every penny you spend. You hunt for sales and swallow your pride when accepting hand-me-downs for your kids. Dinner is, more often than not, pasta. (So what? It's healthy, as long as you're not on the Atkins diet.) A night out on the town now means renting a video from the New Release rack at the local video store instead of a seat at the Super Bowl. In short, your former life seems so impossibly extravagant you can't imagine how you ever spent money so freely. You wonder if you will ever again be able to enjoy what you now consider the luxuries of a distant past.

Unless you are wealthy, it is likely you will need to live on a budget after your divorce. This is especially true if you have been married for a long time or if you have children.

For one thing, you and your ex-spouse each need a home. If there are children and custody is shared, both parents must sustain homes on less money than before. If one parent was accustomed to staying home with the children, that parent might now need to go out and get a job.

If one parent has custody, the other parent will have to help support the children according to his or her state's guidelines, while at the same time maintaining a separate household. This nonresidential parent might be required to provide support he or she feels he can little afford. If the residential parent does not work outside the home, the courts might instruct the working parent to provide spousal maintenance as well. Following divorce, some people start new families and must also help support them. (But beware, the time honored rule in these situation is: You must be financially responsible to your *first* family before you can be generous to your *subsequent* family.)

Sharing the Responsibilities of Your Former Life

In many instances, especially for those who have children, divorce will change your relationship with your former spouse but not sever it. As much as you might wish otherwise, you may still be bound by finances and parental responsibilities for years to come.

Even after you have left the marital home, your children will need your financial support and so might your nonworking ex-spouse (see Chapter 18 for more on spousal support and Chapter 19 for more on child support). What's more, although your support burden will probably be fixed, your earning power can always take a turn for the worse. If you don't get a cost-of-living increase, if you're laid off, or if your expenses are too high, you might have a difficult time making ends meet.

Here's a tale of woe: One evening, after the children had been tucked in and fallen soundly asleep, Helen informed her husband, Henry, that she had lost all feeling for him. No, she hadn't met anyone else, but she wanted to try. The long and the short of it: Their marriage was at an end.

Helen told Henry that she wanted him to move out. Shocked and dazed, he began looking for an apartment nearby.

A computer programmer, Henry had a hard enough time paying the mortgage and bills when his family was intact. Adding a second household to his expenses forced him to moonlight, and his life became nothing but work.

Not that it's any consolation, but things were difficult for Helen, too. Indeed, any parent who maintains a home for young children assumes responsibility for their needs, including all the extra expenses that implies. You might receive a certain amount of help in meeting these responsibilities from your ex-spouse, but more and more, these days, a large part of the financial burden will fall on you. There's no getting around it. On the first of the month, you face a stack of bills that you must pay no matter what your income is.

Helen, for instance, had to go out and work. Her new job, behind the counter at Starbuck's, was tiring and didn't pay much—however, she did earn enough to contribute to the mortgage. She and the children had to cut their expenses precipitously and had far less time together, to boot.

If, like Helen, you have children living with you, you'll find yourself protective not just of your pennies, but also of your time as you juggle school, work, and single parenting. You are no longer just the "chief cook and bottle washer"—you are also the breadwinner, even if that is a role you have not assumed before.

We are not telling you to stay married, and we are certainly not suggesting that Helen would have been better off in a loveless marriage,

> **You Can Do It!**
>
> Juggling finances on a tighter budget requires looking for better prices on purchases, something you may find difficult as you have increasingly less time. But there are solutions. Many people we know have joined discount consumer clubs and buy purchases in bulk. Others shop for deals over the Internet. You can save money, even if your time is limited.

financial perks and all. For Helen, the married state would have been a state of half-life, full of anger and angst. Helen gladly accepted her new challenges in place of the old, and though tired, she had no regrets. For Helen, the new struggles were well worth undertaking in exchange for release from a life sentence with a spouse she didn't love. Nonetheless, it behooves you to understand the difficulties divorce might entail. Each person must decide, individually, which cross he or she can most easily bear.

Taking Stock of Your Finances

As soon as you're faced with the prospect of going it alone financially, call an accountant or divorce financial expert. An accountant especially one familiar with your family's financial situation is in a good position to help you develop a plan to get back on your feet.

If you don't want to go to a professional, you can work to get a handle on financial issues by listing your income, assets, and expenses. (See below for some worksheets to help you.) Then you will know if your current income is adequate, or if you must strive to earn more. Notice that we haven't mentioned putting more debt on your credit card. Adding debt will ultimately lead you into a quagmire. It is better to cut back on unnecessary expenses or increase your income.

Carmen Carrozza, a former bank manager in Chappaqua, New York, has seen many people in the midst of divorce come through the door. The most uncertain are often women whose spouses have been the sole providers while they have been caring for the children. Even though these women worked for a few years before having children, they have been out of the workforce for too long to reenter at the same level, or the work they used to do has changed dramatically.

> **Red Alert**
>
> One friend of ours has refused job after job because she feels the entry-level positions are not commensurate with her age. We have continually suggested she get in touch with reality. While many of her friends from college have been in the workplace for 20 years, she has spent 20 years at home. Her work at home was important, especially to her family, but when it comes to advancement in the workplace, she may have to step back a bit to get her foot in the door. Don't feel you have to take just any job, but be reasonable. It's better to get in the workforce and get some experience under your belt, so you're prepared for that great job when it comes along!

Silver Linings

For those exiting long-term marriages, finding a means of earning enough money to stand on your own can be the most important first step. Very few people are married to partners so well-off they can expect to receive support payments forever. For those whose husband or wife has "made it," you may be eligible for permanent financial support, depending on your state's laws. Anyone in this situation should fight for all they are entitled to.

Looking for Work

If you haven't worked for a number of years, getting back into the workforce will take some time and getting used to. But it can ultimately reward you with far more than financial security. You will begin to feel self-reliant. You will meet new people. And you might even find you are distracted from the problems related to your divorce.

Discover the person you have not yet become. You probably have more resources and talent than you give yourself credit for. To help you identify your natural aptitude, we suggest you list your special interests and abilities in detail. Use the list to help you focus your studies, your job search, and your goals.

You Can Do It!

Before you start looking for a job, make sure you're heading in the right direction. Rank your special interests in such areas as: art, teaching, organizing, cooking, or child-care. Then, if possible, follow these interests as you seek work or build a career. And remember, with adult education courses at your local high school or community college, you should be able to increase your skills and credentials.

Developing a Credit History

According to Carmen Carrozza, one of the most common concerns for those in the midst of divorce involves building personal credit. The task is far easier, of course, for people who can show they have assets or income, by way of steady support or employment.

Good credit is vital. These days, it seems, we can hardly exist in America unless we pull out a credit card to pay the tab. If you have been working all along, your credit rating will not be affected by your divorce, unless you and your spouse had joint accounts and failed to pay those bills on time, or if you stopped paying them after the divorce was filed. If you have been relying on your spouse's income, on the other hand, you will have to establish your own credit history. Although the prospect seems intimidating, it's not as formidable as it sounds.

First, you must be able to identify your assets, like cash accounts, and your sources of income, including salary, interest, and, of course, maintenance (alimony). Because banks are seeking good credit risks, they will be looking not just at your income, but also at debts, credit history, collateral, and stability (how long you've been living in the same place). There's a formula to this, and it's not mysterious: If your income-to-debt ratio is 30 to 40 percent (you use no more than 30 or 40 percent of your income to your pay mortgage, car loans, and the like), banks will generally consider issuing you a credit card.

If you don't have a viable personal credit history, you can start to build one by shopping at stores that give instant credit; department stores, gas stations, and local stores are all good candidates. Begin by making small purchases on credit, and pay your bills promptly. Then, get a Visa or MasterCard. Pay your debts on these cards right away, too. If you've done things right, you should have your own positive credit history in about a year.

Handling Your Debts

In addition to generating income and establishing credit, you will have to come to terms with your debt. You and your spouse most likely have joint debts. These would include a tax debt, a mortgage, a car loan, and credit cards. If you are the non-moneyed spouse, you might have your name on the mortgage or car loan statement anyway; this means you are in debt—even though you have no income to offset the debt.

> **Silver Linings**
>
> If you've been held responsible for a spouse's debt, you may seek recourse in the "Innocent Spouse Rule," a provision in the Internal Revenue Code. Under this rule, if you can show that you are completely ignorant of your spouse's wrong-doing, you might not be held liable. Check with your accountant to see whether you fall into this category.

Third parties, such as the IRS and banks, don't care whether you are getting maintenance or child support. They don't care if you are divorced. They just care about the money you owe them and how they will get it back. They are not bound by the divorce settlement. They will hold both you and your spouse liable for payment.

Jim, for instance, owned a construction company. One year, he hid income by simply not reporting it on his income tax statement. His wife, June, was shocked to learn that the IRS held her as well as her husband liable for his income tax evasion. She was not protected by their divorce settlement because the couple had filed their income tax statement jointly.

CAUTION

Red Alert _____

As far as the credit card companies are concerned, you remain responsible for all the joint credit card debt your spouse incurs, no matter whether you're divorced or think you're protected by a separation agreement. Here's an example: Stephanie, knowing she was planning to leave her husband, Steve, went on a shopping spree before she lowered the boom. She racked up about $5,000 in purchases. Although the judge ordered her to be totally responsible for these debts in the divorce decree, Stephanie never paid them. Instead, she filed for bankruptcy protection. The credit card companies went after Steve for their money. Unfortunately, Steve had no defense. He was jointly liable for "Stephanie's" $5,000 debt.

Selling Your House to Make Ends Meet

If your living situation and financial status have changed for the worse because of your divorce, you might consider liquidating some assets or selling the house (if it was awarded to you) to help with your cash flow. Before you make this decision, be sure to speak with your accountant or a financial planner. Remember, your house is an asset as well as a home. If you have children, their emotional needs must be considered. At the same time, if you've received the house through a divorce settlement or judge's decree while your spouse has gotten the liquid assets, think carefully about whether you have enough cash to live comfortably in the house or whether you should move into less expensive living quarters. If the monthly payments on the house are small, you might as well stay where you are.

Living Within Your Means

You have already created a budget in preparation for your divorce settlement. But now that reality is settling in and your financial status has actually changed, it's a good idea to sit down and parse things out anew, as mentioned in the beginning of this chapter.

As you did before, compare income and expenses, including such occasional items as tax payments, holiday and birthday gifts, and retirement savings.

Now, as you did before, put these two lists side by side. Add the totals for each column. How do they match up? Are you ahead or behind? If you're behind, put a star next to the expenses that are optional or that can be reduced. By how much can they be reduced? Is there any way you can eliminate or reduce expenses that are not starred? If you need help with this, consult your accountant or bank manager.

Sample Income/Expense Statement

Income Source	Amount	Expenses	Amount
Salary (net)	_____	Housing	_____
Child support	_____	Groceries	_____
Babysitting	_____	Clothing	_____
Interest	_____	Entertainment	_____
TOTAL	_____	House repairs	_____
		Car	_____
		Heat, elec., water	_____
		Children's extra-curricular	_____
		Childcare	_____
		Toys, gifts	_____
		Misc. taxes or fees	_____
		Haircuts	_____
		Adult education	_____
		Vacation	_____
		Misc.	_____
		Savings	_____
		TOTAL	_____

The sooner you assess your situation and come to terms with your true financial means, the sooner you will be able to take care of yourself.

The Least You Need to Know

◆ Divorce can mean more expenses on the same or less income. Depending on the facts of your situation—your age, length of marriage, your work history, whether you have young kids, and so forth—you might face the challenge of entering the job market. If so, be prepared to take that step.

◆ Establishing yourself financially means developing a good credit history.

◆ Give yourself some time to weigh all the pros and cons before deciding to sell your home after the divorce.

◆ Creating a new budget will give you a sense of control over your finances.

Part 4

Focus on the Children

Divorce is a time when you are necessarily focused on your own feelings. It is often difficult to think about anything but what is happening to you. Whether you are surprised to find your marriage coming to an end or you've been contemplating a separation for months, severing this relationship is all-encompassing.

If you have children, however, you have a dual responsibility: to yourself, and most importantly, to your kids. Your children know only the security and love they have had with the parents who have nurtured and guided them throughout their short lives. The thought of losing one or even both parents is frightening. The other life changes your children might experience—from changing residences to adjusting to a stepfamily—would disorient even the strongest, most experienced adult. In the chapters that follow, you will learn how to help your children understand and cope with the changes their family is about to undergo.

Chapter 21

Thinking About Custody of the Children

In This Chapter

- ◆ Toward a definition of custody: custody is not ownership
- ◆ Sole custody or joint custody: Which is right for your family?
- ◆ Choosing the children's primary residence
- ◆ Understanding why some mothers forego custody

Once upon a time and long ago, you and your spouse lived together under the same roof as a family. You slept together, ate together, vacationed together, and, most importantly, raised your children together. One, or perhaps both of you, worked outside the home. Sure, you were over-whelmed by household chores; sure, you were tired from too many hours on the job. But there were the compensations: the thrill and sheer idyllic pleasure of weekend soccer or basketball games, the gentle intimacy of an afternoon at the park, the dance recitals, class plays, and rounds of Monopoly or Scrabble on rainy afternoons. You also had some treasured time alone while your spouse went off with the kids for an afternoon.

Now that you are divorcing, things have changed. For half the parents, this means a move to another residence. For these parents the realization that they will likely be seeing the children less often can be painful.

The parent who remains in the home, on the other hand, is faced with the prospect of managing alone. Those who have not been in the labor force since the children were born will have the added burden of looking for work and then juggling work and single parenting.

Before you make these changes, of course, you and your spouse need to put your differences aside to talk about how you will divide your responsibilities and arrange for the custody of your children.

Negotiating Custody

At first, the very concept of negotiating custody might seem alien. When you were a family unit, you both had custody—although you probably never thought of it that way. You were just your children's parents, nothing more, nothing less. Together, you decided where they went to school, what religion they practiced, and whether they would go through the ritual of getting braces or attending camp. It was natural in your family—as in most intact families—for you and your spouse to discuss these things and come to an agreement about what was best.

Once you and your spouse no longer live under the same roof, things will change. Now, the two of you will have to decide just how these decisions are made. Will one parent have the final say? What role will the other parent—the one no longer living with the children most of the time—assume? Will one parent feel overburdened with responsibility? Will the other parent feel cut off from his or her children, painfully disenfranchised from their lives? Or will the children alternate between the two of you, inhabiting different homes and bedrooms from one part of the week to the next? Do you think you can share the task of child-rearing, 50-50, even as you end your marital bond?

You must consider these questions as soon as possible. If you can put your personal animosity aside for the moment, you should be able to arrive at a practical, workable custody arrangement. If you can't (assuming you can afford it), court battles—perhaps lasting until your children are emancipated—might ensue.

Custody Is Not Ownership

Any negotiation, of course, is based on the assumption that you understand precisely what custody is—and what it is not. So let's begin with some definitions:

◆ **Legal custody.** The legal right and responsibility to make decisions for a child.

◆ **Physical custody.** Where a child will live.

◆ **Sole custody.** One parent has the right to make all major decisions regarding the children, and the children reside primarily with that parent. The parent who does not have sole custody is called the "noncustodial parent," and—barring abuse, neglect, or abandonment—will have visitation rights, or "parenting time" with the child.

◆ **Joint custody.** Joint *physical* custody means the children reside with each parent for an equal length of time. Joint *legal* custody means the children reside primarily with one parent, but both parents have an equal right to make major decisions about the children's lives.

> **Divorce Dictionary**
>
> "Custody" is an unfortunate term that can make the non-custodial parent feel diminished as a parent. The terms **time-sharing** and **co-parenting** have become popular with psychologists working in the field of divorce and with many divorced people. The new phraseology emphasizes that both parents are still parents—a crucial concept for making life work after the cataclysm of divorce.

Custody does not mean ownership. Children cannot be owned like a car or a house. What custody does mean is that one (or both) parents have the final say in the decision-making for major issues in child rearing (legal custody). Custody usually also determines with whom the children primarily reside (physical custody).

Although traditional custody guidelines have historically suggested that children live with the noncustodial parent about 20 percent of the time, an increasing trend toward shared or joint custody and more equitable amounts of time means that children will often spend 30 percent to 50 percent of their time with the noncustodial parent.

Understanding Your State's Custody Preference

The advantage of negotiating a divorce settlement when you have children goes beyond saving time, money, and aggravation. It enables you to tailor your living and custody arrangements to your own children's needs without the cookie-cutter results most courts would impose. This fact alone is worth temporarily putting aside your angry or hurt feelings and trying to reach a settlement.

How to begin thinking about the emotional issue of who gets custody? Even if you plan to settle your divorce, it might help to be aware of the form of custody your state prefers or presumes.

For example, in a state that has a presumption of sole custody, if you are not able to come to an agreement with your spouse on custody, and your case goes to court, you will have to prove why joint legal—or maybe even joint physical—custody would be in the best interests of your child, given your family's circumstances. To repeat, this does *not* mean you can't agree to joint legal or physical custody in your own agreement, just that you'll have the burden of proof if you try your case in this situation. In a state that has a presumption of some form of joint custody, on the other hand, if you go before a judge, he or she is likely to order a joint custody arrangement unless you prove it would not work for your family.

It's useful to know your state's preference for custody. You can check in Appendix C in this book for your state's website, which may have links to their laws on custody. Many of the links are listed in Appendix C under "child custody" under a state's name. Barring any mitigating circumstances, judges will generally follow their state's presumption. So, if you are on the wrong side of the presumption, you might be better off negotiating custody based on what you both feel works best.

Foremost in your mind, as you navigate your way through this important decision, should be how you believe your own children—with their individual temperaments, personalities, fears, and needs—will thrive under a particular custodial arrangement. In particular, if you believe you cannot cooperate on a regular basis with your ex-spouse, you should not consider joint custody, no matter what the preference of your state.

Joint or Sole Custody?

For the sake of the children, the goals of divorcing parents should be the same: involvement of both parents in the lives of the children and mitigation of conflict between the parents. These two factors should dominate all others when thinking about custody.

A joint custody solution gives a psychological boost to the parent who would otherwise be the noncustodial parent. But, even in a sole-custody situation, generous time-sharing (combined with open communication between parents) can create an environment where a noncustodial parent is significantly involved in the children's lives.

Is joint custody right for you? That depends a great deal on the ability of you and your spouse to get along. If you are to share decision-making, you must be able to sit down with your former spouse in a noncombative atmosphere and make decisions together. Shared values and parenting styles make this custody style more viable.

Here's what psychologists have found after long-term studies of families in joint custody and sole custody arrangements:

- Joint custody is a viable option only if the parents have an amicable relationship with each other, communicate well, and understand the nuances of their kid's day-to-day routines. Parents in this situation feel more involved in their children's lives than the noncustodial parent in the sole custody arrangement. On the other hand, in a family where one parent says "black" and the other parent says "white," the children are better off with a sole custody arrangement to reduce the possibility that their parents will fight over every decision that must be made on their behalf.

- For parents not on friendly terms, joint legal custody, that is to say, joint decision-making, means more room for disagreement and continuation of conflict. These parents are more likely to return to court than parents who have one decision-maker (sole custody).

- If you're able to communicate about the kids, are willing to live in close proximity to your ex, and have the time and resources to share "possession and access" (as they say in Texas) or "physical custody" (as it's more commonly called), then it can be a great thing for everyone. But generally, only children who tend to be easy-going by nature can adapt well to this kind of living arrangement. Children who do poorly with constant change, have difficulty adjusting to new situations, and seem to need a great deal of stability and security in their lives don't do well with joint physical custody.

In short, if you can agree to most of the following statements, joint custody could work for your family:

I will communicate openly with my ex-spouse regarding the children's needs and activities.

I can be flexible in working with my ex-spouse and put my children's needs first.

I will never bad-mouth my ex-spouse in front of my children. On the contrary, I will show nothing but respect for my children's other parent.

I will respect my ex-spouse's right to have his or her own house rules and not undermine them.

Be honest with yourself. If your feelings don't allow you to accept these guidelines, then get some counseling. If that doesn't work, then joint custody is not a good choice for your family.

When Joint Custody Won't Work

Candace and Bill had been snapping at each other for years by the time they decided to divorce. The manager of a medical clinic in the neighborhood, Bill couldn't keep his eyes off Marion, a lab technician 10 years his junior. Eventually, what had started out as an office flirtation turned into a passionate romance, and Bill asked Candace for a divorce. Of course, Candace was shocked. Despite the fact that she, too, was dissatisfied with the marriage, thinking about Bill moving out—to marry someone else—made Candace's heart race with anxiety.

When Bill decided it was time to work out the details of the divorce, he requested joint legal custody of the two children, Gwen, 14, and Martin, 12. The thought of giving up his role as decision-maker was too much to bear. Candace, humiliated by Bill's abrupt dismissal, wanted as little to do with him as possible and could not imagine sitting down to make mutual decisions for the kids.

In this situation, Candace and Bill would have to transcend their bitterness for joint legal custody to work. As long as the animosity continued, it would not be possible to share decisions about the children. If Candace and Bill's situation continued with ongoing conflict, as many of these situations do, joint legal custody would result in more fighting and perennial visits to court.

Determining the Primary Residence, Whether You Decide on a Sole Custody Arrangement or Joint Legal Custody

Generally, the parent who has been most involved in the daily care of the children will wind up providing their primary home. Traditionally, this has been the mother, though fathers are increasingly assuming the role of primary caretaker either by choice or default. The court will ultimately look to the best interests of the children to make this decision.

Following is a checklist of routine care giving tasks that might help you decide which parent should maintain the primary residence for the children. Custody should go to the parent who has the most checks on the list. Many states use similar criteria. Be honest with yourself when filling out the checklist. Your children will benefit, and you will be more comfortable with the outcome.

Task	Mother	Father
1. Provides meals	❏	❏
2. Holds and comforts children	❏	❏
3. Changes diapers	❏	❏
4. Dresses the children	❏	❏
5. Bathes the children	❏	❏
6. Plays with the children	❏	❏
7. Takes children to the doctor	❏	❏
8. Stays home with sick children	❏	❏
9. Reads stories to children	❏	❏
10. Takes children to school or activities	❏	❏
11. Puts children to sleep	❏	❏
12. Communicates more closely with children	❏	❏
13. Attends more school events	❏	❏
14. Disciplines children	❏	❏
15. Is called by children when they awaken during the night	❏	❏
16. Who the children seek comfort from	❏	❏
17. Arranges playtime with friends	❏	❏

Adapted from Baris, M.A. and Garrity, C.B.: Children of Divorce: A Developmental Approach to Residence and Visitation. Psytec; DeKalb, IL; 1988.

The Noncustodial Parent in a Sole Custody Arrangement

In a sole-custody arrangement, it's only natural for the parent without custody to feel cut out of the family at first. The parent with custody can help bring the other parent back into the picture by offering generous and flexible time with the children in the settlement agreement. If news about the children is freely shared, and the parent without custody goes to after-school activities and other public events, everyone will begin to settle in. The close relationship between both parents and the children can continue, albeit in separate homes.

Remember, even if the children don't live with you, your relationship with your children goes on, no matter what the official custody decision might be. You can and should continue to be involved with your children. If it's important to you, you can continue to share great times and impart the values you embrace. Whether or not you officially have "legal custody" or "physical custody," you can still have a close and involved relationship with your kids.

When a Mother Decides to Give Up Custody

Sometimes, it's difficult for people—male or female—to handle the overwhelming burden of parenting children alone as they work to earn a living. Some women, for the sake of their own personal growth, need the time and space that primary physical custody would simply preclude. A woman who is frustrated about her own life will not be as effective a mother as a woman who is fulfilled. Deciding to relinquish much of the daily childcare responsibilities may end up benefiting the children if they have a happy, self-assured mother and a father who can fulfill the primary nurturing role.

Doreen got married in her first year of college. She had wanted to be a biologist, but she fell in love with her classmate, Brian. Within a year of getting married, she was pregnant with their first child. She loved the role of mother and left school. Doreen then had another child, and for the next five years she devoted her time to caring for the children. Yet, as her marriage to Brian began to deteriorate, Doreen yearned to do something different with her life.

Meanwhile, Brian, an accountant, had moved his practice into their home. When Doreen's unhappiness finally reached the breaking point, she decided to go back to school and renew the life she had abandoned at age 19. She and Brian agreed that Brian would remain in their home with the children and that she would move to a condominium nearby. Brian had primary physical custody, but the children lived with Doreen on the weekends. She was able to pursue her new life and still have a close relationship with her children.

A Parent Is a Parent Is a Parent

Custody is probably the most sensitive issue for parents going through a divorce (unless, of course, they are in agreement on that issue). In most cases, both parents have been putting their greatest effort into their children, so how can one parent be given sole custody, seemingly relegating the other parent to second place? That's why it is so important to emphasize that custody is simply a legal term, one that fails to fully define the profound meaning of parenthood. Difficult though it is to absorb, loss of legal or physical custody does not have to mean a break in the relationship between parent and child.

The Least You Need to Know

- Custody is not ownership. Neither parent "owns" the children. Both parents will always be parents, and the relationship the parents have with their children (absent the intentional alienation of the children to one parent by the other) is usually within their own control.

- Joint legal custody can work if parents are cooperative.

- Joint physical custody can work if both parents want it and agree to live in close proximity.

- The children's primary residence should be with the parent who was the pre-dominant caretaker of the children before the divorce. (That parent will become the physical custodian.)

- Mothers who choose not to be the custodial parent are not necessarily abandoning their children. Many recognize their own personal limitations and need for growth.

Chapter 22

Breaking the News

In This Chapter

- ◆ When to tell your child about your separation and pending divorce
- ◆ What to say
- ◆ Helping your child deal with grief, anger, and rejection
- ◆ Dealing with real abandonment by a parent

If you have children and you haven't yet told them about your intention to separate or divorce, this is the moment you're probably dreading. How can you break such news to your children when they look to you for love and security? What will go through their minds as you begin your discussion with them? How can you ease their fears while being realistic about the enormous changes about to occur?

When to Tell Your Children

As soon as you and your spouse have made the decision to separate, it's time to tell your children, no matter how old they are. Even a toddler can understand, if addressed at his or her level. It is far more injurious to wake up one day with Mommy or Daddy gone than to be told in advance—preferably by both parents together—that one of you is moving out.

Telling your children sooner rather than later will ensure that they don't hear the news from another source or overhear you talking to someone else. Deception can promote fantasies about what is really going on, fears of abandonment, wondering about whether they will ever see their departing parent again, and a lack of understanding of the new realities they are about to face. If your children suspect information is being held back, a breach of trust might develop, becoming difficult, if not impossible, to repair.

How to Tell Your Children

Setting the stage for open, honest communication with your children is your most important job at this stage. Ideally, both parents should be involved in telling children about the divorce. Presenting a united front will help your kids by easing their fears of abandonment and will reduce a loyalty conflict—for example, it's all Mom's fault and Dad is the innocent victim.

If you have more than one child, gather them together for a family meeting to break the news. Having all the children together will give each child support from his or her siblings. Let the children know that both of you are available to talk to each of them individually or together again after the meeting. Be prepared for an avalanche of questions regarding the logistics of the divorce, custody, and visitation. Even money may be of concern to the children.

What to Tell Your Children

As always, your aim is to protect your children while being as open and honest as you can, given the circumstances and their ages and development. So, don't go into all the gory details. However, children who are told nothing about the reasons for their parents' divorce are unnecessarily frustrated and have a more difficult time working things through.

Some children, especially older ones, might not be particularly surprised by the news. Alicia, a 13-year-old, recently had this to say: "My parents had been cold to each other for a long time. Sometimes, they would scream at each other, and all I wanted to do was run away. It came as no surprise when they sat me down and told me they were getting a divorce."

For children who have not been exposed to fighting, an explanation will go a long way toward helping them digest the news. Be as forthcoming as possible about why the marriage is ending, while staying appropriate. When speaking to your children in a group, use language that even the youngest can understand.

Telling the children that you are going to divorce and why is the toughest part of the family meeting. But it is only the beginning. Because children are centered in their own world, they need to have precise and concrete information about how their lives will change. By the end of the discussion with your kids, they should know …

- As much as appropriately possible—given their ages and maturity—about the reasons for the divorce.

- When the separation will take place.

- Where the parent who is leaving will live.

- With which parent they will live.

- When and under what circumstances they will see their other parent.

- Whether they will be moving into a new house or apartment.

- They will have open telephone communication with the parent who is leaving.

Each parent should cover one or two points and then give the other a turn. To see how it works, here is one possible scenario. (Of course, you should modify the specifics depending on the age of your children and your own situation.)

> **Dad:** As you may know, your Mom and I have not been getting along for a while now. Although we were once happy together, we've grown apart. We tried to work things out and have been seeing a marriage counselor for quite a while, but, unfortunately, it hasn't worked.

> We are not getting along, and neither one of us is happy. This makes it uncomfortable for our living together. So we've decided to live separately and then get a divorce. You have done nothing to cause us to divorce. It is not your fault. This is between your mother and me.

> **Mom:** I'm sure you know that we both love you very much. Just because your Dad and I have decided not to live with each other anymore doesn't mean that we don't want to be with you. Parents can divorce each other, but they do not ever divorce their kids. We will be your Mom and Dad forever. We will always be there for you just as before. You will always be taken care of. You will always have a home. Each of us will be with you, just usually not at the same time.

Dad: I have rented an apartment a few blocks away, and I'll be moving there next Saturday. You'll be living with your Mom and coming over to live with me every other weekend. We'll also get together once a week for dinner and home-work help. We'll be sharing each holiday. I'll call you every night after school, and you can call me anytime. You'll have your own room at my apartment, and you can decorate it any way you want. (If the living arrangement is not yet set-tled, you can say, "The details haven't been worked out yet, but we'll let you know as soon as they are.")

Mom: Your family will always be your family, even though Dad and I aren't going to be in the same house. Your grandparents, aunts, uncles, and cousins will still be your family—those relationships won't change.

If you have any questions, you can ask them now, or you can talk to Dad or me later at any time. Remember, we'll always be there for you, and we love you very much.

If you and your spouse are in a heated battle, or if your spouse has left suddenly, a family meeting with both parents will probably be out of the question. Even though you might not know all the details of the living arrangements, you should tell your children whatever information you have, to give them a handle on the changes in their lives—but do not tackle this until you've calmed down.

When talking to your children, set aside your anger. Blaming one parent will only cause confusion. Because your children are emotionally attached to the other parent, they will feel conflicting loyalty. Not only will your child feel torn between his par-ents, but also, eventually, he might react against *you* to defend his relationship with the other parent.

Red Alert

Don't bad-mouth your ex! Your children's relationship with their other parent is separate from yours. Respect their relationship. Trying to be objective about the reasons for your divorce is especially hard if you've been left or if you are battling it out with your spouse. For the children's sake, you must rise to the occasion. Even though it might seem to you that there is an obvious good guy and bad guy—as in the case of the infi-delity of one parent—the reality is almost never that clear-cut.

When 12-year-old Michelle was told by her mother that her Dad had moved out after a final blow-up the night before, Michelle was devastated. Her mother was so angry at her Dad that she blamed him for all the ills of their marriage: She had to do all the housework, even though she worked; he would come home late at night; they never went out because he was too "cheap"; and other complaints.

At first, Michelle was sympathetic to her mother and understood her unhappiness. She felt angry at her Dad for not being more considerate of her mother's feelings. But after a week had passed, Michelle started to feel guilty for having bad thoughts about her father. She missed him. She began to wonder whether her mother had told her the whole truth and even started developing feelings of resentment toward her mother; had her mother, she wondered, been instrumental in driving her father out of the house? The more her mother spoke against her father, the more difficult it was for Michelle to sustain a warm relationship with her.

Helping Children Deal With Intense Emotion and Pain

No matter how "correctly" you explain things to your children, they will still experience a range of emotions, including disbelief, fear, anger, rejection, and grief. The only thing worse for parents than seeing their children suffer is being the cause of that suffering. And parents in the throes of divorce often find themselves in that situation, but they are too tied up in their own pain to take notice.

It is impossible to shield your children from all the hurt life brings. However, the breakup of a family and possibly the loss of one parent is surely one of the toughest hurdles for any child to overcome. This moment and the next year or two will test your emotional strength and your parenting skills to the limit. You think you're not up to the task? You are. You have no choice, and there is a lot of support for you in the community. Friends, family, psychologists, teachers, ministers, priests, rabbis, your lawyer, websites, and books are all there to help you manage this transition. Use whatever resources you need to acquire the knowledge and support necessary to help your children get through the initial shock, adjust to the changes about to begin, and adapt to their new way of living.

No matter how troubled your children might seem in the wake of your divorce, you can help them heal by viewing the world through their eyes. Karen Breunig, co-author (with psychologists Mitchell Baris, Carla Garrity, and Janet R. Johnston) of *Through the Eyes of Children: Healing Stories for Children of Divorce* (Free Press, 1997) notes that parents must be aware of three overriding issues and deal with them up front:

- **Children fear that they will not be allowed to love both parents without interference.** To address this concern, says Breunig, parents must remember that loving the other parent is a child's birthright. A child is partly like each parent, she notes, and "when you tear down your ex-spouse in front of your child, you're tearing down a part of your child."

- **Children harbor the fantasy that their parents will reunite.** Parents must acknowledge that the child has these feelings, Breunig states, at the same time making it clear that reuniting is out of the question. "You must support your child in their grief," she notes, "so that he or she understands it's safe to talk about feelings without fear of rejection. You must listen to the feelings while, at the same time, telling the child that you and your ex will both be there to parent them, but that you cannot promise a reconciliation will ever take place."

- **Children may be emotionally damaged if exposed to too much anger and rage, even if those feelings are not directed at them.** "Emotions run so high in a divorce," says Breunig, "that it takes tremendous adult responsibility to shield children from all the things it would be damaging for them to hear. People can't often control their feelings in the midst of an emotionally damaging divorce, but they can control how they act out those feelings in front of their children. If you've just found out that your spouse has been unfaithful and wants a divorce, it would be very difficult to hide the situation from a child, depending upon age. In such situations, it is not necessarily unhealthy for them to see your grief and sadness. But it can be quite damaging for them to see your rage or hear you lambaste the other parent. Children must be spared the pain of adult emotional business, as much as possible."

Dealing With Fears

Children of divorce are usually most fearful of abandonment and loss of parental love. It is crucial, therefore, that you take every opportunity to reassure your children that their parents love them and will always be there for them. According to psychologist Mitchell Baris, Ph.D., "What differentiates a parent-child relationship from any other kind of relationship is loyalty. Mom will always be Mom, and Dad will always be Dad, and nobody else will ever replace them. Even if the parents remarry, even if they'll be living in two houses, or even if one parent will be living far away, Dad will always be Dad, and Mom will always be Mom."

Let them know (assuming that one parent is not *actually* abandoning the family) that they will have a continuing relationship with both parents—even if, for the moment, you wish you would never see your spouse again! (If you have trouble saying things that you know are in the children's best interests but that stick in your throat, try viewing your spouse as their parent rather than your archenemy. Just for now, put yourself in his or her shoes.)

Dealing With Blame

Children are likely to blame one or both parents for the divorce. Sometimes—and of more concern—children blame themselves. Reassure your children repeatedly that the separation has nothing to do with them. Assure them that although parents can divorce each other, they cannot divorce their children—nor would they ever want to.

Dealing With Anger

Your children might not evidence or express anger until after the shock of the announcement has worn off. Anger, if not constructively channeled, can become outwardly destructive or self-destructive. Hidden feelings can fester and manifest in ways that seem unconnected to the separation.

Eric, for instance, had a close friend, Alex. They saw each other at school every day and often went over to each other's house after school. After Eric's parents announced their separation, he fought with Alex over everything. It seemed that Alex couldn't do anything right. Because Eric kept the news about his parents' divorce to himself, Alex didn't have a clue about what was going wrong. Alex stopped seeing Eric. Eric lost a best friend at a time he needed one the most.

To help your children work through this anger, make yourself available. Children need to know that their feelings count. Listen attentively when your children want to talk. Answer questions as honestly as you can. The more your children can express their feelings, the easier the adjustment will be.

When a Child Is Abandoned

What if, in the worst-case scenario, your spouse announces that he or she plans to abandon the family and have absolutely nothing to do with the children after the divorce?

If possible, it behooves you to convince your partner that the children need him or her in their lives, no matter what. Communicating this urgent message to a spouse who is threatening abandonment might be your best weapon against the devastation of parental loss. Ironically, some parents abandon their children because they, themselves, lack self-esteem. They think their children would do better without them. If your spouse harbors such feelings, you must do your best to explain how crucial he or she is to your child's well-being.

What if, despite your urgings, or completely to your surprise, your spouse actually just up and leaves? If this was a surprise to you, your own shock will make it monumentally more difficult to tell your children. You know intuitively that your children's self-esteem will be affected by your spouse's decision to cut them off. No matter how hard it is for you, it is far more damaging to your children because children don't have an adult's perspective on life or the inner resources to handle such extraordinary rejection and hurt. Your children might experience self-doubt, depression, and regression.

It is your job to pick up the pieces. If you are the parent who has remained, you must be there with all your love and support, making sure your children understand that there's nothing wrong with them. *They* are worthwhile and cherished by you. Instead, it is the parent who left who has the problems.

Remind your children that the flight of their other parent has nothing to do with them; they bear absolutely no blame. Also remind them that they still possess your constant, unconditional love, as well as the love and support of other family and friends. Be cautioned that it is unfair to give the children hope that someday their parent might return.

As the remaining parent, it is also your job to be on the lookout for the psychological side effects of rejection and abandonment. Your children might very well experience strong feelings of low self-esteem, a longing for the departed parent, and eventually anger. If there are any signs of depression after a three-month period, consult a psychologist.

The Least You Need to Know

- Telling your children that your marriage is ending is difficult but not insurmountable. If you and your spouse can manage to share this task, your children will benefit.

- Trust can be achieved by being as open and honest with your children as is appropriate for their age.

- Your children's sense of security will be enhanced if you and your spouse can assure them of a continued relationship with both parents.

- Try to work out the children's future living arrangements before you announce your plans to separate or divorce. Tell the children about these plans when you announce the divorce itself.

- Helping your children handle their grief, anger, and feelings of rejection will be your most important job in the coming months. If you are overwhelmed, seek professional help during this crisis period.

- Actual abandonment by one parent is a difficult scenario for children. Do what you can to prevent it, but if that's not possible, assure your children of your love for them.

Chapter 23

Visitation Schedules That Work for Everyone

In This Chapter

- ◆ Visitation (time-sharing) schedules that work for your kids
- ◆ Working out the kinks
- ◆ Making time-sharing work when parents are at war
- ◆ When kids should have a say

Children of divorce not only suffer the trauma of a family split, they must also adapt to the stress of visiting a parent in a different location. Some adjust well to this involuntary lifestyle change; some have a harder time. In either case, children should understand that each parent is important in their lives, and that the time they spend with the noncustodial parent can be a fun break from the normal routine. But how does visitation succeed in the real world?

When Parents Live Apart

To make shared parenting time work for the kids, it helps if each parent is tuned in to his or her children's individual and developmental needs.

Here are some tips for making co-parenting work:

♦ Cooperate with the other parent as much as possible.

♦ Keep each other informed of what's going on when it comes to a child's schooling, medical care, and social life.

♦ Establish a polite business relationship with the other parent.

> **Silver Linings**
>
> You have a great deal of control over the way your children handle life after divorce. By cooperating with the other parent, you are establishing a life pattern your children can carry into the future.

♦ Be responsible in maintaining the visitation schedule. If a change must be made, work it out with the other parent in advance.

♦ Respect the rules of the other parent's household, just as you respect the rules of school and other public institutions.

♦ Don't send messages to the other parent through your children. Business should be conducted only between parents.

It's All About Attitude

To co-parent successfully, you must maintain a positive attitude. If you see your ex as your children's parent, rather than as your archenemy, you stand a better chance of making co-parenting work.

For example, don't criticize the parenting skills of the other parent. Seven-year-old Melissa's father never failed to comment to Melissa about how wrinkled her clothes were and how messy her hair was when he picked her up from her mother's home. These negative comments about her mom's parenting skills always got the weekend with her dad off to a bad start.

Don't focus on every negative comment your children make about the other parent when they're with you. Check your attitude: Do you secretly relish these comments because you can't stand your ex and hope your kids support your view? Are you in competition with your ex for the kids' loyalty? Unless your children are saying something *very* disturbing about the other parent (physical or mental abuse, alcohol or drug abuse), any negative comments your children might make are often best taken with a grain of salt. Don't blow such comments out of proportion, and remember, your children might resent and distrust you if you cheer them on.

On the other hand, be realistic. Don't overcompensate for your negative feelings toward your ex by bending over backward to paint him or her as perfect. Nothing in life is all good or all bad, so how could it be that way for your children's experience at either home? Children should understand that there will be fun times and boring times, happy times and angry times, with each parent. In any case, portraying your ex as all good will have a false ring to your kids. ("If you like my dad/mom so much, why did you two split up?")

Keep any angry feelings you have toward your ex-spouse between you, your therapist if you have one, and your friends or family. Try to put a lid on your anger when you're with your kids. Sometimes anger comes out indirectly through a negative attitude towards things related to your ex-spouse. This might be confusing and potentially damaging to your kids. It's important to identify unconscious attitudes that you might not realize you express, because your kids' radar will pick them up.

What's your attitude toward your ex? Here's a quick quiz to find out. If you answer "Yes" to two or more of the following items, you need an attitude change!

- I hate my ex so much, I can't stand the thought of my kids being with him (her). _____Yes _____No

- When my kids come back from seeing their other parent, I tell them to take a shower or bath to wash my ex's presence away. _____Yes _____No

- When my kids tell me they had a good time with their other parent, it ties my stomach in knots. _____Yes _____No

- Whenever my kids say nice things about their other parent, my lips start to purse, and I'm silent, or I get the urge to say something really bad. _____Yes _____No

- If my kids report that their other parent is doing well and is happy, I get a sinking feeling in my stomach. _____Yes _____No

- I "accidentally" say things against my ex to friends or family within earshot of my kids. _____Yes _____No

- If asked, I can't come up with one good thing to say about my ex. _____Yes _____No

We hope this little quiz will tune you in to your feelings and bring them to the surface. Not only will this be beneficial to your children, but it might help you deal with some of the anger that is boiling inside you.

Age-Appropriate Visitation

It's a famous biblical story: Two women were fighting over a baby each claimed as her own. Wise King Solomon had the women brought before him. Appearing to rule fairly, he ordered that the baby be cut in half, with one half given to each woman. While the pretender agreed with this decree, the real mother was horrified and screamed, "No! Give the baby to her!" King Solomon then knew that *she* was the real mother.

Although it's important for both parents to maintain a relationship with their children, visitation schedules based simply on dividing up the number of days in a calendar year without regard for the children's age, psychological needs, or temperament can cause unnecessary stress; for very young children, ignoring these factors may cause permanent psychological harm.

For most children, the ability to make transitions from place to place increases with age. For time-sharing to work, both parents must be attuned to their children's unique requirements and needs, as well as the general developmental pattern that most children follow from birth through the teen years.

Infancy to Two-and-a-Half Years

Infancy, psychologists agree, is a time for building an attachment to the primary caretaker. (Attachment to two primary caretakers, a mother and father, is increasingly common, too.) The infant's developmental task is to form trust in the environment. Long separations from the primary caretaker can result in symptoms of depression and regression and later may result in problems with separation and the ability to form relationships.

Toddlers are beginning to develop a sense of independence. They are becoming aware of themselves and begin to speak and walk. They can use symbols to comfort themselves, such as a picture of Mom or a toy she gave them.

Because the successful attainment of these developmental tasks lays the foundation for secure and healthy children, parents should design a schedule that fits a child's needs at this stage. The best schedule, say the experts, is short but frequent time with the noncustodial parent: *short* because infants and toddlers can't maintain the image of their primary caretaker for long and *frequent* to enable them to bond with the noncustodial parent. Most psychologists agree there should be no overnight visitation for very young children.

In cases where both parents share physical custody, frequent daily time with each parent is the ideal.

There are many innovative ways to share parenting responsibility at this stage. We know one couple who bought a second home in the wife's name following the divorce. Their child, a little girl, stayed on in the old house, now in the father's name. The parents shared custody by taking turns staying in the original family homestead. The "off-duty" parent lived in the new house. In short, the child had one stable home; instead, it was the parents who bore the brunt of constant change by moving back and forth. This model is known as "nesting" or "bird nesting" for the obvious reason that the young remain in the nest, as the parents come and go.

Red Alert

If your very young child is grieving for the other parent, he will not be able to focus on his relationship with you. Give your child the time he needs to adjust to separation from his primary caregiver.

Two-and-a-Half to Five Years

This is a time of continued growth and individuality. These young children can now hold the absent parent in mind for longer periods of time. Their language is developed enough to enable these youngsters to express feelings and needs. They have more control over their feelings and bodily functions. This is also the age when children begin to identify more with the same-sex parent.

Although it ultimately depends on the temperament of the individual child, this is typically the age where time away from the primary caretaker can increase, and overnights can be introduced. If the child resists long periods away from her primary caretaker, short but frequent visits should continue until the child is better able to withstand longer separations.

Those who share physical custody must continue to be sensitive to their child's reaction to continual change.

Six to Eight Years

The hallmark of this period is development of peer and community relationships, a moral sense, empathy, and better self-regulation of impulses. Children develop a concept of themselves as they gain competence and master skills.

You Can Do It!

Teenagers often feel displaced in the wake of divorce, and the experts say that support groups of peers can often be particularly helpful. Do look to get your adolescent involved in a well-run support activity to help with the transition.

For children to develop normally, it's important during this age for the noncustodial parent to participate in the activities within the community in which the children live. At this stage, children thrive on consistent contact with friends, school, and extra-curricular activities. Although the length of time away from home can be increased for those aged six to eight, if a child is homesick, most child development experts recommend that the time away should be decreased to a tolerable level.

Nine to Twelve Years

During these years, children develop their academic, athletic, and artistic skills. They become more involved in community activity. There is an increased desire to maintain friendships and seek approval of peers, as well as growing self-awareness as they begin to evaluate their own strengths and weaknesses against the larger arena of the world.

As before, the noncustodial parent is advised to schedule visits, as much as possible, within the orbit of the child's home base. The closer children feel to the noncustodial parent, the more agreeable they will be to segments of time away from community activities and friends.

Thirteen to Eighteen Years

This period marks the beginning of psychological emancipation as children establish their personal identity more strongly than ever before. There is a mourning of the loss of childhood as children relinquish dependency and the protection of the family circle to venture out on their own. Kids at this age are dealing with their sexual feelings. They are also beginning to see how to work within the rules and regulations of society.

At this age, children have generally come to count on a fairly established visitation schedule and routine. Nonetheless, that may change as these teenage children seek to have input into the schedule so that it dovetails with their increasingly complex academic and social lives. It is difficult to force an adolescent into a schedule he or she did not help to create. In fact, if you are divorcing when your child is this age, don't be surprised if the judge meets with him or her to hear what he or she has to say.

Many states allow a judge to *consider* (but not necessarily *defer to*) the preferences of any child over the age of 12, giving due weight to the child's individual maturity and development.

Adopt an attitude of sensitivity and flexibility when it comes to the visitation schedule you establish for your children. If your children are nearing adolescence, their social agenda will be paramount to them. Although spending time with their parents is very important (and sacred for the noncustodial parent), parents who respect their children's needs to develop a social life of their own will be helping them to grow normally.

In situations where physical custody is shared, parents should consider living within a few blocks of each other in the same town. Expecting teens with school, sports, and social lives to "commute" is unfair.

Scheduled for Success

As the years pass, it is normal to revise a schedule so that children spend increasingly more time away from the primary home. As changes are made, however, parents must be sensitive to any signs that a child is being pushed beyond his or her capabilities. Remember that your relationship does not depend on the actual number of hours or days you spend with your children but on the degree of your involvement, concern, and openness to your children's emotional and developmental needs. Don't push your children beyond their temperament and capabilities.

One mother we know was allowed to see her daughter for two hours a week at a local mall, a temporary restrictive agreement that resulted because it was alleged that she used drugs. The mother was told she would have to participate in a 12-step program or some other kind of rehab before more liberal visitation was allowed. The daughter greatly missed her mother and treasured the time. The mother, meanwhile, felt two hours insufficient and, after two months in rehab, petitioned the court for extra hours at the mall. The judge granted the mother four hours at the mall, but so much time trudging around a mall after school was exhausting to the little girl. Though she sorely missed her mother, she began to dread the exertion of the sessions and made excuses so she didn't have to go. The sessions resumed only when the mother promised the girl could go home when two hours were up. Remember, your children may love to see you, and may miss you greatly, but they are still children, and any visitation arrangement must be sensitive to their needs.

Most noncustodial parents, of course, are awarded far more time with their children than this unfortunate mom. Parents with liberal visitation or joint legal custody have been creative and flexible in myriad ways, designing time-sharing schedules that range from alternate weeks at each parent's home, to rotating every other weekend, to living primarily at one parent's home. You know your kids best, so think about what would work for them.

If at First You Don't Succeed ...

Laura and Dan agreed their marriage had reached an impasse. They had a 6-year-old son, Jake, and a 10-year-old daughter, Allison. Laura and Dan made an appointment with a child therapist recommended to them by their marriage counselor. The therapist was experienced in working with children from divorced families, so she was able to provide guidance to Laura and Dan in working out a time-sharing arrangement. Because the parents seemed to get along well, she recommended that they be open-minded about how the plan was working. If it didn't work, she advised, they should meet with her again to modify the plan.

Laura and Dan decided that the children would live with Laura during the week but have dinner with Dan twice during the week. At first, Allison and Jake would live with their father from Saturday morning until Sunday evening. After three months, Friday night at Dad's was to be phased in for Allison, but because Jake was still very young, he wouldn't begin sleeping over on Friday nights for another eight months. Allison and Jake liked this arrangement, and there was no need to change.

Arnold and Melissa weren't as lucky. They had one daughter, Nicole, age four. Arnold wanted Nicole to live with him every other weekend from Friday night until Sunday night. Melissa agreed, but Nicole did not do well with that schedule. She didn't want to leave her mother and would cry incessantly when her father came to pick her up. Even after she spent some time with her father, she was moody and complained that she missed her mother. Bedtime was even worse. Arnold and Melissa tried a few more weekends with this schedule, but Nicole remained unhappy. Arnold agreed to wait a few months and then start with one overnight for a while until Nicole got used to being away from her mother and then work up to the entire weekend when Nicole turned six.

Michael and Anita had a teenage boy, John, who wasn't happy about the divorce. After his parents told him they were separating, John withdrew from both of them in sadness and anger. He just wanted to hang out with his friends and even arranged to stay at his best friend's house every chance he got. Michael and Anita had worked out a schedule where John would live with Michael for two weeks and then Anita for two weeks, but John didn't like the schedule. At first, Michael insisted that John follow the schedule to the letter, but John wouldn't budge.

Michael and Anita consulted an experienced therapist who worked with divorcing families. He suggested that John be included in the decision-making process about where he wanted to live. Michael and Anita talked with John, who by now was getting used to the idea that his parents weren't going to be together any more. John said he wanted to stay mostly in the house where he had grown up, but that he would see his dad on the weekends, as long as he could also hang out with his friends. Michael and Anita agreed to this, and John's new lifestyle eventually became routine.

Silver Linings

According to Dr. Janet Johnston of the Center for the Family in Transition, if a 6-year-old expresses a clear preference about the schedule, parents should try to accommodate those wishes with these caveats: Make sure the child is not just trying to please a parent, and don't let him know it was his idea! Children of this age can't handle the power of making the decision themselves. It's too frightening. Parents should listen to children from ages 9 through 12 and their views should be given consideration. By the time children are teenagers, they can be given more say in determining their visitation schedule, but it is up to the parents to make the final decision.

Keeping the Joy in Holidays Despite the Divorce

Holidays are precious times of the year for many people, and you'll probably want to be with your children on these occasions most of all. Because they are so important, deciding how to divide the time can be difficult. It's essential that you agree on an arrangement that is fair to both parents and to the kids.

Harrison and Susan managed to work things out. They agreed to alternate Christmas Day and Christmas Eve each year. That way, each parent could share gift-giving and a Christmas tree with their children. The kids didn't mind; they got twice as many presents!

David and Vivian shared the Jewish holidays by splitting them up and alternating them. The parent who was not with children for Rosh Hashanah was with them on Yom Kippur. Hanukkah was divided in half, as was Passover. All other holidays were divided up and alternated.

Marion and Will were not very religious, so for them, sharing school vacations was more important than celebrating the religious holidays that fell into those school breaks. They each took one school break and alternated winter and spring break each year.

Long-Distance Parenting

Although moving is sometimes necessary for employment circumstances, it's always better for both parents to stay within reasonable driving distance to the children. Once a parent moves far away, the children will be much less likely to see that parent on a regular basis, and they will probably have a stressful schedule—long summers away from the custodial parent with little contact during the school year. Added to that, they will usually have to travel long distances to see their parent.

The courts understand the negative impact when one parent lives too far from the child to have regular contact. Many states thus prohibit the custodial parent from moving out of state or beyond a certain distance from the noncustodial parent. In recent years such strictures have eased. This change was based on the premise that if the custodial parent is happy, the children will be happy, too. Restrictions against moving are not imposed on the noncustodial parent. Although a judge might refrain from getting involved in such decisions, negotiated divorce settlements can impose restrictions on moving for one or both parents.

Although it's not an ideal situation, if a noncustodial parent moves to another state or even another country, he or she can remain in close contact with the children. Steve moved from New York to Dallas because of a job opportunity he couldn't pass up. But, he still wanted to stay close to his children, Tim, 5, and Alex, 9. Steve called them every night before they went to bed. He also wrote a letter once a week and sent pictures of his new neighborhood. He even sent a video of himself taken by a friend. Steve also came up with some clever ideas for relating to his children while he was not with them. He told them to pick a television program they liked, and he would watch it at the same time. That night, they would talk about the show. He sent puzzles and riddles that the children could finish, and he would ask them how they did. Every six weeks, Steve spent a four-day weekend with Tim and Alex in their town. He also alternated school holidays with his ex-wife, Sharon. In this way, Tim and Alex maintained a pretty close relationship with their dad, even though he lived a couple of thousand miles away.

Managing Visitation in High-Conflict Situations

Evan: I can't take it anymore! Every time I get ready to go over to my Dad's, Mom tells me to make sure to tell Dad he owes her two months' support! Then, Dad tells me to bring a message to my mom that he's paying her too much! I just feel like running away from both of them.

Kate: I know what you mean. I can't stand the way my Dad always asks me who Mom's been seeing. Then, he asks me to find out more about her dates and tell him.

Matthew: My Mom and Dad can't keep from making snide remarks to each other when my Dad comes to pick me up. Why was I so unlucky to get parents who hate each other?

Amy: I always feel pressured to take sides. Why don't they understand I need and love both of them? I don't want to side with one against the other!

Divorce is generally born of conflict. But when extreme conflict persists even after the couple has parted ways, the children of that marriage may find it difficult, if not impossible, to heal. Indeed, when parents cannot put their mutual anger aside, and when they sweep their young children into the conflict, they have ceased to protect their children.

Children of high-conflict divorce, torn between the two most important people in their lives, are often emotionally damaged by the struggle. According to psychologists, such children are often depressed and aggressive. Later, as adults, they often have difficulty maintaining intimate relationships. They are far more likely to divorce than adults who come from intact families or even divorced families at peace.

Because open conflict is most likely to take place at the time the children go from one home to the other, many psychologists specializing in divorced families now recommend that the number of transition times be reduced in high-conflict situations. Here are some specific recommendations for visitation schedules when open warfare rages:

◆ **For moderate conflict:** When parents function well on their own but fight when they are in contact with their ex-spouse, psychologists Mitchell Baris, Ph.D., and Carla Garrity, Ph.D., note that other creative solutions are necessary. Some of these may be minimizing transitions—packaging visitation into one block per week. For very young children, the midweek visits might be eliminated. For older children, the visits might be consolidated each week. These may need to be handled by a neutral third party or take place in neutral places.

- **For moderately severe conflict.** When there is constant litigation, and sometimes even physical threats or abuse between parents, children can suffer extreme emotional scars. In such cases, Baris and Garrity recommend caution. Mental health evaluation is mandatory, and supervised visitation may be recommended if the safety of a child is a concern.

- **For severe conflict.** In this situation, when children are at immediate risk of physical or sexual abuse, visitation should be supervised and a full mental health evaluation conducted.

Children of high-conflict divorce are often hit hardest, even when they seem upbeat on the outside. Parents who fail to notice the warning signs of a child in emotional trouble will pay a high price later. When does your child need help? New York psychologist Michelle Gersten, Ph.D., provides the following guidelines:

- **Maladaptive personality changes of extreme intensity or duration.** If your child has changed in any major way since the separation, trouble may be afoot. Characteristics to examine include inattentiveness, overactivity, aggression, shyness, or fearfulness. Maladaptive behaviors, of course, should set off alarms. Remember, all children involved in divorce will show minor difficulties, including eating and sleeping problems. But if these symptoms are short-lived, you probably don't have to be concerned. On the other hand, if a school-aged child who previously had healthy relations with her peers starts withdrawing from social activities, be on the lookout for trouble.

- **Regression.** If your child has regressed to behaviors from earlier stages of development, seek psychotherapy. Examples might include a 4-year-old who now has frequent accidents, despite successful toilet training previously, or an 8-year-old who speaks in baby talk.

- **Extreme parental conflict.** If the parents continue to fight in front of the child after the initial breakup, therapy may be required. If one parent is manipulative or continually undermines the other, psychotherapy for the child is indicated as well. In one case, a mother consistently failed to inform the father of plans and then told the child the father had simply failed to show. The father, in turn, told the child that the mother "just forgot." The stress of the situation was arduous for the 5-year-old boy, who became confused about his alliances and ultimately needed therapy to successfully relate to his mom and his dad.

The Role of the Parenting Coordinator

Researchers and practitioners, such as Mitchell Baris, Carla Garrity, and Janet Johnston, who work with families in high-conflict divorce situations, have developed the concept of the *parenting coordinator*. The parenting coordinator, who must be familiar with family law, conflict resolution, mediation, family therapy, and child development, is not a mediator or a therapist. Instead, this third party works within the confines of the divorce decree to settle disagreements between parents as they pertain to the children. The parenting coordinator may report regularly to the court and can speak to the children's therapist. The therapist is protected from litigation so that she can work with the children without being pressured or manipulated by either parent.

Divorce Dictionary

A parenting coordinator is an individual, perhaps a psychologist familiar with matrimonial law, who works with both parents to iron out any problems that may arise after the divorce decree is in effect. Sometimes parenting coordinators are assigned by judges, but parents can also voluntarily choose to enlist the aid of a parenting coordinator.

The parenting coordinator can also be a facilitator between parents in high conflict. If one parent wants to send something to the children, he or she can send it to the parenting coordinator to make sure that the children receive it. The parenting coordinator may at times determine when the children are ready for increased visitation, which may have been shortened or curtailed because of the conflict. The parenting coordinator maps out a detailed parenting plan, which is agreed to by all parties. In fact, your state may require parents to file a "parenting plan" if custody is an issue in your divorce. In any case, the more detailed the plan, the less room for conflict.

Points covered in the parenting plan might include …

- ◆ **Visitation schedule.** Sets a drop-off and pick-up time and place, designates a means for transporting children between households, institutes a set plan for handling a refusal to visit, and decides who is responsible when children are sick.

- ◆ **Schedule change requests.** A set protocol for trading days or making last-minute changes.

- ◆ **Phone call policy.** Should they be regulated? Should children be able to initiate phone calls in private at any time?

◆ **Toys and belongings.** Provides guidelines for moving things between two households.

◆ **Boundaries or rules at other household.** Neither parent can tell the other parent what rules to set; if abuse or possible abduction is suspected or concerns about parental judgment persist, the parenting coordinator, judge, or mediator must be contacted.

◆ **Pets.** Establishes rules for moving them back and forth between homes with the children.

Advice from Those Who Know Best

Children of divorce have strong feelings and thoughts about how children should be treated by their parents. A word to the wise—heed the wisdom of the children.

Here are some recommendations to parents from veteran children of divorce:

Recognize that we love and need both parents.

Don't turn us into messengers. Mom and Dad should talk to each other directly.

Don't say bad things about our other parent.

Don't grill us about what is going on at our other parent's home.

Don't ask us to take sides.

Don't make us feel as if we're being disloyal to you if we enjoy being with our other parent.

If you have something angry to say to our other parent, don't say it around us.

Don't purposely forget important clothing or gear when we are going to our other parent's place.

How your children fare in the aftermath of divorce in large part depends on the degree of sensitivity you and your ex-spouse have towards your kids' needs. If you put your children's needs first and are able to take a step back from your own emotional turmoil, you will greatly relieve the stress on your children.

The Least You Need to Know

- One of the most difficult lifestyle changes children undergo as a result of their parents' divorce is moving back and forth between homes instead of living in one stable environment.

- Establish a polite business relationship with the other parent. Share important information about the children's academic, social, and health news.

- Visitation schedules should take the age and temperament of the children into account. The schedule should provide regular and predictable times for the children to be with each parent.

- Monitor your children's progress with the visitation schedule. If they are not adjusting, modify the schedule.

- If you and your ex-spouse cannot stop fighting, consider having a third-party professional—a parenting coordinator or mediator, for example—act as an intermediary and modify the visitation schedule as needed.

- Never put your children in the middle of the fighting. Don't ask them to ally with you against their other parent.

Chapter

24

Two Parents, Two Homes

In This Chapter

- ◆ What transitions look like through the eyes of your children
- ◆ Coping skills for children making the transition
- ◆ Making a smooth exchange
- ◆ How your attitude can help your children
- ◆ What to do if your children refuse to go
- ◆ If you suspect abuse

> **Jimmy:** I hate going back and forth. I feel like a Ping-Pong ball. I just want to stay in one place, in my own room, with my own things.

> **Anna:** I'm glad I get to spend time with my Dad *and* with my Mom. It's a hassle to go back and forth, but it's more important to me to see both my parents.

Transitions are difficult for children, especially young children. (This is also true for many adults, depending on their temperament.) Try to remember what it feels like when you stay at a friend's house; there's the strange bed and bathroom, the likes and dislikes of the individual you're visiting, the different routines. The first night you might feel uncomfortable. You miss your own bed, your carpet, your morning coffee; you long to be free to look really grungy until you've completed your morning routine. Imagine this scenario, and you will begin to understand what your child's back-and-forth experience is like. To your advantage, you are an adult with an adult's perspective. Children, on the other hand, have fewer life experiences and also often experience time differently. What might be just a weekend to you feels more like a month to a child. What might be a two-week summer vacation to you seems like a lifetime to a child.

Although your children love their other parent, the transition between households might still be hard because it is a major change in your children's reality. For children, every reunion is also a separation; every transition is bittersweet. Every "hello" is also a "goodbye."

Each "new" parent should give the children time to adjust to the transition and not get overly concerned with behaviors that seem unusual during the initial period after the change. Be sensitive to your children. Read a book or do some other quiet activity with them. If they seem to need some space, finish what you were doing before they came over. In time, things will get back to normal.

> ### Silver Linings
>
> A child will probably get more one-on-one attention from his parents after the divorce than before the divorce. The working parent who didn't spend much time with the children pre-separation might now spend much more time with them. The custodial parent may feel that this is just a ploy to reduce child support (more time spent might reduce support), but this may be the best news for the children.

Six Strategies for Helping Your Kids with Change

Here are some ideas for helping your kids handle the transition from one parent to the other. You know your children best, so think hard about what makes sense for your family:

- Make a calendar with your children. The calendar should include the highlights of their schedule, including all major activities and especially those times when they will be with the other parent.

- Remind your children that they are leaving the day prior to the visit.

◆ Depending on the age of your children, help them pack their traveling bags the day before they leave. If they are school-aged, make sure that their homework is included. Have a young child choose his or her own traveling bag. His input into this symbol of his transition will help give him a feeling of involvement and control.

◆ To ease the packing and make them feel more comfortable when they are at the other parent's house, let children keep certain basics (toothbrush, comb, pajamas, and so on) at both houses.

◆ Give very young children a traveling bear or other stuffed toy to help provide a sense of security.

◆ Let your child take a picture of the absent parent with him or her.

Making the Exchange Smoothly

If you and your spouse or ex-spouse have a working relationship, the transition from one home to the other is easier on both the parents and the children. Children sense their parents' tacit approval and take with them the good wishes of the parent they are leaving. Even though the sudden change is stressful, knowing that the parent being left supports the departure and will be fine during their absence gives the children the foundation they need to cope.

Seeing Your Ex as Your Child's Parent

We know we've said this before, but it's so important that it bears repeating. Keep your feelings about your ex-spouse to yourself. To lessen the uncomfortable feelings you might have when you face your ex-spouse during the exchange, see him or her through your child's eyes, as your *child's parent*. This technique will help keep your attitude positive during the exchange, which in turn will allow your children to feel okay about leaving you. And you really want your children to feel okay about leaving you. (Don't worry; they'll come back!)

Shielding Your Children from Conflict

If you think you're delivering your children to the enemy, they will sense your tension.

Follow these guidelines for reducing parental conflict:

♦ Communicate only when necessary.

♦ Keep a mental image of your spouse as your children's parent.

♦ Think of your parenting relationship as a business relationship.

♦ Don't get hooked into old patterns of fighting or being goaded into a nasty retort.

♦ Use clear and simple language without taking a judgmental or accusatory stance.

♦ Keep conversations as brief as possible.

♦ End any communication that looks as if it might escalate into a shouting match.

> **CAUTION**
>
> **Red Alert**
>
> If tension is very high, as it might be at the beginning of the separation, it is better to have a third party make the exchange or have one parent drop off the children at school or an after-school activity and the other parent pick them up.

♦ When face-to-face with your ex-spouse during your children's transition from one home to the other, bury your feelings and exchange polite greetings. Keep it short.

♦ Don't discuss arrangements or other business with your ex-spouse during transitions.

♦ Turn the other cheek to any sarcastic or accusatory comments. Excuse yourself as quickly and politely as possible.

♦ Don't exchange checks and money in front of your children.

♦ Don't use children as messengers or delivery people.

♦ Have a positive attitude.

♦ Give a hug and a kiss goodbye to your children; wish them a good time.

♦ Smile. A happy parent makes for secure children.

Children Who Fight Visitation

In some cases, children will refuse to leave to be with the noncustodial parent. Here are some reasons why this might happen:

♦ A parent is not tuned in to the children's interests or is not actively involved with the children during their time together.

- Your children may be very young and anxious about separation from the parent who does the majority of caretaking.

- Open conflict is causing the children to appear to be aligned temporarily with one parent.

- In rare cases, there may be child abuse (which we discuss a little later in the chapter).

If your children don't want to leave their primary home to be with their other parent, having a good heart-to-heart with your ex-spouse should be the first step. The problem may be one that is easy to resolve, such as paying more attention to the children, a change in discipline style, or having more toys or other entertainment at the other home.

Either or both parents may unknowingly be causing the children's refusal to go. Following are two checklists, one for the custodial parent and the other for the noncustodial parent. Be honest. You're the only one looking at this.

Custodial Parent Q&A

I have done my best to encourage my children's visits with their other parent. ____Yes ____No

I do not give double messages to my children about seeing their other parent. ____Yes ____No

I make sure my children know that, although I miss them, I know they will be well taken care of. ____Yes ____No

I tell my children I am fine when they're away. ____Yes ____No

I make sure to pack everything my children need so their time with their other parent goes smoothly. ____Yes ____No

Noncustodial Parent Q&A

I understand it takes a while for my children to adjust to different surroundings, household rules, and customs. I don't pressure them to forget about their other parent when they're with me. ____Yes ____No

I make a mental note if, after a reasonable amount of time with me, my children are not adjusting. ____Yes ____No

I allow my children to speak to their other parent on the phone.
____Yes ____No

I don't do my work when my children are with me and are awake.
____Yes ____No

To stay involved with my children, I participate as much as possible in activities that center on *their* lives (Little League, dance class, play dates, and so on) instead of dragging them to things that are important to *me* but of no interest to them. ____Yes ____No

Go with the Flow

Sara, who was 12 years old, called her father to tell him that she didn't want to go to his house that weekend. She said her girlfriends were having a slumber party, and she didn't want to miss it. Her father insisted that she visit him instead of going to the party.

This wasn't the first time Sara had to miss a social event because that was her weekend to see her father. She felt misunderstood and resented her father for keeping her from her friends. Ultimately, she started feeling as if she didn't want to be with him at all.

If her father and mother had been more flexible with the visitation schedule, on the other hand, Sara could have had her social life and would have felt that her father really understood and cared about her emotional and social needs.

Six months after his parents divorced, nine-year-old Allen began refusing to go to his father's place for the weekend. When asked on several occasions, he wouldn't say why. Finally, he admitted that he was bored because his father would spend most of his time finishing reports for work, and Allen had no one to play with. When Allen opened up about his feelings, his father made sure to do his work after Allen went to sleep and devoted his time to Allen. After that, Allen looked forward to his weekends with his dad.

What's your scenario? If your children are resisting visitation, scrutinize the situation. Perhaps a simple change will turn things around for you, too.

The Anxiety of Transition for the Littlest Children

Refusal to leave the custodial parent is most common in very young children because they are too young to carry a mental image of the parent to whom they are most attached (usually their mother) and fear abandonment.

For these young children, the transition from one parent to the other can set off anxiety about safety and survival. According to Janet Johnston, a foremost researcher in children and high-conflict divorce, children up to six years old may continue to have difficulty if they have had "repeated distressing separations and maintain an anxious attachment to the parent. It is also possible that children under the ages of four or five do not have a sufficient understanding of the concept of time and, for this reason, are confused about the particular visitation schedule. Consequently, they are anxious about when they will be reunited with the primary or custodial parent."

If you and your ex-spouse get along, and your children are very young, the cause of your children's refusal to leave their residential home is likely normal, age-related separation anxiety. A parent's recognition of this and willingness to work with the other parent to ease his or her children's anxiety will go a long way toward building trust and bonding. Insensitivity, on the other hand, can result in continual resistance to leaving the primary residence and the eventual failure of the child-parent relationship.

When a Parent Is Maligned

If you think your ex has begun to wage a serious campaign against you with the kids (engaging in what's now called "Parental Alienation Syndrome" or PAS), you should suggest that your spouse and children see a mental health professional to aid their adjustment to visitation. If your ex refuses to seek help, you might be justified in seeing your attorney to request that the court mandate a mental health intervention, and perhaps a change in physical custody or visitation, depending upon who's alienating whom. Complex situations such as this call for psychological—and perhaps, even legal—intervention for the entire family.

If you are the custodial parent in a heavily litigated case and your children refuse to visit their other parent, make sure that you are not bad-mouthing your ex-spouse in front of your children or sending them negative messages. If you want what's best for your children, you must put aside your feelings toward your ex-spouse and encourage your children to develop or maintain a relationship with their other parent. If your children lose their other parent, their self-esteem will take a nosedive, and they'll suffer feelings of abandonment—even if it now seems that they don't want to be with that parent.

Silver Linings

If you have a good relationship with your children who are old enough to know better, they're generally not going to buy the hard line that you're awful if you're really not. As long as you're totally tuned in to your children, empathetic with their emotional needs, and helping to build their self-esteem, you should be able address any attempt by your ex to alienate you from your kids. But, if you think your children are being "brainwashed," discuss your suspicions calmly with them. You'll get a better feel for the true situation at their other home, and, hopefully, you'll be able to address any issues that arise.

Rebecca's parents separated because her father was seeing another woman. Rebecca was eight years old when her father moved out. Her mother was in shock. When the shock wore off, her mother was filled with rage. She did not hide her feelings from Rebecca. Instead, she told Rebecca that her father couldn't be trusted and that he was insensitive and even cruel.

Rebecca couldn't bear to see her mother so distressed. She aligned herself with her mother against her father. Even though she had been close to her father before the divorce, her angry feelings prevented her from relating to him. She didn't even want to see him.

Red Alert

Participating in open conflict—whether it is screaming at each other or making snide remarks—is the single most damaging thing you can do to your children. Although you have no control over your ex, you do have control over yourself. Don't get dragged into a fight. Stay cool.

Rebecca's father accused her mother of brainwashing Rebecca against him. He went to court to try to gain custody. The litigation was heated and drawn out. Rebecca suffered terribly from the fighting and the insecurity of not knowing where she would be living. She continued to refuse to see her father.

Eventually, her father, who lost the custody battle, became less and less interested in fighting Rebecca's rejections of him. He and his girlfriend married and started a family of their own. As far as Rebecca was concerned, he found it easiest to just drift away.

What could Rebecca's father have done in this situation instead of giving up? For one thing, he might have let Rebecca know the door was always open for her. For instance, he might have continued to send regular postcards or letters, even if Rebecca didn't respond. Perhaps, she would ask to see him again—in her own time.

At the very least, she'd have concrete evidence to prove her dad still cared, despite her refusal to see him.

When your ex maligns you to your child, it puts your relationship at risk. Yet, psychologists note that a hurt, angry ex-spouse cannot always control the expression of powerful, negative emotions. Moreover, they may be unaware of just how much they are damaging the child they love.

How do you handle this situation without drawing the child into the conflict more than he or she already is? According to psychologist Karen Breunig, co-author of *Through the Eyes of a Child*, "the best thing that I would advise is to appeal to the better graces of the offending parent. Explain how damaging this is for the child since the child identifies with *both* parents." It might also be useful for the offending parent to seek therapy.

If your ex remains closed to such suggestions, Breunig says you should discuss the situation with your child. Explain that you are going to try to work the situation out with the other parent and, if appropriate, assure the child that the statements made about you are not true. "Leave the lines of communication open so that your child can feel comfortable about checking these accusations with you, personally," says Breunig.

"Whatever you do," she concludes, "do not fight fire with fire. You will just be turning up the flames on your kid."

If You Suspect Abuse

If your children seem fearful or refuse to visit the other parent on a regular basis, you might have a genuine concern for their safety and even abuse. If this is the case, speak to your lawyer and a mental health professional before making any accusations to your ex-spouse.

The courts have seen a lot of child abuse charges in divorce cases. Many of these accusations turn out to be false statements made by an angry and vengeful spouse, or a parent who wants to limit parental access to the children. For this reason, your lawyer might call you in to discuss the facts behind your

 **Red Alert**

Making a false allegation of child abuse is serious and can even result in a change of custody.

claim of child abuse. Your attorney will explain what constitutes child abuse in your state, according to case law.

On the other hand, if your children are victims of abuse, there must be immediate intervention, including the possible involvement of a psychiatrist, and a change in the visitation arrangement.

The Least You Need to Know

- Children who switch households regularly—different place, different people, different rules—carry a heavy burden. It takes time for them to adjust.

- Prepare your children well in advance of leaving your residence.

- Check your attitude! Your children need a positive relationship with both parents.

- Never engage in conflict with your ex-spouse in front of your children.

- If your children refuse to see their other parent, speak to your children if they're old enough. If necessary, consult with a mental health professional. If you are on good terms with your ex, discuss the problem with him or her. If you are suffering from Parental Alienation Syndrome (PAS), talk to your lawyer.

- If you suspect physical abuse of your children, contact your attorney immediately for advice.

Chapter 25

Single Parenting

In This Chapter

- So you're a single parent—what now?
- The responsibilities of the custodial and noncustodial parents
- Juggling childcare, work, and your social life
- How to nurture your child
- Getting the most out of your time with your child

After the shock of your divorce has dulled a bit, you face the realization that you and your children will be a slightly smaller family. No matter what your child custody arrangement, your family is missing one member—the other parent. This definitely takes a bit of getting used to. In time, new patterns of living will start to feel normal, and the fresh wounds of the family's division will begin to heal for everyone.

A New Beginning: Just You and the Kids

At first, being a single parent might seem overwhelming. Remember how you felt when your first child was born? You were scared but excited. You didn't know what to expect. You were exhausted and awed by your responsibility for this new life. Yet, you rose to the occasion then, and you will again now. Single parenting is simply another time for reorientation, adjustment, and growth—for everyone involved.

If You Are the Custodial Parent (or If You Spend More Time with the Kids)

If you are the *custodial parent*, you will be spending more time than your ex-spouse does getting the kids off to school; buying their clothes; and taking them to the doctor and dentist, after-school activities, and friends' houses. But, hey, you were doing all that before.

What's really different for you now? For one thing, you won't have backup for discipline on a daily basis. You might be the one helping the kids with their homework all the time. If you haven't so far, maybe you will be the one pitching them balls or shooting baskets with them after school.

These changes are not all bad. Your relationship with your children will get even closer than before, when you might have pushed them along to their other parent, so he or she could play his or her role as "mother" or "father." Now, you can explore the other side of parenting.

"But when will I get a break?" you might ask. Your break comes when your kids are with their other parent. That's a nice, solid break. Enjoy it!

Eat, Drink, and Be Merry

It might take some time to adjust to having meals with one parent missing. Not only will it remind you of your new marital state but, after a while, you might crave the company of other adults. What to do? Invite friends or neighbors over for dinner once or twice a week. Take your children out to restaurants so you can be surrounded by people, or just enjoy catching up with your kids' daily activities. Don't park them in front of the TV while they're eating. Have your meals together. That will give all of you a chance to talk about the day's events and will provide a stronger sense of family.

Working Single Parents and "Latch-Key" Kids

Custodial parents who used to stay home to raise the children may now work outside the house to help make ends meet, or even to fulfill their personal or professional aspirations. Either way, this situation increases the number of "latch-key kids"—children who come home from school to an empty home. Of course, the number of families in which both parents work has increased to 68 percent as of 1998, according to the US Census Bureau. So it's not just the children of single parents who let themselves into the house or apartment to care for themselves until a parent gets home. Entire books have been written on this phenomenon and its impact on society. We don't have the space for such analysis here, but we would like to present some basic guidelines:

- Common sense dictates that very young children should never be left alone. Beyond the obvious danger, it's illegal.

- Many states allow children aged 11 and older to stay home alone, but laws differ from state to state. If you are unsure of the laws in your area, contact your local District Attorney's office.

- Even if leaving your child home alone is legal, you must still make sure the circumstances are secure and that your child is comfortable with the idea. Do you live in an apartment building with a doorman the children can call on if there's a problem? Are there adult neighbors your children may contact? As a general rule, children need the security and experience of an adult nearby through the early teen years, especially if the parent will be away for an extended period of time.

- Finally, if you plan to leave your older children home alone, make sure they are armed with emergency phone numbers and strategies for dealing with an array of situations, from physical injury to prank phone calls.

> **You Can Do It!**
>
> As an experienced parent, you have probably checked out the range of organized activities available to your child during after-school hours. If you haven't found anything that works, be sure to contact the local YMCA or Boys and Girls Clubs, your church or synagogue, and your child's school, which may well offer enrichment activities, intramural sports, or clubs. For older children, volunteer activities organized by youth organizations can be ideal.

An Issue of Discipline

Studies have shown that children do best with firm guidance combined with a lot of communication and affection. You may be tempted to overindulge your children to make up for the pain they are going through because of your divorce. This approach has been shown to have the worst outcome for children. Frankly, a stricter attitude toward discipline (we're not promoting hitting here!) seems to help children and teenagers more than an overly permissive style. At this unsettled time, children need definite boundaries and limits combined with a lot of patience, love, and understanding.

Caring for Yourself

One of the most important things you can do to support your kids is to take care of yourself. If you are an unhappy parent, it will have a major effect on your children. They look to you for strength and support. It's frightening to children of any age to see a parent lost to depression and thus removed from them emotionally; for many, the situation provokes anxious feelings of losing that parent as well, something especially painful at the time of divorce. To help them, help yourself by:

♦ Getting enough rest and exercise, and eating healthily.

♦ Putting yourself in places where you can meet new people.

♦ Getting busy with renovating your new life; start with renovating your house or apartment, even if it's just a fresh coat of paint and some new throw rugs!

♦ Taking an adult education class or volunteering.

♦ If necessary, going into psychotherapy for a while.

Silver Linings

If you and your spouse had been battling it out for custody and visitation, be grateful now that the other spouse wants to be active in your children's lives. While you might fear the times when your children are away from you and you are denied access to them, you will come to realize that the time they spend with their other parent gives you a much-needed break, allows your children to have both parents in their lives, and gives you help with the monumental tasks of parenting.

If you are the custodial parent, you have a lot on your plate. As long as your ex-spouse is in the picture, however, you are not entirely alone in raising your children.

If You Are the Noncustodial Parent (or If You Spend Less Time with the Kids)

The noncustodial parent will also be facing new challenges. Much of what is true for the parent with physical custody is also true for the noncustodial parent. The good news is that you have time for entertainment and your errands when the kids are with their other parent. Then, when the kids are with you, you can really devote that solid block of time to them. If you used to give little time to your children because you were too tired when you came home from work, you might not have developed the kind of fulfilling relationship you can now enjoy with the free time that comes from splitting the parenting duties post-divorce.

The noncustodial parent, often the dad, must make a special effort to maintain a close and loving relationship with the children. Jack Feuer, a journalist, a divorced and dedicated father, and the author of several books for divorced dads, has some winning strategies for forging bonds when a parent is not in daily contact with the kids:

♦ Put a phone line in your child's room so you can call without going through your ex-spouse.

♦ Send them photos of your time together.

♦ Volunteer to coach your child's youth sports team.

♦ Baby-sit when your spouse must go out.

♦ Avoid the "Disney Dad" syndrome—the tendency of noncustodial dads to make every second with their children extraordinary. These fathers are continually taking them to expensive amusement parks among other special places, buying them everything they ask for, in short, turning the visit into one big playtime, Feuer says. Yet children need normality, so try to establish an ordinary post-divorce life with your child.

♦ Share discipline with your spouse. Noncustodial dads are often reluctant to share in the discipline, Feuer notes. But it is important that dads participate in the discipline process and that they develop, with their ex-spouse, a style of discipline that is consistent in both homes, if possible. "My son goes to bed

30 minutes later on school nights at my house than he does at his mom's," says Feuer, "but if he misbehaves at school, the punishment is the same at both houses. And if she says he cannot see videos because he misbehaved at school, he does not see them at my house, either."

You Can Do It!

Spending quality time with your children is the greatest gift you can give them. Communicating in a genuine way—really listening to them—will not only solidify your relationship, but it will also help them—and you!—get through this tough time.

Red Alert

It's best if both parents can agree on a single disciplinary policy. But the reality is often different. If you've punished or docked your children at your residence, don't expect the other parent to uphold your disciplinary measures at his or her home. Do continue with your punishment when your children return, if that's the deal.

♦ Give your children a sense of possibility, establish horizons, and teach values.

♦ Come to terms with your divorce so you don't communicate feelings of anger and hostility to your children. If you are having trouble dealing with your emotions, seek counseling. "Because many men do not know how to experience strong emotions when they feel them," Feuer says, "they might have the impulse to flee, removing themselves from the emotional lives of their children in the process." Because this is the worst mistake a divorced father can make, Feuer suggests therapy as a viable alternative.

♦ Treat your ex-spouse as a business partner. "Be civil and courteous," Feuer says. "The research on the impact of divorce on children is often ambiguous, but there is one thing on which everyone agrees: The degree of hostility and amount of conflict between parents has a direct impact on how children will grow up. Do not ever fight with your ex-wife in front of the kids for any reason."

"Your job as a parent is the most important you will ever have," says Feuer, "and you must live up to your end of the responsibility. Be a dependable parenting partner, and remember, the kids come first."

Don't Overdo It

You've probably heard the cliché about "weekend dads" (or moms) who spoil their kids by entertaining them at expensive places and buying more toys and gifts than they could ever hope to see at their other parent's home. This is a mistake. Your children need *you*, not amusement parks, shows, toy stores, and other places that might assuage your guilt or show them what a great parent you are. Occasional trips are fine, but your children will appreciate "hanging out" time much more.

Your Enormous Responsibilities

What are your practical responsibilities as a noncustodial parent? You don't have to buy the clothes for your children, but if you can afford it (even if you are paying your ex-spouse support), it might be a good idea to have a spare outfit or two at your place. Buying some toys for the younger kids is a must. If you cook, provide your kids with home-cooked meals, or even have them share in the cooking. If you're not into cooking find great take-out.

Regarding discipline, the same is true at your home as for the primary residence. Firm discipline with a loving touch yields the best results.

What if your very young children are having a hard time being away from their custodial parent? If you can't comfort your small children after a reasonable amount of time, be flexible and hope your ex-spouse will be as well. Bring your children back and try again soon, maybe for a shorter time but more frequently. In the end, you will have earned your children's trust in you, and you won't have risked their emotional well-being.

The Ultimate Balancing Act: Parenting, Work, and a Life of Your Own

Being a single parent is, indeed, a juggling act. If you didn't work when you were married, and you do after the divorce, you will most likely have to put major time and effort into developing your career. You will also need help with the kids when you aren't home. Depending on their ages and your financial situation, you might need a full- or part-time babysitter and day care or nursery school. For older children, if you can afford it, having someone at home for their arrival will give them a feeling of security. Even young teenagers—although they won't admit it—feel more at ease if they know someone is looking after them.

Especially if you have primary custody of your children, you'll have to shop whenever you have a spare moment and have dinner ready for your hungry bunch. For both parents, spending time with your kids after dinner playing games, reading, and doing homework is the rewarding part of parenting. This is especially true for divorced parents, whose time with their children is limited to the hours and days that the children live with you. Cherish it.

You Need Friends, Too

At some point during the healing process, you will be ready to meet new people (unless the reason for your divorce was that you had a new love in your life). How do you fit a social life into your busy schedule, and how will it affect your children?

The best time to become socially active is when your kids are with their other parent. That way, you'll be free to be you, not your kids' parent.

Red Alert

Children whose parents have divorced may be skittish about new romantic involvement for Mom and Dad. Many children fantasize that Mom and Dad will reconcile, or they might see your new "friend" as taking time away from them. Finally, if children become attached to your new friend and it doesn't work out, they will experience another loss. The bottom line: be careful about when you introduce a new romantic partner to your children. Establish your relationship first—make sure it's what *you* want before involving your kids.

The Importance of Optimism

We know you might not believe it, but eventually, you will get your life together. In our most optimistic moments, we love to point to Lori—a recently divorced friend of ours who has done an admirable job.

Lori, the mother of a 7-year-old boy, Ari, and a 10-year-old boy, Jesse, recently divorced. Her main occupation had been raising her two sons, although she had begun a singing career before she had her first son. After the divorce, she decided to go back to music school so she could become a teacher. Meanwhile, she had some savings to live on but elected to work part-time as well.

Her children went to school on an early bus every morning. Lori had one class in the morning, did some shopping after the class, then went to her job selling designer eyewear. A classmate of hers agreed to be at her home every afternoon when her children got home from school. When Lori got home, she made dinner, worked with her kids on their homework, and read to them before bed. After they were asleep, she did her own homework. Sometimes, she fell asleep before she put on her pajamas.

When Ari and Jesse were with their father, Lori did more school work, ran all her errands, and took in dinner and a movie with a friend. A year after the divorce, she forced herself to go on a date. She made it a point to fit one singles event into her schedule every month. She also joined a fitness club and worked out on her free weekends.

Lori is still single, but today, she's a success. Ari and Jesse, now in the 9th and 12th grades, are top students as well as athletes. They both have an abundance of friends. And Lori is a music teacher who feels pride in her children, her own professional accomplishments, personal independence, and new circle of friends.

Needs Water and Sunlight: Nurturing Your Kids

Byron's daughter, six-year-old Michelle, lived with him three days each week, every other weekend, and one evening each week. Michelle was more important to him than any other part of his life. He was lucky to have a job as a bank teller, where he could be home at 5:30 p.m. every day with no take-home work. When he picked up Michelle on Friday evening, he always took her to her favorite Japanese restaurant. She could count on it. Michelle ordered the same dish, tempura, every time. When they got to Byron's home, it was time for Michelle's bath and a story. Before Michelle went to sleep, Byron would help her call her mother to wish her a good night.

The rest of the weekend was always spent on activities together both indoors and out. Sometimes, Byron would invite some friends of his who had children, and Michelle would play with them for a while. But mostly, because Byron's time with Michelle was precious to him, he was one-on-one with Michelle. On Mondays, Byron took Michelle to her kindergarten class. Because he was still at work when she was finished, he had a standing arrangement with a neighbor's 17-year-old daughter to pick up Michelle and stay with her until he got home from work. Then, Byron cooked dinner and put Michelle to bed. The next morning, Byron took Michelle to school. After school, her mother picked up Michelle and took her home.

Whether you're the custodial or noncustodial parent, or if you share the time with your children equally, your kids need nurturing. As divorced parents, both you and your ex-spouse have to be mindful of your kids' needs at all times. Each of you is responsible for their physical, emotional, and spiritual health and well-being when they are with you—including giving hugs and kisses (number one on the list), goofing around, teaching them right from wrong, feeding them, making sure that they brush their teeth twice a day, and taking care of them when they're sick.

Once the wounds of the divorce process have healed and you have gotten used to the new family arrangement, everything will fall into place and become less overwhelming. Generally, much of the anxiety you have felt during this trying time will disappear after the legal issues are settled. Working out your new daily life will become easier as time goes on, until it becomes routine. Then who knows what new and exciting people and adventures await you!…

The Least You Need to Know

- Parenting post-divorce is a challenge, but with good organization and support, you can make it a successful routine.

- Single parents must be mindful of their children's needs during the delicate post-divorce transition time.

- The most successful disciplinary approach is firmness and consistency, with a lot of communication and affection.

- If you are dating, do so when you are not with your children. Don't introduce your new significant other to the children until you know you're serious, if the kids are young.

- To get the most out of your time with your children, focus on *them*. Do activities you all enjoy, take care of their physical, emotional, and spiritual needs, keep the communication lines open, and give them a lot of affection.

Chapter 26

Redefining the Family

In This Chapter

- ◆ The new stepparent: helping your child adjust
- ◆ Stepparents have feelings, too!
- ◆ The blended family: half-siblings, stepsiblings, and the new baby

Most likely, children whose parents are divorced will be living in both of their parents' homes. They will be dealing with a larger number of authority figures, different lifestyles, different rules, and different personalities. Sometimes, one or both parents will remarry. They might marry someone who already has children. They might have another child with their new partner. When parents divorce, get remarried, and then start new families, it has a profound impact on the children. At a minimum, everyone involved will have to make a lot of adjustments.

In the best of all worlds, the two families will be supportive and nurturing to the children, opening up new vistas of experience, providing more interaction, and adding significant people to the children's lives.

Helping Your Kids Accept Your New Spouse

If you and your significant other have gotten to the point where you both think it's time to live together and even marry, you must take steps to prepare your children for the change. Think about it: they will have to accept the fact that you and your ex-spouse will never be reunited, that you will have a new spouse or live-in partner, and that, potentially, they will have new stepbrothers or stepsisters. That is a lot to digest! Go slowly and proceed with caution.

Phasing in are the key words here. As we mentioned in Chapter 25, don't introduce your children to your new partner until you are sure about *your own* feelings about him or her. In many instances, your children will still be digesting the loss of your marriage—the family unit as they knew it. To see one of their parents with a new love interest can cause stress in the early period after divorce, so be sensitive and aware of their psychological needs. Even teenagers can be profoundly disturbed by a parent's interest in someone outside the original family. Take a reading on your kids from time to time by discussing similar situations—such as a TV show or perhaps another divorced family where one or both parents remarried—so that you can judge their emotional readiness.

When you are ready to introduce your kids to your new partner, take it slowly. Going to a neutral place, such as the movies, a restaurant, the playground, or an amusement park, might be the best way to ease into this difficult introduction. Let your kids gradually get to know your new partner over a period of time. When it feels right, open a discussion about your intention to marry or live together. Your kids might even initiate the conversation.

Don't expect them to welcome this new person (perhaps, interloper, in their eyes) with open arms. And don't be surprised if their reaction continues to be negative for quite a while. Accepting your new partner will take time. The more relaxed you are about it, the easier it will be for your kids to adjust.

Silver Linings

Take your time to carefully integrate the new addition(s) to your children's lives. Realize that, from their perspective, they have not only witnessed the dissolution of the only family they have known, but they are being asked to accept that their parent's love will be going to a stranger now instead of to their other parent. If you put yourself in your children's place, you will better understand how to handle this difficult adjustment.

At some point after your children get to know your new partner, the time will be right to introduce his or her children to your children, if there are any. You and your new partner can decide on an appropriate time.

The Dynamics of the Stepfamily

There was a time when being part of a stepfamily set you apart. But that was in the distant past. A study by Bumpass, Raley, and Sweet (1995), using data from 1987–1988 estimates that 23 percent of children are living in legally married stepfamily households. If you add cohabiting households to the mix, the number is 30 percent.

Although the stepfamily is an increasingly common institution, living in a stepfamily is not always easy. Each participant—the new parent(s), possibly the new step-siblings, and perhaps eventually new half-siblings—adds to a changing dynamic within the stepfamily. Each will be coming to the family with their own emotional perspective and needs.

> **Red Alert** _____
>
> Negativity toward an ex is extremely damaging to children under any circumstance. In instances where a stepparent is involved, any anger or criticism of the other biological parent can make the situation especially difficult and complex. When ex-spouses bad-mouth each other, children are caught in the middle and feelings of guilt can emerge. This will make it more difficult than ever for the child to forge a relationship with the step-parent, even if that step-parent never says a negative word about the absent parent.

According to stepfamily counselor Jeannette Lofas, as a new stepfamily adjusts, everyone is susceptible to feeling like an outsider as family members take on new relationships and roles. Just when you think you found your seat, someone else is sitting in it. For instance, a 15-year-old girl might be used to sitting in the front seat of the car with Daddy, but when Daddy has a girlfriend, where should the girl sit? She will try to protect her territory.

If the stepparent also has children, there's the interaction of the children with the stepparent's children. Are they compatible—even superficially—not to speak of jealousies, turf-guarding, and other sundry emotions.

How about mixing and matching discipline styles? Is step-dad a pushover compared to biological dad? Or the opposite? Have the children who just moved into your house been raised to stay up to all hours while you expect your kids to go to bed at 10:30 P.M.? How will you set the rules so the new children and your children adjust to living under one roof?

It's easy to see that recreating the happy-go-lucky Brady Bunch might be a little optimistic.

But Jeannette Lofas, who was born into a stepfamily and also married into a stepfamily, sees hope. She imparts some of her most valuable tips for the new, blended family:

> ### You Can Do It!
>
> You can't force a new stepparent or stepfamily down your kids' throats. Especially around this sensitive issue, pay attention to your children's cues—if they are subtle. (They may not be subtle at all!)

- Go slowly. Learn to partner with a new husband or wife through the creation of structure and discipline and the accumulation of couple strength. For instance, when a man has parented alone, he might allow the kids to stay up late or order dinner in. The new wife might not feel these things are appropriate, but if she tries to change things, the stepchildren will simply ignore her. She can easily slip into the role of "the bad guy," even if she states her point of view as gently as possible.

- The stepfather or stepmother should not attempt to be parents to their stepchildren, even if the biological parent has died. Nor should they assume the role of friend. Instead, they should be seen as male or female head of household and a partner to the biological parent.

- The stepparent must not impose discipline on his or her own without the support of the biological parent. To do so always creates dissension, rendering the stepparent "the bad guy" in a flash.

- Stepparents should attempt to bond with stepchildren by filling in where the biological parent cannot. For instance, a stepfather might play one-on-one basketball with a stepson or take stepchildren to see a movie; these are activities one can share without assuming the parental role.

How to Make Your Children Feel Welcome in Your New Family

Let's summarize some of the things you can do to help your kids adjust to their new family structure:

◆ Be sensitive to your children's feelings about your having a new partner.

◆ If your child seems hostile, withdrawn, or is just not behaving as usual, insecurity about her or his relationship with you might be the cause. Reassure your child that your love for him or her has never been in doubt.

◆ Integrating everyone into a new stepfamily will require patience. The relationship between your children and their stepparent must grow naturally. Expecting too much too soon is bound to ruffle feathers. New roles within the blended family will be created as relationships take shape.

How Stepparents See It

Judy, a 48-year-old social worker who had never been married, was introduced to Arthur, a 55-year-old divorced man who was the owner of a clothing manufacturing company. He had two adult children—Alice, 22, and Michael, 25. Arthur was still very close to his children even though they were grown. His children enjoyed their time with their father. They would see him every other weekend for dinner and enjoyed summer vacations with him at his lake house.

Judy and Arthur were getting along very well and quickly became serious about their relationship. Alice sensed this and began to develop resentful feelings towards Judy for the attention Judy was getting from her father. Alice became "clingy" for a 22-year-old. She asked her father if she could stay in his apartment on some weekends. It was hard for Arthur to say "No." After a few months, Arthur asked Judy to move in with him. She agreed.

Judy found life with her new companion more complicated than she had anticipated. Alice made frequent visits to her father's home while Judy was there. Judy was uncomfortable occupying the same space as Alice in Arthur's apartment, and more often than not, she felt as if she and Alice were competing for his attention and time.

Both Arthur and Judy had to preserve the integrity and growth of their own relationship while still understanding Alice's feelings. It is up to Arthur—not Judy—to set the boundaries for his daughter. Although Alice is also an adult, she is still Arthur's child and is in a parent/child relationship with him. But because she is an adult, she should be able to understand more readily than a child that her father is entitled to make decisions for his own life. Judy is in an intimate adult relationship with Arthur. She is *not* Alice's parent. But because she is an older adult, she will have to be patient while Alice adjusts to her father's new relationship.

Judy's frustration and anger are valid responses to this circumstance. They are not uncommon for new stepparents. Open communication between the new couple and between parent and child is the best way to navigate these rough waters. Arthur and Judy will have to be patient, yet united, as Alice, an adult child, recognizes that her role as Arthur's daughter is not threatened by Judy's new role as his spouse and companion.

Half-Siblings, Stepsiblings, and the New Baby

It is no longer unusual for children of divorce to have many new relationships when their parents remarry. Although getting used to being part of a blended family is not easy, there are many positives. If parents have the right attitude, and sibling and stepsibling rivalries are worked out, having additional close relationships can be enriching to your children.

Half-siblings, who are biologically related through one parent only, often have closer ties than stepsiblings, who are not biologically related. That doesn't mean stepsiblings can't develop close relationships. Age, sex, life experience, and temperament have a lot to do with the way the new family interacts.

Some specific issues come up with half-siblings and stepsiblings in a blended family:

- **Jealousy over parents.** Whose dad/mom is it?

- **Sharing space—children's need for their own space and privacy.** Whose home is it? Whose room is it? Whose drawers are they? Whose bathroom is it?

- **Need for respect.** Children's individuality should be respected. They should not be taken for granted, such as assuming older children will baby-sit for the younger ones. Children's wishes should be considered when making plans, and they should be told when plans are changed. Children should sense that you trust them and respect their place in the family.

◆ **Sexuality between your older children and their older stepsiblings.** Because stepsiblings are not related biologically, sometimes issues of intimacy can arise for adolescents and teenagers.

◆ **A new baby.** Children in a stepfamily are often challenged by the arrival of a new baby—the product of one of their parents and their stepparent. This can be met with excitement or jealousy or both. The baby can be seen as eating up all their parent's time, a nuisance, and possibly an embarrassment if they think their parent is over the hill. Other children are able to enjoy the new baby and see themselves as the big brother or sister.

Each of these special issues should be handled carefully. Creating an atmosphere where communication is facilitated so feelings don't get bottled up is key. Making sure your children have the physical space, privacy, and respect they need to feel comfortable and secure will help prevent problems before they develop.

Silver Linings

A blended family can be an asset to your children if everyone has the right attitude. Additional family relationships will enrich your children. Children close in age with their step or half-siblings can become fast friends and provide mutual support to each other throughout their lives. Stepparents can be positive role models who can give love and added perspective to your children's world view. As long as the children have adjusted to their new family structure, they can begin to accept and even enjoy the new additions to their world.

In short, being aware of the feelings of your children, your new spouse or significant other, and his or her children, if there are any, is the first step toward making it all work. If problems arise, listen carefully and try to think things through. Although it won't always be possible to please everyone in every case, sensitively negotiating with everyone involved will go a long way toward promoting harmony.

The Least You Need to Know

◆ When you have met the person you think will be your next spouse or live-in partner, introduce him or her to your children and let them get to know each other over a period of time. Allow their relationship to grow naturally.

◆ If your children feel that their importance to you has been overshadowed by your new family, reassure them that their relationship with you is special and that nothing and no one can replace them.

◆ Children should be parented by their biological parent, unless there is an emergency. The stepparent should not take on the role of the children's parent.

◆ Blended families thrive when everyone—including the children—has his or her own space and privacy and is treated with respect.

◆ Mutual respect, consideration, and understanding, as well as ample communication, will ease the way for your new blended family.

Chapter 27

Parting Words: Facing Your Feelings

In This Chapter

- Dealing with grief, rejection, guilt, loneliness, and anger
- Regaining control of your emotions and your life
- How to cope with missing your former life
- Living with your decision: how to stop second-guessing your situation and move on without regret

Your spouse has moved out, you've negotiated a settlement, and signed all the documents. The final divorce decree has arrived in the mail, and even your attorney has gone off to fight other battles.

You've been to another country—the land of the divorcing—but now your flight has landed, and you're coming home. Having divested yourself of the luggage of dysfunction and pain, you are about to deplane free and clear, ready to enter the world of regular people—those untethered by lawyers' phone calls, judicial decisions, visitation squabbles, or battles over the ownership of the crystal chandelier. After all, your spouse is now legally your ex; the war you have waged for so long, during your marriage, and again in your effort to untie the knot, is over.

Or is it? The truth is, on an emotional plane, you might still have some vital issues to resolve. Much of the time, the newly divorced suffer residual effects from the experience. Only after you have truly severed the emotional ties of your marriage, not just the legal ones, are you free to rebuild your sense of identity and begin anew.

The Heart of Darkness

Along with a feeling of relief, you might continue to harbor guilt, pain, and anger. You must resolve these feelings so you can move on.

Feelings of pain and anger following divorce are quite natural. The ability to feel pain—as long as it doesn't go on endlessly—may be the measure of your emotional depth. Rest assured that once the pain ends, you will have the ability to love again. But to dwell on these feelings would be doing yourself a disservice by sustaining a relationship—at least in your mind—with a partner who has probably already let you go. It is time to move on.

CAUTION

Red Alert

Some people have so much trouble coping with the pain of divorce that they resort to alcohol or drugs. Often, these people are immersing themselves in emotional numbness to escape their feelings. A word to the wise: it's better to feel the pain and get through it, beginning life anew, than to linger in emotional limbo. If you are having problems along these lines, seek support from your community or congregation, your friends, website support groups, or, if all else fails, get professional help.

Into the Light

For some people, the feelings of rejection they experience in the aftermath of divorce are simply overpowering. Although you should give yourself plenty of time to heal, if you are still suffering mightily by the time the papers are signed, you should seek professional help.

"As you look into your feelings with the help of a professional," states psychologist Mitchell Baris, "you may even find that the problem is deeper than the divorce itself." Perhaps you are unable to recover because of a particularly difficult experience during childhood. Perhaps there is a long-standing reason, unrelated to your marriage, for your sense of failure and low self-esteem, if that's what you're feeling. If so, take this opportunity to learn about yourself. You deserve it!

> ### Silver Linings
>
> It's common to pass through life without stopping to consider the consequences of our actions or being truly introspective. Given the stress of life today, exploring the inner self is often a luxury we feel we cannot afford. In the wake of divorce, it behooves you to go through such exploration. This is a gift—it may be painful at first, but it will enrich you in the long run.

A Life of Your Own

Our friend Shanna spent five years in a marriage trying to please an irascible, critical husband who found fault with everything—her eating habits, what she read, her clothes and weight, her philosophy of life, and her friends. Fortunately for Shanna, she had no children, and after a year of therapy, she felt ready to sever the bond. For six months after her divorce was finalized, Shanna lived in a studio apartment. For furniture, she used cardboard chests. Her bed was a cot, picked up on sale. For art, she had a single cartoon hanging on the wall: the picture of an Earth man, surrounded by aliens, in a bar in some godforsaken section of the cosmos. The caption: "When I've made it, I'll go back to Earth."

To Shanna, that said it all. She couldn't help feelings of anger, even rage, at her ex. At the same time, she felt a twinge of guilt: Her husband couldn't help his nature, and he had been truly devastated when she walked out.

Shanna eventually moved back to the town she grew up in to be close to her family, but not before she had bolstered her emotional resources. She had many issues to deal with in the aftermath of her divorce, and it took months before she was able, in the truest sense of the word, to return to the "singles" world to which she now belongs.

> ### You Can Do It!
>
> Sometimes, you *can* go home again. In the wake of divorce, it may be helpful to return to your roots. There, you might find the nurturing of old friends and family as well as inner strength you thought you had lost. You might also find some insight into your own role in the break-up of your marriage.

Silver Linings

Yes, you're divorced from your spouse. But your emotional self might still be in the process of letting go. Here are three helpful tips for regaining yourself:

◆ See people and events based on their own contexts and avoid the tendency to project your past relationship onto these new experiences.

◆ If you feel exhausted or overwhelmed by your divorce, give yourself some time and space before jumping into another relationship.

◆ After the divorce is final, sit back and reflect on what went wrong in your marriage. Perhaps if you can really understand what happened, you will be less likely to repeat the mistake.

Rediscovering Your Sense of Self

The issue for Shanna and most other survivors of divorce was a true loss of identity. After years, or sometimes decades, of living with another person, it is easy to accept, without question, *their* sense of who you are. In Shanna's case, that meant seeing herself as somehow stupid and lazy.

For Matt, a commodities trader on Wall Street, it meant something else. Addicted to creature comforts, he left his house in his black BMW for the commuter train at 7 each morning, and after a day of tussling in the trenches, he returned each night at 8. Ursula, his wife, seemed to spend her day working out at the gym and cleaning the house. She met Matt at the door with a cocktail and chatter about the neighbors while classical music drifted out from the stereo in the den. Sure, they had two kids—Samantha and Jordan—but organized Ursula had them in bed and asleep before Matt walked in.

Ursula convinced him he could not navigate the complexities of what she called "real life"—buying the groceries, meeting with teachers, going to the dry cleaners, and even boiling eggs. "He's great with numbers but clueless about surviving," she often told their friends. With a taste for the most expensive furniture, clothing, cars, and vacations, Ursula prided herself in what she referred to as "class." Despite Matt's advanced degrees and high-powered income, Ursula insisted, he did not know the difference between true quality and "crap."

Ultimately, Matt came to agree with the classification. A working-class boy from Queens, he had, he often thought, ascended to a kind of royalty in his marriage to

Ursula. When it came to the art of elegant living, he told himself, she would be his guide. He dressed the part with enthusiasm, and although he'd once loved his family and friends, he now felt justified in shunning them as "crude" and "low class."

One idyllic summer day, Matt sat on his deck, mimosa on the table and cigar in hand. It was the perfect backdrop for Ursula's announcement; he had to leave immediately because her affair with Samantha's piano teacher was, as she put it, "a symphony of passion I can no longer control." There could be no discussion and no resolution, Ursula said. "I never loved you anyway, from the moment I married you. You're overweight, you're boring, you're nervous, and you have no taste."

That was it. After 15 years of marriage, Matt was out and the piano teacher was in. To Matt, it was like being cast out of the castle. He would now descend, he thought, to the wretched, untouchable world from which he had sprung.

In short, it was difficult for Matt to see value in what were once his virtues—his honesty, grittiness, long-term friendships, and his ability to work like a dog. Instead, despite his high-powered career, he saw himself through Ursula's lens—a clumsy, inept pauper who had aspired too high and now must take the fall.

Matt's image problem was typical. "After years of living with a spouse, you tend to internalize the labels and messages that you've heard repeated over time," says New York clinical psychologist Ellen Littman, a member of the faculty at Pace University and an expert on intimacy and self-image, among other issues. "Messages like 'You're no good' and 'You're incompetent' tend to reverberate in your mind. If you've let your spouse define who you are, you are faced with the tremendous task of redefining yourself in a divorce."

Your new task: Shedding the labels and creating new ones that fit the image of the person you have become.

Often, Littman notes, "people choose spouses who have qualities in common with people in the family of origin. Your role in your new family may echo your role in the old. Even if the labels are unpleasant, they can, therefore, feel safe." In a strange way, this was even true of Matt—whose parents suffered a lack of self-confidence, which they managed to instill in their kids. When Ursula reiterated that sense of inadequacy, it was all too easy for Matt to agree.

> **Silver Linings**
>
> Once you consider how your marriage has perpetuated the worst in you, you may well view your divorce as the chance of a lifetime. When you finally get out of the environment in which negative images of you have been reinforced, you can start to view yourself in a new light, reflecting on your strengths and weaknesses, free of outside expectations.

The trick, of course, is to replace a negative image with one that is more positive—and probably more realistic—instead of sliding back, once more, into old patterns. After all, if you are changing your life, this should be the place to start.

Now That It's Over, It's Okay to Feel Angry

When do you get a chance to face your anger and express it, and who is it appropriate to express it to? "A tremendous amount of anger builds as a marriage dissolves," Littman says, "yet it's not wise to express that anger in front of your children or to your spouse. In fact, being in touch with all the anger might even be dangerous for you. Nonetheless, this high level of anger is inside you and often gets turned inward in the form of self-blame."

In Matt's case, for instance, his wife had clearly been unfaithful. Yet she blamed the situation on his deficits, and this, in turn, overwhelmed him with self-doubt. Didn't he deserve this treatment? Wasn't he disgusting? Hadn't he aspired for more than he deserved?

Matt was lucky, at least in one sense. Already seeing a therapist, he explored his anger and his self-esteem issues before venturing out for romance again. He came to understand that he was shouldering more than his fair share of the blame, and, without fear of repercussion in the therapist's office, expressed his inner rage.

Divorce Dictionary

When you face your anger, you will be able to let go of it eventually. As you let go of your anger, you should be able to release all the negative definitions of yourself your spouse had convinced you were true.

"Directing your anger at the perpetrator rather than yourself is the first step toward recovery," Littman states. "Many people are frightened by the intensity of their rage and feel that it is in some way unacceptable. They need to know that rage is an acceptable response when the very moorings of your life have been shaken, and you have had very little control over the destruction."

By purging his anger and examining the constraints Ursula had imposed on him, Matt was able to move on. A year after the day he'd been "kicked out," he was fathering his children as he never had when he lived at home. Able to return to a looser style far more natural to him, he often kept the kids up late—by Ursula's standards, anyway—on weekend sleepovers, watching movies and playing games. Now, when he was with his children, he was really with them—not blitzed out on classical music and a drink.

For the next couple of years, Matt, now 40, was on a mission: Part excavation and part exploration, he pieced together a self he never could have been with Ursula in tow. He joined the Sierra Club and took hikes into the mountains; he reconnected with his family and friends from the old 'hood. (Happily, he discovered that many of these so-called "classless characters" had become major success stories—in business as well as the arts.) And he joined a community theater group, becoming a member of the chorus in a series of musicals.

Says Littman: "The goal is creation of a new identity based on wisdom gained from the journey. This new identity should embrace your unique set of gifts."

There is a postscript to this story: Matt remarried and, unfortunately, divorced yet again. But the second time around, he never relinquished his new sense of self, and through it all, he sustained an ever-stronger relationship with his children. As for Ursula, she moved the piano teacher into the house she once shared with Matt, still playing classical in the den and serving cocktails each night at 7.

Red Alert

To sacrifice your needs for someone else is contrary to the concept of personal growth. Ultimately, a successful relationship must be built upon a foundation where both people are coming from the position of positive personal growth and supporting each other's journey, together!

Dealing With Feelings of Guilt

Self-righteous to the end, Ursula never suffered a moment of guilt for cutting off Matt so quickly or for lying to him for a full five years. But that is unusual. Most people feel terribly guilty for rejecting their spouses and hurting them deeply, not to mention destroying the nuclear family for their children.

You would be guilty—not just *feeling* guilty—if you brushed aside your spouse and recklessly caused your children harm by leaving the marriage without seriously trying to work things out. You made a commitment when you married, and if you had children, took on profound responsibility.

On the other hand, if you *and* your spouse—because the near-failure of a marriage is never entirely one-sided—made a strong effort to reconstruct your relationship, with professional help if necessary, then your guilt is unfounded. The option of staying in a marriage with children for the sake of the children has worked for some. This route requires strength, patience, and perhaps in your mind, sacrifice. But if you are the victim of relentless mental or physical abuse, or if, despite your best effort (including counseling), you cannot find satisfaction in your marriage, there is no reason to feel guilty. Such a marriage must be dissolved.

The Life You Left Behind

Even when you're well out of your marriage, it's natural to miss your life—afternoons in the yard, evenings with friends, and especially the kids. Brian, for instance, left his primary home to his wife and children. He found himself paying for their life in the house, however, even though he had no access to the premises and limited contact with his kids. "I just feel overwhelmed," he told us. "I'm 45 years old, and I'm experiencing a loss of alternatives. My money is committed, and I'm working to sustain a family I'm not even living with—and I don't get any of the positives."

> **You Can Do It!**
>
> Remember, if you are the noncustodial parent, feelings of loss can be repaired by throwing yourself into making a home for the children when they are with you. Think of things to do with your children that are ongoing and constant, something that they want to come to your home to do. How about taking a cooking class together and then re-creating the recipes at your place Or, get a knock-hockey table and start a competition, or a 100-piece jigsaw puzzle that stays put until the next time the kids come over.

Brian is frustrated, but he is not really seeing the reality of the situation, at least regarding his kids. He may not be living with his children, but he probably will be spending a good deal of time with them. He can have the same closeness as before, and perhaps the bond will even deepen now that he is taking care of them on his own.

As for his social problems, one solution for Brian is to get out into the world and meet new people. If he cannot make ends meet financially, he should be thinking about working toward a new career by going back to school—a good place to find new friends and interests while increasing his earning potential.

He might also want to develop additional parenting skills now that he will be taking care of his children without backup. He can take child development classes and read up on child safety issues. These classes are also a good place to make new friends.

When Doubt Lingers

It's not unusual, in the aftermath of divorce, to wonder whether you have done the right thing. In fact, unless your marriage has been complete hell—and that is not usually the case—you will still harbor residual feelings of affection for your spouse and the happy moments you spent together.

"Unless it's a situation of utter relief from the most adverse possible circumstances," says Dr. Mitchell Baris, "ambivalent feelings are likely to linger."

There is, quite simply, a period of wondering whether you could have worked it out or whether you simply gave up too soon.

Red Alert _____

The temptation to be drawn back into the circle of your past relationship and all that it represents is real. Once the divorce is final, make it your business to establish your own life and center of activity. Make it your goal to move on.

One friend of ours began harboring such feelings, especially after his ex started calling him and asking him to be open, at least, to trying again. Her requests were especially tempting to him because she had been the one to end the relationship and push for the divorce in the first place. Just a year ago, he had pleaded with her to give the marriage a shot, and now, miraculously, she was doing just that.

But for our friend, things had changed. The experience had revealed to him his wife's fickle, callous side, and he had started dating someone new. Not only was he basically content again, but also he had no desire to plunge himself into the pain he had experienced as recently as a year before.

What should he do? A therapist wisely advised him to get together with his ex-spouse. "Don't be afraid," the psychiatrist told him. "You're thinking very clearly now, and you'll see things for what they really are."

Indeed he did. His ex-wife claimed she wanted a reunion, but within minutes of their meeting at a local coffee shop, she was commenting on his tie (too loud) and his hair (too short).

Our friend was cordial throughout the meeting but was able to walk away from it understanding he was well out of a relationship that meant nothing but pain. He had looked into the eye of the monster, after all, and he had prevailed.

The moral of the story: After your divorce, face your ambivalence head on. If your spouse has really been a louse or is just not right for you, you'll have the ability to see that, even if in your weaker moments you're still not sure.

How to Be Friendly with Your Ex

The divorce has been finalized and you're on your own. Your marriage, and all the pain it represents, is part of your past. Yet part of moving forward, for many, is learning to deal in a friendly, amicable way with their ex.

It seems like an oxymoron—two angry, divorced people ending up friends. Yet it is possible, according to Bill Ferguson, an attorney-turned-divorce consultant and author of *Heal the Hurt That Runs Your Life* (1996) and *Miracles Are Guaranteed* (1992). The key, says Ferguson, is to end the cycle of conflict and restore the feeling of love. By love, this does not necessarily mean "the husband and wife kind of love," he says, "but the kind of love that one human being extends to another."

> **⚠ CAUTION**
>
> **Red Alert**
>
> The divorce courts are full of people who love each other. You may still love your ex, even after the divorce. This does not mean you should try to put your marriage together. Instead, remember that the goal is literally putting your divorce together, so that you can move on with your separate lives as friends.

This can seem like a daunting task if you are in the midst of conflict and angry feelings. How does one begin?

The first step, says Ferguson, is the realization that love is never enough to make a relationship work. In addition to love, a marriage also requires such elements as appreciation and acceptance—what Ferguson terms "the experience of love." That experience is destroyed by judgmental, critical behavior, he notes. Although it might be impossible to hold back such attitudes during the marriage, when the marriage is over, the cycle can end.

"To create and maintain this cycle of conflict," says Ferguson, "there must be two people participating, like a tennis match. When one person stops playing the game—when one person stops the non-acceptance—the cycle ends."

The key, he notes, is truthfully seeing your ex for what he or she is. "That person is the way he or she is, like it or not," says Ferguson. "When you can be at peace with the truth, you can see what you need to do. Maybe you need to move on."

Yet how do you break the cycle of conflict when you're hurt? "The first step," says Ferguson, "is realizing where the hurt is coming from." His notion is amazingly simple: "Your upset was caused not by what happened between you and your ex, but by your resistance to what happened. Now you must take your focus off what happened and, instead, work on healing the hurt that was triggered when the cycle of conflict began. Your anger and resentment are avoidance of the hurt. By facing the hurt, and coming to a place of forgiveness, it will be easier to be friends in the years to come."

"Trusting is one of the keys to letting go and being free inside," Ferguson adds. "However, this doesn't mean to trust that life will turn out like you want it to. Often life doesn't. The key is understanding that however life turns out, you will be fine."

The Least You Need to Know

- Allow yourself to experience the pain. It's something you've got to get through, but don't hold onto it indefinitely.

- After the divorce is final, sit back and reflect on what went wrong in your marriage. Perhaps if you can really understand what happened, you will be less likely to repeat the mistake again.

- After your divorce, face your ambivalence about your spouse head on.

- In moments of loneliness, it is tempting to succumb to the fantasy that you can once more find comfort and love with your ex. While this is certainly possible, beware of this notion as a common, unrealistic wish among the newly divorced.

The Complete Divorce Lexicon

abandonment   The departure of one spouse from the marital home without the consent of the other spouse. In some states, this may constitute grounds for divorce.

action   A lawsuit. In matrimonial matters, it is usually a lawsuit for a divorce, an annulment, or a legal separation.

adultery   Engaging in sexual relations with someone other than one's spouse. In some states, this may constitute grounds for divorce.

affidavit   A sworn statement of facts. Affidavits usually accompany motions and are used to avoid having to personally appear in court to testify. However, sometimes you might have to appear in court even though you have prepared an affidavit.

alimony or **maintenance** or **spousal support**   Payments made by one spouse to the other to assist with the support of the recipient spouse. Payments usually terminate upon the earlier of the death of either spouse, the remarriage of the recipient spouse, or a date decided by a judge or agreed upon by the husband and wife. Payments received are usually taxable to the recipient spouse and tax-deductible by the paying spouse.

appeal   A presentation, usually in writing, but sometimes supplemented by lawyers' oral arguments in court, to a court a level above the court that has decided an issue. The purpose of the appeal is to have the higher court reverse or in some way modify what the lower court did.

appellant   The person who brings the appeal.

billing rate   The rate at which an attorney bills a client for work performed. Many attorneys bill on an hourly basis, charging a certain amount of money per hour. Some attorneys bill per project, regardless of how much or little time it takes to do the work. This is also referred to as "unbundling" fees.

brief   A written presentation of a party's position. Lawyers most often submit briefs to argue appeals. Lawyers also submit briefs to support points of law made at the trial court level.

child support   A sum of money to be paid by one parent to the other to assist with the support of the couple's children. Child support is sometimes paid directly to a third party, such as a private school or a healthcare provider, rather than to a parent. In some jurisdictions, child support is paid to a state support collection unit, which in turn pays it to the recipient spouse. Child support usually terminates upon a child's emancipation. Unlike alimony, child support is not taxed as income to the recipient.

cohabitation   The act of living with someone. In some states, cohabitation may be grounds for the termination of support. In addition, some husbands and wives may agree when settling their case that cohabitation for a period of time (such as six months on a substantially continuous basis) will cause support to be terminated.

community property state   A state where all property (and typically income) acquired during the marriage is presumed to belong equally to both parties.

constructive abandonment   The refusal of one spouse to engage in sexual relations with the other. In some states, this may constitute grounds for divorce.

contempt   The act of willfully violating a court order. Nonpayment of support when a spouse has the means to pay such support frequently gives rise to contempt adjudications in divorce cases.

cross-examination   The act of being questioned by the attorney representing the person on whose behalf the witness is not testifying.

decision   The judge's reasoning for why he or she directed something to be done or not done. Decisions usually accompany orders. Findings of fact and conclusions of law are the same as a decision. Decisions are sometimes referred to as "opinions."

defendant   The person who defends the lawsuit.

deposition   Answering questions under oath. In matrimonial matters, a deposition usually centers on a party's finances or child custody issues and is conducted in a lawyer's office or in the courthouse, but a judge will not be present. In some jurisdictions, the grounds for divorce may also be the subject of the deposition. A stenographer takes down everything that is said and later types it up for review by the parties and their attorneys.

direct examination   The act of being questioned under oath by the attorney representing the person on whose behalf the witness is testifying.

discovery   The act of revealing information so that both parties are fully informed of facts before trial. Discovery can pertain to finances or to one's physical or mental condition when those issues are relevant, such as when a spouse claims an inability to work due to an injury. Depending on the jurisdiction, other areas may be discoverable as well. Discovery methods include taking depositions, answering interrogatories, producing documents, and undergoing a physical.

dissolution   In many states, divorce is now called dissolution.

emancipation   The age at which a parent is no longer responsible for a child's support. The age varies by state. In some states, it may be 18; in others, 21. In addition, other events, such as a child getting married, joining the armed forces, or working full-time, if such events occur before the emancipation age, may also be deemed emancipation events.

equitable distribution   A system of dividing property between spouses based upon what the judge considers to be fair. The law and precedent provide the judge with the factors to consider in making that determination.

exclusive use and occupancy of the marital residence   The right one spouse has to reside in the home in which the parties had previously lived together. Such right may be agreed upon or may be directed by a judge while an action is pending.

forensic   The term refers to applying scientific methods to legal matters and is sometimes used when an accountant performs a valuation of a business or a professional practice for distribution in a divorce. It can also refer to the process where a psychologist, psychiatrist, social worker, or other mental health professional is appointed to interview the parents and their children and make a recommendation to the court about who would be the better custodial parent. The mental health expert may also interview child caretakers, grandparents, teachers, and anyone else who has frequent contact with the children.

garnishment   A mechanism whereby support is sent by the paying spouse's employer directly to the recipient spouse and is deducted from the paying spouse's paycheck.

grounds   The legally sufficient reasons why a person is entitled to a divorce. Although many states are no-fault states—where no grounds need to be asserted other than incompatibility or irreconcilable differences—other states require the plaintiff to prove grounds, such as adultery, abandonment, or mental cruelty.

interrogatories   A series of questions that must be answered under oath, within a certain period of time, usually designed to ascertain a person's financial holdings and means of earning income or to address child custody issues.

joint custody Sharing of the responsibilities for raising children despite a divorce. Joint *legal* custody can mean the children will live with one parent most of the time, but both parents will make major decisions. If the children divide their time equally between the two parents' homes, this is called "joint physical custody."

judgment of divorce The written document that states that a husband and wife are divorced. In some states, this may be called a decree of dissolution. Typically, lawyers draft the judgment of divorce for the judge to review and sign. This document can contain a name change for one or both parties.

law guardian A person, usually a lawyer, selected by the judge and assigned to represent the children of the divorcing parents or an incapacitated adult.

marital property In general, property a husband and wife acquired during the marriage. Such property may also be called joint property. In some jurisdictions, inheritances, disability awards, and gifts received from a third party (that is, not the spouse) are not considered marital or joint property, even if a spouse received them during the marriage. Other exceptions may exist as well.

motion A request made of a judge at a time an action is pending or at trial. Motions can be made in writing for the court to consider, or orally, such as at trial. In matrimonial cases, motions are typically made for temporary support, temporary custody, visitation rights, or to enjoin someone from taking money or property.

noncustodial parent The parent with whom the children do not live. Such a parent might not make day-to-day decisions but, depending on the definition of legal custody, can have a great deal to say about decisions regarding the children.

order A ruling or "decree" by a judge, made orally or in writing, directing someone to do or refrain from doing something.

order of protection An order directing one spouse to refrain from harassing or contacting the other. Violation of an order of protection can result in arrest and imprisonment.

perjury The act of lying under oath.

petitioner The person who first goes to court to file a request or petition for some kind of relief. Sometimes called the "plaintiff."

plaintiff The person who starts a lawsuit. Sometimes called the "petitioner."

postnuptial agreement or **separation agreement** A written contract entered into by a husband and wife, which sets forth all their present and future rights in the event of a divorce or a spouse's death. The parties may or may not be involved in divorce litigation at the time they sign such an agreement.

precedent The use of previous decisions in cases factually similar to the case before a judge in order for the judge to decide how to adjudicate the present case.

prenuptial agreement   A written contract entered into by a couple who intend to marry but want to establish, before marriage, their rights in the event of a death or divorce after marriage. The validity of such agreements depends on state law.

pro se **divorce**   A divorce that is handled by the individual seeking the divorce rather than with the aid of an attorney.

record   All the evidence (testimony, documents, and exhibits) upon which a judge based his or her decision. When a party appeals a decision, it is necessary to compile all the papers and transcripts of testimony that the lower court used to decide the case and present that information to the higher court.

respondent   The person who has to defend or object to the appeal. The respondent also responds to the petition in the trial court and, in that case, may also be referred to as the "defendant."

retainer   A payment made to an attorney to secure his or her services. As the attorney works, charges are deducted from the retainer until the money is depleted. At that time, the attorney will bill on a weekly or monthly basis or ask for a new retainer.

retainer agreement   A contract signed by an attorney and client setting forth the billing arrangement to be instituted between the lawyer and the client. Some states require that a client's "bill of rights" be included in a retainer.

separate property   Property a spouse acquires before the marriage and after an action for divorce has begun. In some jurisdictions, inheritance, disability awards, and gifts received during the marriage by one party are considered separate property. Other exceptions may exist as well.

sole custody   One parent has the right to make the major decisions concerning the children. Even where one parent has sole custody, the other parent often has the right to be informed, consulted, and to offer an opinion about the decision. Major decisions include religion, education, and health issues. Day-to-day decisions, such as the child's daily routine, are made by the parent who is caring for the child at the time. Under sole custody the child's residence is with the custodian, and the noncustodial parent has "visitation rights" (also called "parenting time" among other names).

transcript   The written presentation of testimony given at trial or in a deposition.

The Divorce Network: A Guide to Divorce Organizations

Given the number of divorces, it's no surprise that thousands of divorce organizations exist around the United States. Some are for single parents, and some are just for singles. Some cater to the needs of parents without custody, others to the political agendas of divorced women and moms or divorced men and dads. We cannot list every organization in this appendix. However, we hope that the broad spectrum of national groups presented will enable you to link, either directly or through referral, to the information, support, and friendship that you need in your local area.

Children and Divorce

National Association of Child Advocates
1522 K Street, NW, Suite 600, Washington, D.C. 20005
Eve Brooks, President
Phone: 202-289-0777
Fax: 202-289-0776
Email: naca@childadvocacy.org
Website: www.childadvocacy.org

NACA strives to change policy in areas of healthcare, education, childcare, child support, and juvenile justice. Although NACA and its 44 member organizations do not provide individual services, they can provide information on the most current legislation and policy. You can reach member organizations around the country by calling or faxing the Washington office. Link from there to local groups devoted to child support enforcement, single parents, noncustodial parents, stepfamilies, and father's rights.

Children's Rights Council
6200 Editors Park Drive, Suite 103
Hyattsville, MD 20782
Phone: 301-559-3120
Fax: 301-559-3124
Website: www.gocrc.com

A national nonprofit organization dedicated to assisting children of separation and divorce through advocacy and parenting education.

Association for Children for Enforcement of Support (ACES)
2260 Upton Avenue
Toledo, OH 43606
Geraldine Jensen, President
Phone: 1-800-738-ACES (2237)
Fax: 1-800-739-2237
Website: www.childsupport-ACES.org

This self-help, nonprofit child-support organization teaches custodial parents what they need to do to collect child support. The association has 350 chapters located all across the United States. Call, write, or fax for information on how to contact a chapter in your area.

National Center for Missing and Exploited Children
Charles B. Wang International Children's Building
699 Prince Street
Alexandria, Virginia 22314-3175
Phone: 1-800-THE-LOST (Hotline); 703-274-3900 (Office)
Fax: 703-274-2200
Website: www.missingkids.com

NCMEC gives legal and technical assistance and can look into parental abduction cases if the parent reporting the abduction has custody and if the child has been entered into their computer system as a missing juvenile. If the child has not been entered, that should be done first before a listing can be made. NCMEC also publishes a list of local nonprofit organizations involved in recovering missing children throughout the United States.

Find the Children
2656 29th Street, #203
Santa Monica, CA 90405
Phone: 1-888-477-6721
Website: www.findthechildren.com

A national nonprofit organization dedicated to the prevention, location, and recovery of missing and abducted children. This group provides educational materials and training, registers missing children, and manages specific cases by distributing photographs and descriptive information about missing children, working with other organizations in the field, maintaining a referral list of professionals all over the country who can help families of missing children, providing emotional support to families of missing children, and giving referrals for post-recovery counseling. All services to victim families and their children are provided free of charge.

Legal Resources

For matrimonial attorneys, mediation, conciliation, and dispute resolution, contact:

American Academy of Matrimonial Lawyers
150 N. Michigan Avenue, Suite 2040
Chicago, IL 60601
Sandra Murphy, President
Phone: 312-263-6477
Fax: 312-263-7682
Website: www.aaml.org

This organization provides referrals to board-certified attorneys specializing in matrimonial and family law. Chapters are located all over the United States and in other countries.

American Bar Association
750 N. Lake Shore Drive
Chicago, IL 60611
Robert A. Stein, Executive Director
Phone: 312-988-5000
Fax: 312-988-6281
Website: www.abanet.org/family/home.html

This organization of 400,000 members can provide a list of state bar associations and can also provide numbers for referral services by state.

Association of Family and Conciliation Courts
6515 Grand Teton Plaza, Suite 210
Madison, WI 53719

Phone: 608-664-3750
Fax: 608-664-3751
Website: www.afccnet.org

This international association of judges, lawyers, counselors, custody evaluators, and mediators maintains a library of videos, pamphlets, and other publications on custody and visitation issues, child support, mediation, and more. Some titles include *Guide for Stepparents*, *Twenty Questions Divorcing Parents Ask About Their Children*, and *Preparing for Your Custody Evaluation*. This group also sponsors parent education programs and conferences on a wide range of child welfare issues.

Kayama
1363 Coney Island Avenue
Brooklyn, New York 11230
Phone: 1-800-932-8589
or in New York, 718-692-1876
Website: www.kayama.org

A non-profit organization that provides information and assistance for obtaining a Jewish divorce ("get").

Single Parents

For issues relating to single parents, contact:

Parents Without Partners
1650 South Dixie Highway, Suite 510
Boca Raton, FL 33432
Phone: 561-391-8833
Fax: 561-395-8557
Website: www.parentswithoutpartners.org

The organization provides information on child support and custody issues for both custodial and noncustodial parents. Resources are provided through local chapters.

Divorce Care
P.O. Box 1739
Wake Forest, NC 27588-1739
Phone: 1-800-489-7778;
Website: www.divorcecare.com

A series of support groups and seminars conducted by people who understand what you are experiencing.

Single Parents Network
Website: singleparentsnetwork.com

A "hub" consisting of links to relevant single parent websites, articles, information and support boards for those looking for single parent information and support.

Parents World
Website: www.parentsworld.com/index.php

A website for single parents, including articles, message boards, books, and games.

Moms and Divorce

National Women's Law Center
11 Dupont Circle NW, Suite 800
Washington, DC 20036
Nancy Duff Campbell, Co-President
Phone: 202-588-5180
Website: www.nwlc.org

This group works to guarantee equality for women under the law and to seek protection and advancement of their legal rights and issues at all levels. Areas of interest include child support enforcement, dependent care, and the family.

Women's Law Project
125 S. 9th St., Suite 300
Philadelphia, PA 19107
Carol Tracy, Executive Director
Phone: 215-928-9801
Fax: 215-928-9848
Website: www.womenslawproject.org/AboutWLP.htm

This nonprofit feminist law firm challenges sex discrimination in the law and in legal and social institutions. This group also maintains telephone counseling and referral services on women's legal rights concerns and community education.

National Organization of Single Mothers
Box 68
Midland, NC 28107
Phone: 704-888-MOMS
Website: www.singlemothers.org

A website consisting of relevant links on for single mothers, covering such topics as financial help, dating, Christian mothers, parent resources, and child support, surrogate mothers, sperm banks, and divorce lawyers.

Dads and Divorce

National Fatherhood Initiative
101 Lake Forest Boulevard, Suite 360
Gaithersburg, Maryland 20877
Phone: 301-948-0599
Fax: 301-948-4325
Website: www.fatherhood.org

Organization whose objective is to improve fathers' involvement in their children's lives.

Fathering Magazine
Website: www.fathermag.com/SingleFather.shtml

Practical childcare tips for the single dad.

Single & Custodial Fathers Network, Inc.
Website: www.scfn.org

A website devoted to support and information for single fathers. Includes a message board and information, staffed by veteran single fathers.

Domestic Abuse

National Coalition Against Domestic Violence
P.O. Box 18749
Denver, CO 80218
Phone: 303-839-1852
Fax: 303-831-9251
The National Domestic Violence Hotline: 1-800-799-SAFE (7233)
Website: www.ncadv.org

The National Coalition Against Domestic Violence works in the political realm to support legislation to advocate for victims of domestic violence. It aids in the establishment of shelters for battered women. NCADV serves as a national information and referral center for the general public, media, battered women and their children, allied and member agencies and organizations. To locate an organization that offers support and services in your area, contact your state coalition.

Domestic Abuse Project
204 West Franklin Avenue
Minneapolis, MN 55404
Phone: 1-800-793-5975; 612-874-7063
Fax: 612-874-8445
Website: www.mndap.org

The Domestic Abuse Project seeks to remedy domestic abuse through legal advocacy, therapy, training, as well as research and evaluation. Their goal is to provide safety to survivors and their children, to hold abusers accountable for the violence, and to build programs that serve as models for communities around the nation.

AMEND (Abusive Men Exploring New Directions)
2727 Bryant Street, Suite #350
Denver, CO 80211
Phone: 303-832-6363
Fax: 303-832-6364
Website: www.amendinc.org

This organization provides therapy for abusive men and advocacy for women as well as violence prevention programs in schools. It can also provide specific information on help resources for women in violent relationships.

Child Abuse Listening and Mediation (CALM)
P.O. Box 90754
Santa Barbara, CA 93190
Phone: 805-965-2376; 24-hour listening service (bilingual): 805-569-2255
Website: www.calm4kids.org

This group helps parents who are having difficulty coping with stress in their lives and are afraid they might hurt their children. It provides counseling for families in which abuse has occurred and for families at risk for abuse to occur. The organization provides support groups for parents of children who have been abused and for children who have been abused by a family member. It also provides support groups to educate parents and improve relationships between parents and children. Respite care is available. Referrals are provided to other organizations and services.

Child Welfare League of America
440 1st Street, NW, Suite 310
Washington, DC 20001
Phone: 202-638-2952
Fax: 202-638-4004
Website: www.cwla.org

This group consists of more than 800 member agencies in the United States and Canada. Call, write, or fax to obtain information on how to contact a group in your area.

Rape, Abuse and Incest National Network
635-B Pennsylvania Ave., SE
Washington, DC 20003
National Sexual Assault Hotline: 1-800-656-HOPE
Phone: 202-544-1034 or 1-800-656-4673 ext. 3
Fax: 202-544-3556
Website: www.rainn.org

This organization operates the National Sexual Assault Hotline at 1.800.656.HOPE. It offers programs to prevent sexual assault, help victims, and attempts to ensure that rapists are apprehended, convicted and punished.

American Bar Association Commission on Domestic Violence
ABA Commission on Domestic Violence
740 15th Street, NW, 9th Floor
Washington, DC, 20005-1022
Phone: 312-988-5000
Website: www.abanet.org/domviol/home.html

The Commission seeks to assure an adequate legal response to domestic violence, sexual assault, and stalking. It seeks to mobilize the legal profession to increase access to justice for victims of domestic violence.

Blended Family Support

For issues related to stepparents and their spouses, contact:

Stepfamily Association of America
650 J Street, Suite 205
Lincoln, NE 68508
Phone: 1-800-735-0329
Website: www.stepfam.org

This organization focuses on supporting stepfamilies. It provides educational information and resources to help with any issues that might come up as a result of stepfamily life.

Stepfamily Foundation
333 West End Avenue
New York, NY 10023
Phone: 212-877-3244
Fax: 212-362-7030
Email: staff@stepfamily.org
Website: www.stepfamily.org/index.html

Provides counseling, on the telephone and in person, and information to create a successful step relationship.

Financial Resources

For issues regarding finances and divorce, contact:

Older Women's League
1750 New York Avenue, NW, Suite 350
Washington, DC 20006

Phone: 202-783-6686; 1-800-825-3695
Fax: 1-202-629-0458
Website: www.owl-national.org

This group provides support and information on issues important to midlife and older women, including the effects of divorce on older women.

Pension Rights Center
1350 Connecticut Ave. NW, Suite 206
Washington, DC 20036
Phone: 202-296-3776
Website: www.pensionrights.org

This group provides everything you wanted to know about pensions—in particular, information concerning how divorce affects pensions—and offers a lawyer referral service.

National Foundation for Consumer Credit
801 Roeder Road, Suite 900
Silver Spring, Maryland 20910
Phone: 800-388-2227 or 800-682-9832 (Spanish assistance); 301-589-5600; 301-576-2519
Fax: 301-495-5623
Website: www.nfcc.org

A nonprofit membership organization whose purpose is to educate, counsel, and promote the wise use of credit, NFCC serves as an umbrella group for 200 member services with more than 1,100 counseling offices throughout the United States, Puerto Rico, and Canada. NFCC offers free or low-cost professional money-management counseling and educational services to consumers nationwide.

Psychological Support

For emotional help groups for divorce, contact:

Ackerman Institute for Family Therapy
149 E. 78th St.
New York, NY 10021
Phone: 212-879-4900
Fax: 212-744-0206
Website: www.ackerman.org/

This organization provides family and couples treatment and helps divorcing partners resolve issues of childcare—such as how to tell children about a divorce and how to keep the child from the center of conflict.

International Association for Marriage and Family Counselors

Dr. Robert Smith, Executive Director
Texas A&M University—Corpus Christi
College of Education
6300 Ocean Drive
Corpus Christi, TX 78412
Phone: 361-825-2307
Website: www.iamfc.com

IAMFC promotes excellence in the practice of couples and family counseling by creating and disseminating first-class publications and media products, providing a forum for exploration of family-related issues, involving a diverse group of dedicated professionals in their activities, and emphasizing collaborative efforts. IAMFC is a division of the American Counseling Association (ACA), which embraces a multicultural approach in support of the worth, dignity, potential, and uniqueness of the families we serve.

Mental Help.net
www.mentalhelp.net

Mental Help.Net is dedicated to educating the public about mental health, wellness, and family and relationship issues and concerns. The website is designed and maintained by clinical psychologists to provide news, articles, reviewed links, interactive tests, book reviews, self-help resources, therapist and job listings and videos.

A Guide to National and State Divorce Laws on the Internet

Divorce laws can vary so much from state to state and change so rapidly that it would be impossible to include them in this book; many of the laws we report would be inaccurate a month after publication. Instead, we created an Internet roadmap for finding the most up-to-date versions of codes, statutes, and case decisions.

The appendix is divided into two major sections. The first section focuses on search engines, law libraries, and other general resources on divorce. The second section covers the divorce laws for each of the 50 United States. Remember that online material varies from state to state, so one jurisdiction might have much more information available for its residents than another. We know some of these Internet addresses are long and complex; unfortunately, government filing systems remain arcane, even on the Web.

Please note that Internet addresses change frequently, and it is possible that some of these links will expire by the time you read this section. If so, use the search engines.

A General Guide to Divorce Law on the Internet

The Best Legal Search

FindLaw
www.findlaw.com

LawCrawler
web.lawcrawler.com

Search Law Reviews
www.lawreview.org

The Law Libraries

World Wide Web Virtual Law Library
www.law.indiana.edu/law/v-lib

Cornell Legal Information Institute
www.law.cornell.edu

U.S. Divorce Law from Cornell
www.law.cornell.edu/topics/divorce.html

Divorce-Related Websites and Resources on the Internet

Divorce Central
www.divorcecentral.com

Divorce Source
www.divorcesource.com

DivorceNet
www.divorcenet.com

Divorce Magazine
www.divorcemag.com

DivorceLinks.com
www.divorcelinks.com

Divorceprocess.com
www.divorceprocess.com

Social Security Administration
www.ssa.gov

National Child Support Enforcement Association
www.ncsea.org

National Conference of State Legislatures
www.ncsl.org

Family Law Issues Overview
www.ncsl.org/programs/cyf/fl.htm

Domestic Violence Overview
www.ncsl.org/programs/cyf/dvbookintro.htm

U.S. State Department on Child Abduction
travel.state.gov/family/abduction.html

Important Federal Laws

Parental Kidnapping Prevention Act
dept.fvtc.edu/ojjdp/AmberAlert/federal.pdf

Hague Convention on Child Abduction
www.loc.gov/law/public/reports/child_abduction.pdf

Internal Revenue Code
www.fourmilab.ch/ustax/www/contents.html

National Legal and Bar Associations

American Bar Association
www.abanet.org

Canadian Bar Association
www.cba.org

Association of Trial Lawyers of America
www.atla.org

Federal Bar Association
www.fedbar.org

American Civil Liberties Union
www.aclu.org

American Association of Law Libraries
www.aallnet.org

Electronic Frontier Foundation
www.eff.org

Electronic Privacy Information Center
www.epic.org

National Association of Legal Assistants
www.nala.org

National Court Reporters Association
www.nvra.org

National Federation of Paralegal Associations
www.paralegals.org

National Lawyers Guild
www.nlg.org

Practicing Law Institute
www.pli.edu

Washington Legal Foundation
www.wlf.org

Federal Office of Child Support
www.acf.dhhs.gov/ACFPrograms/CSE/index.html

A State-by-State Roadmap to Divorce Laws and Legal Resources on the Internet

This listing provides links to all state governments. Where available, we have included the state family laws, information on child support and custody, domestic violence, and the state attorney bar association. Keep in mind that these websites may be updated or changed at any time, so links may not work.

Alabama

Alabama State Government
www.alabama.gov

Marriage
www.legislature.state.al.us/CodeofAlabama/1975/50692.htm

Divorce and Alimony
www.legislature.state.al.us/CodeofAlabama/1975/50752.htm

Husband and Wife
www.legislature.state.al.us/CodeofAlabama/1975/51069.htm

Child Custody and Support
www.legislature.state.al.us/CodeofAlabama/1975/50821.htm

Protection from Abuse
www.legislature.state.al.us/CodeofAlabama/1975/51269.htm

Family Violence Protection Order Enforcement
www.legislature.state.al.us/CodeofAlabama/1975/51306.htm

Domestic Violence Facilities
www.legislature.state.al.us/CodeofAlabama/1975/51333.htm

Alabama Bar Association
www.alabar.org

Alaska

Alaska State Government
www.state.ak.us

Alaska Family Law Citations
www.state.ak.us/courts/shclaws.htm

Child Support Services Division
www.csed.state.ak.us/

Divorce and Dissolution
alaskalawhelp.org/AK
(then click on "Family and Life Planning" and then "Divorce and Dissolution")

Alaska Court System
www.state.ak.us/courts

Domestic Violence
www.state.ak.us/courts/shcdv.htm

Alaska Bar Association
www.alaskabar.org

Arizona

Arizona State Government
az.gov/webapp/portal

Uniform Marriage and Divorce Act
www.supreme.state.az.us/dr (Use search feature for specific queries, such as "child custody.")

Child Support
www.azdes.gov/dcse/default.asp

Marriage Workshops/Skills
www.azdes.gov/marriage

Domestic Violence
www.supreme.state.az.us/dr/dv/dv.htm

Arizona Bar Association
www.azbar.or

Arkansas

Arkansas State Government Family Resources
www.accessarkansas.org/family.php

Arkansas Statutes (searchable)
170.94.58.9/NXT/gateway.dll?f=templates&fn=default.htm&vid=blr:code

Arkansas Child Support Overview
courts.state.ar.us/courts/acs_guidelines.html

Child Support Enforcement
www.arkansas.gov/dfa/child_support/ocse_index.html

Domestic Violence
www.accardv.uams.edu/

Arkansas Bar Association
www.arkbar.com

California

California State Government
www.ca.gov/state/portal/myca_homepage.jsp

Family Codes
www.leginfo.ca.gov/cgi-bin/calawquery?codesection=fam&codebody=&hits=20

Uniform Divorce Recognition Act
www.leginfo.ca.gov/cgi-bin/displaycode?section=fam&group=02001-03000&file=2090-2093

California Courts and Judicial System
www.courtinfo.ca.gov

Child Support Services
www.childsup.cahwnet.gov

Domestic Violence
www.courtinfo.ca.gov/selfhelp/protection/dv/

California Bar Association
www.calbar.org

Colorado

Colorado State Government
www.colorado.gov

Colorado Statutes (searchable)
198.187.128.12/colorado/lpext.dll?f=templates&fn=fs-main.htm&2.0

Colorado Child Support Enforcement
www.childsupport.state.co.us/home/indexIndex.jsp

Colorado State Legal Forms
www.courts.state.co.us/chs/court/forms/selfhelpcenter.htm

Domestic Violence
www.cdhs.state.co.us/OPI/domestic_violence_in_colorado.htm

Colorado Bar Association
www.cobar.org

Connecticut

Connecticut State Government
www.ct.gov

Family Law Statutes (If link doesn't work, go to above link and click on "Browse." Then look
for Family Law.)
www.cga.ct.gov/2005/pub/Title46b.htm

Family Court Forms
www.jud2.state.ct.us/webforms

Child Support
www.dss.state.ct.us/csrc/csrc.htm?ctportalPNavCtr=127345I#27350

Domestic Violence
www.jud.state.ct.us/lawlib/Notebooks/Pathfinders/DomesticViolence/domviolence.htm

Connecticut Bar Association
www.ctbar.org

District of Columbia

District of Columbia Government
www.dc.gov

District of Columbia Pro Se Form
www.dcbar.org/for_the_public/legal_information/family/family_court_forms/index.cfm

Child Support Services Division
csed.dc.gov/csed

Domestic Violence
dhs.dc.gov/dhs/lib/dhs/pdfs/target_services/dom_violence.pdf

District of Columbia Bar Association
www.dcbar.org

Delaware

Delaware State Government
www.delaware.gov

Delaware Domestic Relations Laws
www.delcode.state.de.us/title13

Family Court System
courts.state.de.us

Child Support Overview
www.state.de.us/dhss/dcse/ovrvw.html

Division of Child Support Enforcement
www.state.de.us/dhss/dcse

Domestic Violence
www.state.de.us/dsp/domestic.htm

Delaware Bar Association
www.dsba.org

Florida

Florida State Government
www.myflorida.com/

Florida Statutes
www.flsenate.gov/Statutes

Court System
www.flcourts.org

Child Support
www.myflorida.com/dor/childsupport

Domestic Violence
www.doh.state.fl.us/family/svpp/domestic.html

Florida Bar Association
www.flabar.org/newflabar/lawpractice/adreg/adguide.html

Georgia

Georgia State Government
www.georgia.gov

Official Code of Georgia
www.legis.state.ga.us
Click "Georgia code" and search for your key word.

Grounds for Divorce
www.ganet.state.ga.us/cgi-bin/pub/ocode/ocgsearch?docname=OCode/G/19/5/
3&highlight=marriage

Alimony
www.ganet.state.ga.us/cgi-bin/pub/ocode/ocgsearch?docname=OCode/
G/19/6/5&highlight=marriage

Child Custody
www.ganet.state.ga.us/cgi-
bin/pub/ocode/ocgsearch?docname=OCode/G/19/9/3&highlight=marriage

Child Support
www.ganet.state.ga.us/cgi-bin/pub/ocode/ocgsearch?docname=OCode/G/19/11/
43&highlight=marriage

Domestic Violence/Dispute Resolution
www.godr.org/domviol.html

Supreme Court of Georgia
www.gasupreme.us

Department of Human Resources
www.state.ga.us/Departments/DHR/dfcs.html

Georgia General Assembly
www.state.ga.us/Legis

Atlanta Legal Aid
www.atlantalegalaid.org

Atlanta Volunteer Lawyers Foundation
avlf.org

Georgia Bar Association
www.gabar.org

Atlanta Bar Association
www.atlantabar.org

Hawaii

Hawaii State Government
www.hawaii.gov/portal

Hawaii State Divorce Information
www.courts.state.hi.us (then click on "Self-Help" and then "Divorce")

Hawaii Uncontested Divorce Packet
www.hawaii.gov/jud/Oahu/Family/uncondiv.pdf

Hawaii Child Support
www.hawaii.gov/csea/csea.htm

Domestic Violence
www.honolulupd.org/info/dv.htm

Hawaii Bar Association
www.hsba.org

Idaho

Idaho State Government Website
www.accessidaho.org

Child Support and Online Child Support Payment

(online payment is on the right-hand side)
www.healthandwelfare.idaho.gov/portal/alias__Rainbow/lang__en-US/tabID__3337/
DesktopDefault.aspx

Idaho Divorce Forms
www2.state.id.us/cao/courtforms.asp

http://www.isc.idaho.gov/rulesfrm.htm

Domestic Violence
http://www.isc.idaho.gov/rulesfrm.htm

Idaho Bar Association
www2.state.id.us/isb

Illinois

Illinois State Government
www.illinois.gov (searchable)

Marital Law Statutes
www.ilga.gov/legislation/ilcs/ilcs2.asp?ChapterID=59

Supreme and Appellate Court Opinions
Child Support Enforcement
www.19thcircuitcourt.state.il.us/rules/rules12.htm

Department of Children and Family Services
www.state.il.us/dcfs

Domestic Violence
ag.state.il.us/dvsa/violence_Victims.htm

Illinois Legal Aid
www.illinoislegalaid.org (searchable)

Supreme Court of Illinois
www.state.il.us/court

Illinois Bar Association
www.illinoisbar.org

Chicago Bar Association
www.chicagobar.org

Indiana

Indiana State Government
www.state.in.us (searchable)

Child Support
www.in.gov/fssa/children/support/index.html

Parenting Time Guidelines
www.in.gov/judiciary/rules/parenting

Domestic Violence
www.in.gov/icw/violence.html

Attorney General
www.ai.org/atty_gen/index.html

Indiana Bar Association
www.inbar.org/

Iowa

Iowa State Government
www.iowa.gov/state/main/index.html

Iowa Statutes
www.legis.state.ia.us/Current/tablesandindex/Skeleton_Index.pdf (Look for
your keyword.)

Iowa State Government Judicial Branch/Families and Children
(Includes Child Support)
www.judicial.state.ia.us/families

Domestic Violence
www.judicial.state.ia.us/families/domviol/dvlaws.asp

Iowa Bar Association
www.iowabar.org/main.nsf

Kansas

Kansas State Government
www.accesskansas.org

Kansas State Government Marriage and Dissolution Notice
www.kdhe.state.ks.us/hci/as03/AS03MARR.PDF

Kansas Child Support Enforcement
www.srskansas.org/cse/cse.htm

Domestic Violence
www.kdhe.state.ks.us/dva/safety_planning.html

Kansas Attorney General
www.accesskansas.org/ksag/

Kansas Bar Association
www.ink.org/public/cybar

Kentucky

Kentucky State Government
http://kentucky.gov

Title XXXV Domestic Relations
www.lrc.state.ky.us/krs/titles.htm

Child Support Enforcement Division
ag.ky.gov/childsupport

Domestic Violence
ag.ky.gov/victims/domestic.htm

Kentucky Bar Association
www.kybar.org

Louisiana

Louisiana State Government
www.louisiana.gov/wps/portal

Statutes
www.legis.state.la.us/lss/tsrssearch.htm

Child Support Guidelines (Louisiana Department of Social Services)
www.dss.state.la.us/departments/ofs/Child_Support_Award_Guidelines.html

Child Support Enforcement
www.dss.state.la.us/departments/ofs/Support_Enforcement_Services.html

Visitation and Access to Child
www.dss.state.la.us/Documents/OFS/Access_and_Visitatio.pdf

Domestic Violence
www.4woman.gov/violence/StateResourcesDetail.cfm?ID=3745

www.state.la.us/opb/pub/exec-bud99/01-exec/01-exec.18.html

Louisiana Bar Association
www.lsba.org

Maine

Maine State Government
www.state.me.us

Domestic Relations Statutes
www.maine.gov/portal/government/legislature.html

Child Support Overview
www.maine.gov/dhhs/bfi/dser/

Maine Judicial Branch/Family Division
www.courts.state.me.us/mainecourts/familydiv/

Maine Courts/Divorce Frequently Asked Questions
www.courts.state.me.us/faq/divorce.html

Domestic Violence
www.state.me.us/ag/index.php?r=crimeandvictims&s=domesticviolence

Maine Bar Association
www.mainebar.org

Maryland

Maryland State Government
Maryland.gov

Department of Family Administration (including forms)
www.courts.state.md.us/family/forms/index.html

Child Support Overview
www.dhr.state.md.us/csea

Domestic Violence
www.dhr.state.md.us/victim/dvp.htm

Maryland State Bar Association
www.msba.org

Massachusetts

Massachusetts State Government
mass.gov

Massachusetts Statutes
www.state.ma.us/legis/laws/mgl/index.htm

Child Support Guidelines
www.cse.state.ma.us/parents/cseguide.htm

Massachusetts Child Support Enforcement Case Manager
https://ecse.cse.state.ma.us/ECSE/Login/login.asp

Domestic Violence
www.lawlib.state.ma.us/domestic_violence.html

Massachusetts Bar Association
www.massbar.org

Michigan

Michigan State Government
michigan.gov

Statutes (searchable)
courts.michigan.gov/scao/services/focb/legis.htm

Domestic Relations Forms
courts.michigan.gov/scao/courtforms/domesticrelations/drindex.htm

Michigan Child Support
www.michigan.gov/dhs (then click on "Assistance Programs" and then "Child Support")

Domestic Violence
www.michigan.gov/dhs/0,1607,7-124-5460_7261---,00.html

Supreme Court
www.supremecourt.state.mi.us

Michigan Bar Association
www.michbar.org

Minnesota

Minnesota State Government
www.state.mn.us

Marriage Dissolution
www.revisor.leg.state.mn.us/stats/518

Uniform Interstate Family Support Act
www.revisor.leg.state.mn.us/stats/518C

Rights and Privileges of Married Persons
www.revisor.leg.state.mn.us/stats/519

Child Support
www.childsupport.dhs.state.mn.us/Action/Welcome

Court Forms
www.courts.state.mn.us/forms/?pageID=138

Domestic Violence
www.revisor.leg.state.mn.us/stats/518B

Minnesota Center Against Violence and Abuse: www.mincava.umn.edu/

Minnesota Bar Association
www.mnbar.org

Mississippi

Mississippi State Government
mississippi.gov

Family Law
www.msbar.org/10_family_law.php

Division of Child Support Enforcement
www.mdhs.state.ms.us/cse.html

Domestic Violence
www.dps.state.ms.us/dps/dps.nsf/divpages/ps2ojp-stop?OpenDocument

Mississippi Bar Association
www.msbar.org

Missouri

Missouri State Government
missouri.gov

The Statutes (Searchable)
www.moga.state.mo.us/homestat.htm

Child Support Enforcement
www.dss.mo.gov/cse

Domestic Violence
ago.missouri.gov/publications/domesticviolence.pdf
dss.missouri.gov/mis/apprpsum/famspprt/fsddomvl/dvlncfs.html

Missouri Bar Association
www.mobar.org

Montana

Montana State Government Website
www.discoveringmontana.com/default.asp

Divorce Forms
www.lawlibrary.state.mt.us/dscgi/ds.py/View/Collection-5210

Child Support Guidelines
www.dphhs.mt.gov/aboutus/divisions/childsupportenforcement/index.shtml

Domestic Violence
www.doj.state.mt.us/victims/domesticviolence.asp

Montana Bar Association
www.montanabar.org

Nebraska

Nebraska State Government
nebraska.gov

Divorce Statutes (searchable)
statutes.unicam.state.ne.us

Divorce Certificates
www.hhs.state.ne.us/ced/dicert.htm

Child Support Guidelines
www.court.state.ne.us/rules/childsupp.htm
www.nol.org/home/DC8/CSTemplate.html

Child Support Enforcement
www.hhs.state.ne.us/cse/cseindex.htm
www.hhs.state.ne.us/cse/chsuenf.htm

Domestic Violence
court.nol.org/public/self_help/domestic_violence/protection_order.html

Nebraska Bar Association
www.nebar.com

Nevada

Nevada State Government
www.nv.gov

Dissolution of Marriage
leg.state.nv.us/nrs/nrs%2D125.html

Court Forms for Divorce
nvsupremecourt.us/general/gen_forms.html#frms_divorce

Custody and Visitation
leg.state.nv.us/nrs/nrs%2D125c.html

Child Support
www.leg.state.nv.us/NRS/NRS-125B.html

Child Support Enforcement
www.welfare.state.nv.us/child.htm

Domestic Violence
nvsupremecourt.us/general/gen_forms.html#frms_domestic

Nevada Bar Association
www.nvbar.org

New Hampshire

New Hampshire State Government
www.state.nh.us/

New Hampshire Courts Family Division
www.courts.state.nh.us/fdpp/index.htm

Divorce Self-Help
www.courts.state.nh.us/superior/selfhelp/index.htm

Child Support Overview
www.dhhs.nh.gov/DHHS/DCSS/default.htm

Domestic Violence
www.doj.nh.gov/victim/domvioworkplace.html

New Hampshire Bar Association
www.nhbar.org

New Jersey

New Jersey State Government
www.state.nj.us

Family Court
www.judiciary.state.nj.us/directive/family.htm

Ten Steps to Divorce
www.judiciary.state.nj.us/essex/family/tensteps.htm

Divorce, nullity, and separate mainteinanc
www.judiciary.state.nj.us/rules/r5-7.htm

Child Support Guidelines
www.judiciary.state.nj.us/csguide/98r56a.htm

Child Support Enforcement
www.judiciary.state.nj.us/essex/probation/enforcement.htm

Parent Education Program for Divorcing Parents
www.judiciary.state.nj.us/essex/family/parenteducation.htm

Domestic Violence
www.judiciary.state.nj.us/essex/family/famviolence.htm
www.judiciary.state.nj.us/rules/r5-7a.htm

New Jersey Bar Association
www.njsba.com

New Mexico

New Mexico State Government
www.state.nm.us/

Statutes
www.state.nm.us/category/governmentnm.html#laws (Click on "Statutes and Constitution …,"
then search for dissolution of marriage.)

Child Support Overview
https://elink.hsd.state.nm.us/clink/

Domestic Violence
www.nmcadv.org

New Mexico Bar Association
www.nmbar.org

New York

New York State Government
www.state.ny.us

Divorce Statutes (search for Domestic Relations)
public.legifo.state.ny.us/menugetf.cgi

Consolidated Laws (search for Domestic Relations)
http://assembly.state.ny.us/leg/?cl=29

Uncontested Divorce and Forms
www.courts.state.ny.us/litigants/divorce/index.shtml

Child Support Overview
https://newyorkchildsupport.com/custodial_parent_info.html#3

Child Support Enforcement
https://newyorkchildsupport.com/home.html

Domestic Violence
www.opdv.state.ny.us/victims/index.html

"Court Help"
Answers to frequently asked questions about divorce.
www.courts.state.ny.us/courthelp/qa_familylaw.html

New York Bar Association
www.nysba.org

North Carolina

North Carolina State Government
www.ncgov.com

Family Court
www.nccourts.org/Citizens/CPrograms/Family/Default.asp

Pro Se Divorce Packet
www.nccourts.org/County/Durham/Courts/Family/Domestic/Divorce.asp

Family Financial Settlement
www.nccourts.org/Citizens/CPrograms/FFS

Child Custody Mediation
www.nccourts.org/Citizens/CPrograms/Child/Default.asp

Child Support Guidelines
https://nddhacts01.dhhs.state.nc.us/home.jsp?TargetScreen=WorkSheet.jsp

Child Support Enforcement
www.ncchildsupport.com

Domestic Violence
www.doa.state.nc.us/cfw/cfw.htm

North Carolina Bar Association
www.ncbar.org/index.aspx

North Dakota

North Dakota State Government
discovernd.com

Statute
www.state.nd.us/lr/cencode/t14.html

North Dakota Supreme Court
For decisions relating to divorce, click on "Opinion" on the left-hand sidebar
and use search feature.
www.court.state.nd.us

Child Support
www.state.nd.us/humanservices/services/childsupport/online.html

Domestic Violence
www.ndcaws.org/violence/violenceindex.asp

North Dakota Bar Association
www.sband.org

Ohio

Ohio State Government
ohio.gov

Divorce Statutes
onlinedocs.andersonpublishing.com/oh/lpExt.dll?f=templates&fn=main-h.htm&cp=PORC
(Look for Domestic Relations and click on it.)

Standards of Practice for Family and Divorce Mediation
www.sconet.state.oh.us/Dispute_Resolution/divorce/divorce.pdf

Office of Child Support
jfs.ohio.gov/Ocs/services.stm

How to Apply for Child Support
jfs.ohio.gov/Ocs/howtoapply.stm

Ohio Supreme Court Task Force on Family Law and Children
www.sconet.state.oh.us/Judicial_and_Court_Services/taskforce

Family Court History
www.sconet.state.oh.us/Judicial_and_Court_Services/family_court/vol1num1.pdf

Domestic Violence
www.odvn.org

Ohio Bar Association
www.ohiobar.org

Oklahoma

Oklahoma State Government
www.ok.gov

Oklahoma Legal Research System
oklegal.onenet.net

Oklahoma Bar Association "Is Divorce the Answer for You?"
okbar.org/public/brochures/divbroc.htm

Child Support Enforcement
www.okdhs.org/childsupport

Early Childhood Visitation Guidelines
www.health.state.ok.us/program/mchecd/divbook.pdf

Domestic Violence
Statutes: www.womenslaw.org/OK/OK_statutes.htm
Organization: www.ocadvsa.org

Oklahoma Bar Association
okbar.org

Oregon

Oregon State Government
oregon.gov

Searchable Index
landru.leg.state.or.us/ors

Dissolution of Marriage
www.ojd.state.or.us/osca/cpsd/courtimprovement/familylaw/flpacket1.htm

Child Custody
www.osbar.org/public/legalinfo/1133.htm

Child Support
www.oregon.gov/DAS/IRMD/EGOV/children.shtml

Domestic Violence
www.dhs.state.or.us/abuse/domestic

Oregon Bar Association
www.osbar.org

Pennsylvania

Pennsylvania State Government
www.state.pa.us

State Government Searchable Website
www.state.pa.us/PAPower/site/default.asp

Child Support Program
www.humanservices.state.pa.us/childsupport/pgm/asp/index.asp

Domestic Violence
www.dpw.state.pa.us/Family/DomesticViolence/003670180.htm

Pennsylvania Bar Association
www.pabar.org

Rhode Island

Rhode Island State Government
www.state.ri.us

Statutes
www.rilin.state.ri.us/Statutes/TITLE15/INDEX.HTM

Child Support Guidelines and Formula
www.supportguidelines.com/glines/rics_order.html

Child Support Enforcement
www.childsupportliens.com

Family Court
www.courts.state.ri.us/family/defaultfamily.htm

Domestic Violence
www.courts.state.ri.us/domesticnew/default.htm

Rhode Island Bar Association
www.ribar.com

South Carolina

South Carolina State Governmentwww.myscgov.com/SCSGPortal/static/home_tem4.html (searchable)

South Carolina Legislature
www.scstatehouse.net (searchable)

Child Support Enforcement
www.state.sc.us/dss/csed/faqs.htm

Domestic Violence
www.state.sc.us/dss/aps/fv.htm

Organizations:
www.sccadvasa.org
hadm.sph.sc.edu/Students/KBelew/FVPlan.htm

South Carolina Bar Association
www.scbar.org

South Dakota

South Dakota State Government
www.state.sd.us

South Dakota Statutes
legis.state.sd.us/statutes/
Index.cfm?FuseAction=DisplayStatute&FindType=Statute&txtStatute=25

South Dakota Division of Child Support
www.state.sd.us/social/CSE/index.htm

Domestic Violence
www.state.sd.us/social/ASA/domesticabuse

South Dakota Bar Association
www.sdbar.org

Tennessee

Tennessee State Government
www.tennesseeanytime.org/

Domestic Relations Law
www.state.tn.us/tccy/tnchild/t36/t_36.htm

Child Custody
www.state.tn.us/tccy/tnchild/t36/t_36_ch_6.htm

Child Support
www.state.tn.us/humanserv/child-support.htm

Tennessee Supreme Court
tscaoc.tsc.state.tn.us

Domestic Violence
www2.state.tn.us/health/Downloads/domestic_violence.pdf

Tennessee Bar Association
www.tba.org

County Bar Associations
www.tba.org/Resources/net_tnbars.html

Texas

Texas State Government
www.state.tx.us

Statutes
www.capitol.state.tx.us/statutes/fatoc.html

Child Support
www.oag.state.tx.us/child/index.shtml

Domestic Violence
www.dhs.state.tx.us/programs/familyviolence/

Texas Bar Association
www.texasbar.com

Utah

Utah State Government
utah.gov

Utah Laws (searchable)
www.utah.gov/government/utahlaws.html

Divorce Information
www.utahbar.org/bars/slcbar/html/divorce.html

Child Support
www.hsors.utah.gov/faq.htm

Domestic Violence
attorneygeneral.utah.gov/domesticviolence.html

Utah State Bar Association
www.utahbar.org

Vermont

Vermont State Government
vermont.gov

Domestic Relations Statutes
www.leg.state.vt.us/statutes/chapters.cfm?Title=15

Vermont Family Court
www.ocs.state.vt.us//handbook/famCourts.htm

Vermont Office of Child Support
www.ocs.state.vt.us/default.asp

Child Support Guideline Software
www.vermontjudiciary.org/Resources/docs/csdownloadpage.htm

Domestic Violence
www.path.state.vt.us/cwyj/dvu

Vermont Bar Association
www.vtbar.org

Virginia

Virginia State Government
virginia.gov

Searchable Statutes
leg1.state.va.us/000/src.htm

Child Support
www.dss.state.va.us/family/dcse.html

Juvenile & Domestic District Court Forms
www.courts.state.va.us/forms/district/jdr.html

Domestic Violence
www.oag.state.va.us/Protecting/Domestic_Violence/

Virginia Bar Association
www.vsb.org

Washington

Washington State Government
access.wa.gov

Divorce Information
www.courts.wa.gov/selfhelp/index.cfm?fa=selfhelp.display&fileID=ds

Domestic Relations Forms
www.courts.wa.gov/forms/?fa=forms.compress

Child Custody
www.courts.wa.gov/selfhelp/index.cfm?fa=selfhelp.display&fileID=cc

Child Support
www1.dshs.wa.gov/dcs/index.shtml

Domestic Violence Program
www1.dshs.wa.gov/basicneeds/an2dvp.html

Washington State Bar Association
www.wsba.org

West Virginia

West Virginia State Government
wv.gov

Child Support
www.wv.gov/offsite.aspx?u=www.wvdhhr.org/bcse (Links on the right panel of this web page also contain marriage statutes.)

Domestic Violence
www.wvdhhr.org/bcf/children_adult/dv/

West Virginia Bar Association
www.wvbar.org

Wisconsin

Wisconsin State Government
wisconsin.gov

Wisconsin Statutes
www.legis.state.wi.us (then click on "Wisconsin Law" and then "Statutes")

Child Support (searchable)
www.dwd.state.wi.us/bcs

Domestic Violence
dhfs.wisconsin.gov/Children/DomV/INDEX.HTM

Wisconsin State Bar Association
www.wisbar.org

Wyoming

Wyoming State Government
wyoming.gov

Statutes
legisweb.state.wy.us/statutes/sub20.htm

Child Support
dfsweb.state.wy.us/cse_enforce.html

Domestic Violence
www.uwyo.edu/ces/FAMILY/LIFE/Marriage/COUPLES/Domestic_Violence.htm

Wyoming Bar Association
www.wyomingbar.org

Suggested Reading

Books on Divorce

Here we list just a few of the many valuable books on divorce. Check your library or local bookstore for more. The more recent the publication date, the better—but some of the "classics" are well worth the read.

General

Boomer's Guide to Divorce (and a New Life), Marlene M. Browne, Esq. Indianapolis: Alpha Books, 2004.

Addressed to the "baby boomer," this guide to divorce covers everything from the cultural times we lived in then and live in now to nitty gritty details of divorce and life after divorce. Easy reading written by an experienced divorce attorney.

Ex-Etiquette for Parents: Good Behavior After a Divorce or Separation, Jann Blackstone-Ford, Sharyl Jupe. Chicago: Chicago Review Press, 2004.

This book helps you with defining and practicing good behavior after divorce or separation, parenting and family building, and managing the formalities. These topics generally are not covered in other divorce books, but they are vital!

New Life After Divorce, Bill Butterworth. Colorado Springs: WaterBrook Press, 2005.

A Christian-based book offering support and hope for those going through divorce.

Surviving Separation and Divorce: Regaining Control, Building Strength and Confidence, Securing a Financial Future, Lorian Hoff Oberlin. Avon, MA: Adams Media Corporation, 2005.

Provides a general discussion of all aspects of divorce, including legal, financial, child, and emotional issues.

We're Still Family: What Grown Children Have to Say About Their Parents' Divorce, Constance Ahrons. New York: Perennial, 2005.

Constance Ahrons presents the results of a follow-up study of now-adult children of divorce. Her conclusion is that divorce does not destroy children, as some psychologists have said. The majority of the people Ahrons interviewed believed that divorce was a positive move on their parents' parts.

Understanding the Divorce Cycle: The Children of Divorce in Their Own Marriages, Nicholas H. Wolfinger. Cambridge, UK: Cambridge University Press, 2005.

Wolfinger discusses the impact of divorce on people's lives, observes the cycle of divorce over generations, and compares marriages of children of intact families with those of divorced families.

Heart of Divorce: Advice from a Judge, Susan P. Baker. Austin: Eakin Press, 2004.

The author has spent more than 20 years working with families and children in crisis. She was moved to write this book after witnessing the heartbreak and meanness of litigation.

For Better or For Worse: Divorce Reconsidered, E. Mavis Hetherington and John Kelly. New York: W. W. Norton and Co., Inc., 2003.

The author, Professor Emeritus of Psychology at the University of Virginia, has conducted research on 1,400 families over almost three decades. In this book she presents a new interpretation of her findings with a more nuanced, positive spin on outcomes of divorce.

A Client's Guide to Limited Legal Services, M. Sue Talis. Danville, California: The Nexus Publishing Company, 1997.

Written in plain English, this book explains how people can keep their legal fees low by only using a lawyer in a very limited way. It includes questionnaires to help you decide if you are a good candidate.

How to Heal a Painful Relationship: And if Necessary, How to Part as Friends, Bill Ferguson. Houston: Return to the Heart, 1999.

Learn how to end the cycle of conflict, heal the hurt, resolve issues, and restore the love.

Second Chances: Men, Women, and Children a Decade After Divorce, Judith S. Wallerstein and Sandra Blakeslee. New York: Ticknor & Fields, 1989.

Renowned divorce researchers Wallerstein and Blakeslee report on what happened to selected families during, after, and long after divorce, based on a 10-year study of 60 middle-class families. Some of the findings are controversial because the sample size was so small, but it's a classic study from the '80s and one of the few long-term studies in existence.

Children and Divorce

What About the Kids? Raising Your Children Before, During, and After Divorce, Judith S. Wallerstein and Sandra Blakeslee. New York: Hyperion, 2003.

Renowned divorce researchers advise parents on helping children at each developmental stage with divorce.

The Unexpected Legacy of Divorce: The 25 Year Landmark Study, Judith Wallerstein, Julia Lewis, Sandra Blakeslee. New York: Hyperion, 2000.

Following the lives of children and families of divorced and intact families, the authors conclude that the effects of divorce are seen into adulthood.

Helping Your Kids Cope with Divorce the Sandcastles Way, M. Gary Neuman, Patricia Romanowski. New York: Random House, 1999.

A comprehensive book on helping your kids cope with divorce.

Voices of Children of Divorce, David Royko. New York: Golden Books, 1999.

Through the voices of children of all ages, this book provides observations and insights on what it is like for the young victims of divorce.

Mom's House, Dad's House: A Complete Guide for Parents Who Are Separated, Divorced, or Remarried, Isolina Ricci. New York: Simon & Schuster, 1997.

Creative options and commonsense advice for dealing with the legal, emotional, and practical realities of creating two happy and stable homes for your children.

"Why Did You Have to Get a Divorce? and When Can I Get a Hamster?" A Guide to Parenting Through Divorce, Anthony E. Wolf. New York: Noonday Press, 1998.

How to tell your children about the divorce, how to keep your children from being caught between you and your ex-partner, and how to help children cope with new partners or new siblings.

Rocking the Cradle of Sexual Politics, Louise Armstrong. Reading, Massachusetts: Addison-Wesley, 1994.

Explores the politics of incest and child sexual abuse.

Caught in the Middle: Protecting the Children of High-Conflict Divorce, Carla B. Garrity and Mitchell A. Baris. New York: Lexington Books, 1994.

Provides parents embroiled in conflict—and the professionals who work with them—with tools to reduce tension and remove children from the center of fire.

For the Sake of the Children, Kris Kline and Stephen Pew, Ph.D. Rocklin, California: Prima Publishing, 1992.

How to share your children with your ex-spouse in spite of your anger.

Surviving the Breakup: How Children and Parents Cope with Divorce, Judith S. Wallerstein. New York: Basic Books, 1980.

Based on the Children of Divorce Project, a landmark study of 60 families during the first five years after divorce. Note: *Second Chances*, mentioned earlier, is the sequel to this book.

Children of Divorce: A Developmental Approach to Residence and Visitation, Mitchell A. Baris, Ph.D. and Carla B. Garrity, Ph.D. DeKalb, Illinois: Psytec, 1988.

Drs. Baris and Garrity outline their recommendations for age-appropriate time-sharing for parents who are separating and divorcing.

Parent vs. Parent: How You and Your Child Can Survive the Custody Battle, Stephen P. Herman. New York: Pantheon Books, 1990.

Child psychiatrist and court-appointed psychiatric evaluator, Dr. Herman, focuses on what to expect during litigated cases.

Family Abduction: How to Prevent an Abduction and What to Do if Your Child Is Abducted, P. Hoff. Arlington, Virginia: National Center for Missing and Exploited Children, 1994.

This book tells parents what steps to take to reduce the risk of abduction when separation is imminent.

Single Parenting

Successful Single Parenting, Gary Richmond. Eugene, Oregon: Harvest House Publishers, 1998.

Divorce can be tough for children, but the effects don't have to be long-term. This Christian-oriented book provides answers to tough questions single parents face about how to soften the blow of divorce for their children.

Divorce and New Beginnings: An Authoritative Guide to Recovery and Growth, Solo Parenting, and Stepfamilies, Genevieve Clapp. New York: John Wiley and Sons, 1992.

Takes parents and children step-by-step through each stage of divorce and discusses rebuilding a successful family by handling daily problems and long-term concerns.

Moms and Divorce

The Complete Single Mother: Reassuring Answers to Your Most Challenging Concerns, 2nd ed, Andrea Engber and Leah Klungness. Avon, Mass: Adams Media Corporation, 2000.

A lively guide for single mothers, whether divorced or never married. The book covers most parenting issues unique to single mothers. A "how to" book on raising happy and productive children despite the missing spouse.

Dads and Divorce

Dad Alone, How to Rebuild Your Life and Remain an Involved Father After Divorce, Phil Clavel. Montreal: Vehicule Press, 2004.

A handy reference for single dads recovering from divorce.

Good Men: A Practical Handbook for Divorced Dads, Jack Feuer. New York: Avon Books, 1997.

Deals with single parenting from a man's point of view. Practical information on a wide variety of concerns—whether you are a divorced man seeking sole custody, joint custody, or visitation rights, or whether you are still fighting with your ex for the right to see your kids.

Live-Away Dads: Staying a Part of Your Children's Lives When They Aren't a Part of Your Home, William C. Klatte. New York: Penguin Books, 1999.

Covers taking care of yourself, getting along with your children's mother and others, navigating the court system, fathering your children, and building a network of support.

Fathers After Divorce: Building a New Life and Becoming a Successful Separated Parent, Michael Green. Lane Cove, Australia: Finch Publishing Pty, Ltd., 2002.

A complete guide for dads.

Divorced Dads: Shattering the Myths, Sanford L. Braver, Dianne O'Connell. New York: Tarcher/Putnam, 1998.

A non-traditional view of the role of divorced fathers.

Stepfamilies

Two Happy Homes: A Working Guide for Parents & Stepparents After Divorce and Remarriage, Shirley Thomas, Ph.D. Longmont, Colo: Springboard Publications, 2005.

The title says it all.

7 Steps to Bonding with Your Stepchild, Susan J. Zieghan. New York: St. Martin's Press, 2001.

Recognizing different relationships, understanding your partner's and stepchild's view, and how to begin bonding with your stepchild.

Stepfamilies: Love, Marriage, and Parenting in the First Decade, James H. Bray. New York: Broadway Books/Random House, 1998.

Based on a longitudinal study, a detailed guide to easing the conflicts of stepfamily life and healing the scars of divorce.

The Enlightened Stepmother: Revolutionizing the Role, Perdita Kirkness Norwood, Teri Wingencher. New York: Avon Books, 1999.

Written from the stepmother's point of view, this book discusses what works and what doesn't when it comes to being a stepmom.

The Courage to Be a Stepmom: Finding Your Place Without Losing Yourself, Sue Patton Thoele. Berkeley, California: Wildcat Canyon Press, 2003.

Hands-on advice and practical skills for women who want to be good stepmothers while taking care of themselves.

Blending Families, Elaine Fantle Shimberg. New York: Berkeley Publishing Group/Penguin Putnam, 1999.

A guide to the complex situation of bringing families together.

Just for Children

It's Not Your Fault, Koko Bear: A Read Together Book for Parents and Young Children,
Vicki Lansky. Minnetonka, Minnesota: Book Peddlers, 1998.

A picture book for kids whose parents are going through divorce.

Steptrouble: A Survival Guide For Teenagers with Stepparents, William L. Coleman.
Minneapolis, Minnesota: CompCare Publishers, 1993.

A product of divorce himself, Coleman writes in a teen-friendly way about coping
with divorce and a new stepfamily situation.

Dinosaurs Divorce: A Guide for Changing Families, Laurence Brown and Marc Brown.
Boston: Little Brown & Co., 1988.

This children's classic will bring comfort to any child of divorce.

Women and Divorce

From Ex-Wife to Exceptional Life: A Woman's Journey through Divorce, Donna F. Ferber.
Farmington, CT: Purple Lotus Press, LLC, 2005.

Drawing on 20 years of counseling experience, Ferber offers women valuable tools,
guidance, and emotional support for handling all aspects of divorce.

Fair Share Divorce For Women, Kathleen Miller. Bellevue, Washington: Miller, Bird
Advisers, Inc., 1995.

This book arms women with the information and techniques they need to protect
their assets.

What Every Woman Should Know About Divorce and Custody, Gayle Rosenwald Smith,
J.D. and Sally Abrahms. New York: Perigee, 1998.

What women need to know to come out ahead in divorce and custody battles.

Grandparents and Divorce

The Essential Grandparent's Guide to Divorce: Making a Difference in the Family, Lillian
Carson. Deerfield Beach, Florida: Health Communications, Inc., 1999.

Clinical psychologist Lillian Carson offers advice to grandparents who are going
through divorce or whose children are divorcing.

Grandparenting Redefined, Irene M. Endicott. Lynnwood, Washington: Aglow
Publications, 1992.

A book targeted at grandparents who are raising their grandchildren. Discusses child-rearing problems due to divorce and remarriage and drug and child abuse.

Domestic Abuse

Why Does He Do That?: Inside the Minds of Angry and Controlling Men, Lundy Bancroft. New York: The Berkeley Publishing Group, 2002.

Learn the early warning signs, abusive personality types, the role of drugs and alcohol, what you can fix and what you can't, and how to get out of a relationship safely.

Healing the Trauma of Domestic Violence: A Workbook for Women, Edward S. Kubany, Ph.D., et al. Oakland, California: New Harbinger Publications, Inc., 2003.

A program for recovery after being freed from domestic violence.

Legal Issues

Your Divorce Advisor: A Lawyer and a Psychologist Guide You Through the Legal and Emotional Landscape of Divorce, Diana Mercer, J.D., and Marsha Kline Pruett, Ph.D. New York: Fireside, 2001.

Explores the legal and emotional landscape of divorce.

Between Love and Hate: A Guide to Civilized Divorce, Lois Gold. New York: Plume Books, 1996.

An experienced mediator, Gold advises readers on getting through their divorce as civilly as possible.

Divorce Yourself, 6th Edition: The National Divorce Kit, Dietrich Orlow. Carbondale, IL: Nova Publishing Company, 2005.

This book contains forms, questionnaires, checklists, and courtroom guidelines designed for all 50 states.

Financial Books and Articles

Survival Manual to Divorce: Your Guide to Financial Confidence & Prosperity, Carol Ann Wilson. Marketplace Books, Inc., 2005.

A reference book on the financial aspects of a divorce settlement.

Dividing Pensions in Divorce, Gary A. Shulman. New York: Aspen Law & Business Publishers, 2004.

A book for professionals, though do-it-yourselfers may want to use this book as a reference. Get it from your library ... it's expensive!

Divorce and Money: How to Make the Best Financial Decision During Divorce, 7th Edition, Violet Woodhouse and Victoria Felton-Collins. Berkeley: Nolo Press, 2004.

A practical guide to evaluating assets during divorce.

The Pension Answer Book, Stephen J. Krass, Esq. New York: Aspen Law and Business, 2005.

Priced and designed for the professional, this book includes chapters on pension and retirement plans, life insurance and death benefits, 40l(k) plans, IRAs, rollovers, annuities, and more.

Bankruptcy and Divorce: Support and Property Division, Judith K. Fitzgerald and Ramona M. Arena. New York: Aspen Publishers, 1998.

Intended for professionals, this book covers such issues as bankruptcy and divorce, child support, property settlement, estate problems, pensions and retirement funds, and premarital agreements.

Psychological Support

Mars and Venus Starting Over: A Practical Guide for Finding Love Again After a Painful Breakup, Divorce, or the Loss of a Loved One, John Gray. New York: Harper Collins, 2002.

The author of *Men Are from Mars, Women Are from Venus* tackles finding love again.

The Psychotherapist As Parent Coordinator in High-Conflict Divorce: Strategies and Techniques, Susan M. Boyan and Ann Marie Termini. Binghamton, New York: Haworth Press, 2004.

A book for psychotherapists interested in helping parents in high-conflict divorce. Although written for professionals, this book might help those going through a high-conflict divorce.

Heal the Hurt That Runs Your Life, Bill Ferguson. Houston: Return to the Heart, 1996.

Discover and heal the inner issues that destroy love and sabotage your life.

Getting Up, Getting Over, Getting on: A Twelve Step Guide to Divorce Recovery, Micki McWade. Beverly Hills, California: Champion Press, 1999.

Tools for recovering from divorce.

Index